BEST
BABY NAMES
FOR
JEWISH
CHILDREN

AMI • ARI • ARIEL • AVI • CHANA
• DODI • DOR • DORON • GIORA •
HADAR • HADAS • KEREN • LIOR
• MAL   AZAL •
NILI •   OFRA •
ORLI •   RON •
SHOSE   • TALI
• TAL   KVA •
TZIPO   DEN •
ZOHA   L • AVI
• CHA   DORON
• GIO   DAS •
KERE   ACH •

BEST
BABY NAMES
FOR
JEWISH
CHILDREN

❖

Alfred J. Kolatch

MALKA • MAZAL • NILI • NIREL
• NOAM • OFRA • ORLI • RON •
RONI • SHARON • SHOSHAN •
SIMCHA • TAL • TALI • TALYA
• TAMAR • TIKVA • TZIPOR •
TZOFI • YARDEN • ZOHAR • AMI

JONATHAN DAVID PUBLISHERS, INC.
68-22 ELIOT AVE. • MIDDLE VILLAGE, NEW YORK 11379

BEST BABY NAMES
FOR JEWISH CHILDREN

Jonathan David Publishers, Inc.
68-22 Eliot Avenue
Middle Village, New York 11379
www.jdbooks.com

4 6 8 10 9 7 5

Library of Congress Cataloging-in-Publication Data

Kolatch, Alfred J.
        The best baby names for Jewish children / by Alfred J. Kolatch.
                p. cm.
". . . contains a large assortment of names . . . selected from my earlier books"— ref.
ISBN 0-8246-0406-7
1. Names, Personal—Jewish. 2. Names, Personal — English.
3. English language—Etymology—Names. 4. Names, Personal—Hebrew.
I. Title.
CS3010.K66   1998
929.4'4'089924—dc21   97-40038
                                                        CIP

Cover design by Dorothy Wachtenheim Design
Text design and composition by John Reinhardt Book Design

Printed in the United States of America

For
Alyssa, Joshua, Jordan,
Jessica, and Brandon

PREFACE

Dear Mom and Pop:

This handy volume offers a wide assortment of names from which to select an appealing one for your child. The entries have been selected from my earlier books, published over the last fifty years, including *These Are the Names* (1948), *The Name Dictionary* (1966), *The Jonathan David Dictionary of First Names* (1980), *The Complete Dictionary of English and Hebrew First Names* (1984), *Today's Best Baby Names* (1986), and *The New Name Dictionary* (1989).

Best Baby Names for Jewish Children provides the origin and definition of each entry and suggests one Hebrew name equivalent. A great many more suggestions can be found in *The New Name Dictionary*, which contains an appendix that gives the correct spelling, in Hebrew characters, of each Hebrew and Yiddish name.

Those seeking more historical information about a particular biblical or talmudic name should consult *The Complete Dictionary of English and Hebrew First Names*. In *The Jonathan David Dictionary of First Names*, much anecdotal material is presented along with the names of outstanding personalities in various fields of endeavor who have borne a particular cognomen.

You will find, perhaps to your surprise, that the same name sometimes appears in both the masculine and feminine sections. In the past few decades, almost 200 Hebrew unisex names have come into being. These include Ami, Ari, Ariel, Avi, Chana, Dodi,

Dor, Doron, Giora, Hadar, Hadas, Keren, Lior, Malach, Malka, Mazal, Nili, Nirel, Noam, Ofra, Orli, Ron, Roni, Sharon, Shoshan, Simcha, Tal, Tali, Talya, Tamar, Tikva, Tzipor, Tzofi, Yarden, and Zohar.

A child's name selection may be based on meaning, sound, or parents' creativity—as many of the names in this volume show. The name Adiela, for example, was created by a couple who liked the masculine Hebrew name Adiel, meaning "adorned by God." When the newborn turned out to be a girl, the couple quickly feminized their name selection from Adiel to Adiela.

Some parents exhibit creativity by inventing a new form or spelling for an established name. Thus, Molly becomes Mollye or Molli; Sarah becomes Sara or Sari or Suri; Jonathan becomes Jon-Jon, Jonji, or Jonni; and Ephraim becomes Efrem or Effi.

The wise King Solomon, reputed to be the author of the Book of Ecclesiastes (Kohelet), wrote these beautiful lines (7:1):

Tov sheim mi-shemen tov.

A good name is better than fragrant oil.

May the name you choose for your child bring much joy and good cheer into your lives.

ALFRED J. KOLATCH

BEST
BABY NAMES
FOR
JEWISH
CHILDREN

MASCULINE

Aaron The Anglicized form of Aharon.

Abahu From the Aramaic, meaning "God is my father."
HEBREW EQUIVALENT: Abahu.

Aba'ye From the Aramaic, meaning "little father." HEBREW
EQUIVALENT: Aba'ye.

Abba From the Aramaic, meaning "father." HEBREW
EQUIVALENT: Abba.

Abbe, Abbey From the Old French and Latin, meaning "an
abbot." HEBREW EQUIVALENT: Abba.

Abbie A variant spelling of Abbey.

Abbot, Abbott Greek and Latin forms of the Aramaic Abba.

Abe A pet form of Abraham.

Abel From the Hebrew, meaning "breath." HEBREW
EQUIVALENT: Hevel.

Abelard From the Anglo-Saxon, meaning "noble." HEBREW
EQUIVALENT: Achiram.

Aberlin A Yiddish form of Abraham.

Abi A pet form of Abraham.

Abie A pet form of Abraham.

Abin A variant spelling of Avin.

Abina A variant spelling of Avina.

Abir From the Hebrew, meaning "hero, strong." HEBREW
EQUIVALENT: Abir.

Abiram A variant spelling of Aviram.

Abiri From the Hebrew, meaning "my hero." HEBREW
EQUIVALENT: Abiri.

Able A variant spelling of Abel.

Abner A variant spelling of Avner.

Abraham The Anglicized spelling of Avraham.

Abram A variant spelling of Avram.

Absalom A variant form of Avshalom.

Adad A variant form of Hadad.

Adael From the Hebrew, meaning "adorned by God."
HEBREW EQUIVALENT: Ada'el.

Adair From the Celtic, meaning "ford near the oak tree."
HEBREW EQUIVALENT: Oren.

Adam From the Hebrew, meaning "earth." HEBREW
EQUIVALENT: Adam.

Adar From the Hebrew, meaning "noble, exalted." HEBREW
EQUIVALENT: Adar.

Adelbert A variant form of the Old High German,
meaning "noble" and "bright." HEBREW EQUIVALENT:
Nadav.

Adi, Addi, Addie From the Hebrew, meaning "my
adornment." HEBREW EQUIVALENT: Adi.

Adiel From the Hebrew, meaning "God is my adornment."
HEBREW EQUIVALENT: Adiel.

Adif From the Hebrew, meaning "excellent." HEBREW
EQUIVALENT: Adif.

Adin From the Hebrew, meaning "beautiful, pleasant."
HEBREW EQUIVALENT: Adin.

Adir From the Hebrew, meaning "noble, majestic." HEBREW
EQUIVALENT: Adir.

Adiv From the Hebrew and Arabic, meaning "pleasant,
gently-mannered." HEBREW EQUIVALENT: Adiv.

Adlai From the Aramaic, meaning "refuge of God."
HEBREW EQUIVALENT: Adlai.

Adler From the German, meaning "eagle." HEBREW
EQUIVALENT: Da'ya.

Admon From the Hebrew *adom*, meaning "red." HEBREW
EQUIVALENT: Admon.

Adna, Adnah From the Aramaic, meaning "good fortune"
or "adorned." HEBREW EQUIVALENT: Adna.

Adni From the Hebrew, meaning "my delight." HEBREW
EQUIVALENT: Adni.

Adolf, Adolfo Variant German forms of Adolph.

Adolph From the Old German, meaning "noble helper."
HEBREW EQUIVALENT: Ezra.

Adon From the Hebrew "master." HEBREW EQUIVALENT:
Adon.

Adoniya From the Hebrew, meaning "the Lord is my God."
HEBREW EQUIVALENT: Adoniya.

Adoram From the Hebrew, meaning "God is exalted."
HEBREW EQUIVALENT: Adoram.

Adrian A short form of the Latin Hadrian. From the Greek,
meaning "rich." HEBREW EQUIVALENT: Adar.

Adriel From the Hebrew, meaning "God is my majesty."
HEBREW EQUIVALENT: Adriel.

Afek From the Hebrew, meaning "water channel." HEBREW
EQUIVALENT: Afeik.

Afik A variant form of Afek. HEBREW EQUIVALENT: Afik.

Agel From the Hebrew, meaning "I will rejoice." HEBREW
EQUIVALENT: Agel.

Agil A variant form of Agel. HEBREW EQUIVALENT: Agil.

Agmon From the Hebrew, meaning "reed." HEBREW
EQUIVALENT: Agmon.

Agur From the Hebrew, meaning "knowledgeable,
learned." HEBREW EQUIVALENT: Agur.

Aharon From the Hebrew, meaning "mountain." HEBREW
EQUIVALENT: Aharon.

Ahava, Ahavah From the Hebrew, meaning "love." HEBREW
EQUIVALENT: Ahava.

Akavya The Aramaic form of Akiva.

Akevy The Hungarian form of Jacob.

Akiba A variant spelling of Akiva.

Akim A Russian short form of Yehoyakim.

Akiva A variant form of Ya'akov (Jacob). HEBREW
EQUIVALENT: Akiva.

Aksel From the old German, meaning "small oak tree."
HEBREW EQUIVALENT: Alon.

Al A pet name for many first names, including Alan, Albert, Alfred, and Alexander.

Alan, Allan From the Celtic, meaning "harmony, peace." HEBREW EQUIVALENT: Avshalom.

Alard, Allard From the Old German, meaning "of noble ancestry." HEBREW EQUIVALENT: Yisrael.

Alastair From the Greek, meaning "the avenger." HEBREW EQUIVALENT: Elnakam.

Alban From the Latin, meaning "white." HEBREW EQUIVALENT: Lavan.

Albert A French form of Adelbrecht, meaning "noble, nobility." HEBREW EQUIVALENT: Adir.

Albie A pet form of Albert.

Albin A variant spelling of Alban.

Albion A variant form of Alban.

Albrecht An early German form of Albert.

Aldan A variant spelling of Alden.

Alden From the Middle English, meaning "antiquated, aged." HEBREW EQUIVALENT: Kadmiel.

Alder From the Old English, meaning "old." HEBREW EQUIVALENT: Alon.

Aldo An Old German and Italian form of Alder.

Aldon A variant spelling of Alden.

Aldous A variant spelling of Aldus.

Aldred From the Old English, meaning "old, wise counsel." HEBREW EQUIVALENT: Bina.

Aldus A Latinized form of the Old German Aldo.

Aldwin From the Old English, meaning "old friend." HEBREW EQUIVALENT: Amitan.

Alec, Aleck Short forms of Alexander.

Alef, Aleph From the Hebrew, meaning "number one" or "leader." HEBREW EQUIVALENT: Alef.

Alemet From the Hebrew, meaning "concealed, hidden." HEBREW EQUIVALENT: Alemet.

Alex A popular short form of Alexander.

Alexander From the Greek, meaning "protector of men." HEBREW EQUIVALENT: Aleksonder.

Alexis A form of Alexander.

Alf, Alfeo, Alfie Pet forms of Alfred.

Alfonse, Alfonso, Alfonzo Variant spellings of Alphonso.

Alfred From the Old English, meaning "old, wise counsel."
HEBREW EQUIVALENT: Navon.

Alfredo The Spanish form of Alfred.

Alger From the Anglo-Saxon, meaning "warrior." HEBREW
EQUIVALENT: Avicha'yil.

Ali From the Arabic, meaning "exalted." HEBREW
EQUIVALENT: Atalya.

Alistair A variant spelling of Alastair.

Alitz From the Hebrew, meaning "joy." HEBREW
EQUIVALENT: Alitz.

Alix A variant spelling of Alex.

Aliz From the Hebrew, meaning "joy, joyful." HEBREW
EQUIVALENT: Aliz.

Allen A popular variant spelling of Alan.

Allison A masculine name derived from Alice, meaning
"Alice's son."

Allistair A variant spelling of Alastair.

Allister A variant form of Alastair.

Allix A variant spelling of Alex.

Almagor From the Hebrew, meaning "fearless." HEBREW
EQUIVALENT: Almagor.

Alman A variant form of Almon. HEBREW EQUIVALENT:
Alman.

Almog From the Hebrew, meaning "coral." HEBREW
EQUIVALENT: Almog.

Almon From the Hebrew, meaning, "forsaken." HEBREW
EQUIVALENT: Almon.

Alon, Allon From the Hebrew, meaning "oak tree." HEBREW
EQUIVALENT: Alon.

Alphonse The French form of Alphonso.

Alphonso From the Old High German, meaning "of noble
family." HEBREW EQUIVALENT: Achiram.

Alpin From the Latin, meaning "high mountain." HEBREW
EQUIVALENT: Aharon.

Alroy From the Old English, meaning "royalty, ruler."
HEBREW EQUIVALENT: Aluf.

Alson From the Anglo-Saxon, meaning "noble stone."
HEBREW EQUIVALENT: Tzuriel.

Alta From the Latin and Spanish, meaning "tall, high."
HEBREW EQUIVALENT: Aharon.

Alter From the Old High German, meaning "old one."
Popular as a Yiddish name. HEBREW EQUIVALENT: Yashish.

Alton From the Old English, meaning "old town." HEBREW
EQUIVALENT: Kadmiel.

Altus A variant form of Alta.

Aluf, Aluph From the Hebrew, meaning "prince, leader."
HEBREW EQUIVALENT: Aluf.

Alva From the Latin, meaning "white, bright." HEBREW
EQUIVALENT: Lavan.

Alvan From the Old English, meaning "beloved friend."
HEBREW EQUIVALENT: Ahuv.

Alvin A variant form of Alvan.

Alvis From the Old Norse, meaning "wise." HEBREW
EQUIVALENT: Haskel.

Alwin, Alwyn From the Old English, meaning "old, noble
friend." HEBREW EQUIVALENT: Eldad.

Alyn, Allyn Variant spellings of Alan.

Amadore From the Italian, meaning "gift of love." HEBREW
EQUIVALENT: Achiman.

Amal From the Hebrew, meaning "work, toil." HEBREW
EQUIVALENT: Amal.

Amali A variant form of Amal. HEBREW EQUIVALENT: Amali.

Amand A French form of the Latin Amandus, meaning
"worthy of love." HEBREW EQUIVALENT: Ahuvya.

Amania A variant spelling of Amanya.

Amanya From the Hebrew, meaning "loyal to the Lord."
HEBREW EQUIVALENT: Amanya.

Ambler From the Old French, meaning "one who walks
leisurely." HEBREW EQUIVALENT: Darkon.

Ambrose From the Greek, meaning "divine" or "immortal."
HEBREW EQUIVALENT: Amiad.

Amel A variant form of Amal. HEBREW EQUIVALENT: Amel.

Amery A variant spelling of Emory.

Ami From the Hebrew, meaning "my people." HEBREW EQUIVALENT: Ami.

Amiaz From the Hebrew, meaning "my nation is mighty." HEBREW EQUIVALENT: Amiaz.

Amichai From the Hebrew, meaning "my nation lives." HEBREW EQUIVALENT: Amichai.

Amidan From the Hebrew, meaning "my people is righteous." HEBREW EQUIVALENT: Amidan.

Amidar From the Hebrew, meaning "my nation is alive." HEBREW EQUIVALENT: Amidar.

Amidor From the Hebrew, meaning "my generation of people." HEBREW EQUIVALENT: Amidor.

Amidror From the Hebrew, meaning "my nation is free." HEBREW EQUIVALENT: Amidror.

Amiel From the Hebrew, meaning "God of my people." HEBREW EQUIVALENT: Amiel.

Amihud From the Hebrew, meaning "my nation is glorious." HEBREW EQUIVALENT: Amihud.

Amin From the Hebrew, meaning "trustworthy." HEBREW EQUIVALENT: Amin.

Amior From the Hebrew, meaning "my nation is a light, a beacon." HEBREW EQUIVALENT: Amior.

Amir From the Hebrew, meaning "top branch of a tree." HEBREW EQUIVALENT: Amir.

Amiram From the Hebrew, meaning "my nation is exalted." HEBREW EQUIVALENT: Amiram.

Amiran A variant form of Amiron. HEBREW EQUIVALENT: Amiran.

Amiron From the Hebrew, meaning "my nation is a song." HEBREW EQUIVALENT: Amiron.

Amit From the Hebrew, meaning "friend." HEBREW EQUIVALENT: Amit.

Amitai From the Aramaic, meaning "true, faithful." HEBREW EQUIVALENT: Amitai.

Amitan From the Hebrew, meaning "true, faithful." HEBREW EQUIVALENT: Amitan.

Amiti A variant form of Amit.

Ammi A variant spelling of Ami.

Ammiel A variant spelling of Amiel.

Ammos A variant spelling of Amos.

Amnon From the Hebrew, meaning "faithful." HEBREW EQUIVALENT: Amnon.

Amon From the Hebrew meaning "hidden." HEBREW EQUIVALENT: Amon.

Amory A variant spelling of Emery.

Amos From the Hebrew, meaning "burdened, troubled." HEBREW EQUIVALENT: Amos.

Amram From the Hebrew, meaning "mighty nation." HEBREW EQUIVALENT: Amram.

Anan From the Hebrew, meaning "cloud." HEBREW EQUIVALENT: Anan.

Anani A variant form of Anan. HEBREW EQUIVALENT: Anani.

Ananiel From the Hebrew, meaning "God is my cloud [protector]." HEBREW EQUIVALENT: Ananiel.

Anatole From the Greek, meaning "rising of the sun" or "from the east." HEBREW EQUIVALENT: Shimshon.

Anatoly A Russian form of Anatole.

Anav From the Hebrew, meaning "grape." HEBREW EQUIVALENT: Anav.

Anavi From the Hebrew, meaning "my grape." HEBREW EQUIVALENT: Anavi.

Ancel From the Old German, meaning "god, godlike." HEBREW EQUIVALENT: Adon.

Anchel, Anchelle Variant spellings of Anshel.

Anders A patronymic form of Andrew, meaning "son of Andew."

Andi A variant spelling of Andy.

Andor A variant form of Andrew.

André A French form of Andrew.

Andrew From the Greek, meaning "manly, strong, courageous." HEBREW EQUIVALENT: Gavriel.

Andy A pet form of Andrew.

Angel, Angell From the Greek, meaning "messenger" or "saintly person." HEBREW EQUIVALENT: Arel.

Angus From the Gaelic and Irish, meaning "exceptional, outstanding." HEBREW EQUIVALENT: Ben-Tziyon.

Anschel A variant spelling of Anshel.

Ansel, Anselm From the Old German, meaning "divine helmet." HEBREW EQUIVALENT: Avigdor.

Anshel A Yiddish form of Asher.

Anson, Ansonia From the Anglo-Saxon, meaning "the son of Hans."

Antal A form of Anatole.

Anthony From the Greek, meaning "flourishing." HEBREW EQUIVALENT: Efra'yim.

Anton, Antone, Antonin Variant forms of Antony.

Antony A variant form of Anthony.

Ara From the Hebrew, meaning "to pluck, gather." HEBREW EQUIVALENT: Ara.

Arad From the Hebrew, meaning "wild ox." HEBREW EQUIVALENT: Arad.

Aram From the Assyrian, meaning "high, heights." HEBREW EQUIVALENT: Aram.

Aran From the Assyrian and Arabic, meaning "chest, sarcophagus." HEBREW EQUIVALENT: Aran.

Arba From the Hebrew, meaning "four." HEBREW EQUIVALENT: Arba.

Arbel From the Hebrew, meaning "sieve." HEBREW EQUIVALENT: Arbel.

Arbie Probably from the Old French, meaning "crossbow." HEBREW EQUIVALENT: Kashti.

Arch A short form of Archibald.

Archibald From the Anglo-Saxon, meaning "bold" or "holy prince." HEBREW EQUIVALENT: Arye.

Ard A variant form of Adar.

Arden From the Latin, meaning "to burn." HEBREW EQUIVALENT: Aviur.

Ardon From the Hebrew, meaning "bronze." HEBREW EQUIVALENT: Ardon.

Arel From the Hebrew, meaning "lion of God." HEBREW EQUIVALENT: Arel.

Areli A variant form of Arel. HEBREW EQUIVALENT: Areli.

Argus From the Greek, meaning "bright." HEBREW EQUIVALENT: Avner.

Ari From the Hebrew, meaning "lion." HEBREW EQUIVALENT: Ari.

Aric, Arick Early German forms of Richard.

Arie A variant spelling of Ari.

Arieh A variant spelling of Aryeh.

Ariel From the Hebrew, meaning "lion of God." HEBREW EQUIVALENT: Ariel.

Arik A pet form of Ariel and Aryeh.

Ario A variant form of Ari.

Arky A pet form of Archibald.

Arlando A variant form of Orlando.

Arlen The Celtic form of the name Arles, meaning "pledge." HEBREW EQUIVALENT: Nidri.

Arlin A variant spelling of Arlen.

Arlo Probably from the Old English, meaning "fortified hill." HEBREW EQUIVALENT: Aharon.

Arlyn A variant spelling of Arlin.

Armand The French and Italian form of the Old German Hermann, meaning "warrior." HEBREW EQUIVALENT: Mordechai.

Armando The Spanish form of Armand.

Armen, Armin Variant forms of Armand.

Armon From the Hebrew, meaning "castle, palace." HEBREW EQUIVALENT: Armon.

Armond A variant spelling of Armand.

Armoni A variant form of Armon. HEBREW EQUIVALENT: Armoni.

Arnan From the Arabic, meaning "lotus fruit," and, from the Hebrew, meaning "roaring stream." HEBREW EQUIVALENT: Arnan.

Arne A variant form of Arnold.

Arni, Arnie Pet forms of Arnold.

Arno A pet form of Arnold.

Arnold From the Old German, meaning "power of an eagle." HEBREW EQUIVALENT: Nesher.

Arnon From the Hebrew, meaning "roaring stream." HEBREW EQUIVALENT: Arnon.

Arnoni A variant form of Arnon.

Arny A pet form of Arnold.

Aron A variant form of Aharon (Aaron).

Arsen From the Greek, meaning "manly, strong." HEBREW EQUIVALENT: Amiram.

Art A pet form of Arthur.

Arthur From the Gaelic, meaning "rock, rocky hill," and the Celtic, meaning "bear." HEBREW EQUIVALENT: Aharon.

Artie A pet form of Arthur.

Arty A pet form of Arthur.

Artza From the Hebrew, meaning "earth, land." HEBREW EQUIVALENT: Artza.

Artzi A variant form of Artza.

Arvid From the Anglo-Saxon, meaning "friend of the people." HEBREW EQUIVALENT: Amitai.

Arvin A variant form of Arvid.

Ary A variant spelling of Ari.

Arye, Aryeh From the Hebrew, meaning "lion." HEBREW EQUIVALENT: Aryei.

Aryel, Aryell Variant spellings of Ariel.

Arzi From the Hebrew, meaning "my cedar." HEBREW EQUIVALENT: Arzi.

Arzon A variant form of Arzi. HEBREW EQUIVALENT: Arzon.

Asa From the Aramaic and Arabic, meaning "create" or "heal." HEBREW EQUIVALENT: Asa.

Asael From the Hebrew, meaning "God created." HEBREW EQUIVALENT: Asael.

Asaf From the Hebrew, meaning "gather." HEBREW EQUIVALENT: Asaf.

Aser A variant spelling of Asher.

Ash From the Old Norse and the Middle English, meaning "tree of the olive family." HEBREW EQUIVALENT: Eshel.

Asher From the Hebrew, meaning "blessed, fortunate, happy." HEBREW EQUIVALENT: Asher.

Ashley From the Old English, meaning "field of ash trees." HEBREW EQUIVALENT: Eshel.

Asie A variant form of Asael. HEBREW EQUIVALENT: Asiel.

Asir From the Arabic, and Aramaic, meaning "bound up, imprisoned." HEBREW EQUIVALENT: Asir.

Asis, Asiss From the Hebrew, meaning "juice." HEBREW EQUIVALENT: Asis.

Asriel From the Hebrew, meaning "prince of God." HEBREW EQUIVALENT: Asriel.

Asser A variant form of Asher.

Assi From the Aramaic, meaning "doctor." HEBREW EQUIVALENT: Assi.

Atar From the Hebrew, meaning "to pray." HEBREW EQUIVALENT: Atar.

Atid From the Hebrew, meaning "the future." HEBREW EQUIVALENT: Atid.

Atir From the Hebrew, meaning "wreath, crown, ornament." HEBREW EQUIVALENT: Atir.

Atzmon From the Hebrew, meaning "strength." HEBREW EQUIVALENT: Atzmon.

Aubrey From the Anglo-Saxon, meaning "[elf] ruler." HEBREW EQUIVALENT: Avraham.

August A variant form of Augustus.

Augustus From the Latin, meaning "revered, exalted." HEBREW EQUIVALENT: Segev.

Aurel From the Latin and French, meaning "gold, golden." HEBREW EQUIVALENT: Ofar.

Austen, Austin Variant Anglicized forms of Augustus.

Av From the Hebrew, meaning "father." HEBREW EQUIVALENT: Av.

Avahu From the Hebrew, meaning "God is my father." HEBREW EQUIVALENT: Avahu.

Avdan From the Hebrew, meaning "father is judge."
HEBREW EQUIVALENT: Avdan.

Averel, Averell From the Anglo-Saxon, meaning "to open,"
connoting springtime. HEBREW EQUIVALENT: Aviv.

Averil, Averill Variant spellings of Averel.

Avery A variant form of Aubrey.

Avi From the Hebrew, meaning "my father." HEBREW
EQUIVALENT: Avi.

Avia A variant spelling of Aviya.

Aviad From the Hebrew, meaning "my father is eternal."
HEBREW EQUIVALENT: Aviad.

Aviah A variant spelling of Avia.

Aviam From the Hebrew, meaning "father of a nation."
HEBREW EQUIVALENT: Aviam.

Aviasaf From the Hebrew, meaning "father of a multitude."
HEBREW EQUIVALENT: Aviasaf.

Aviav From the Hebrew, meaning "grandfather." HEBREW
EQUIVALENT: Aviav.

Aviaz From the Hebrew, meaning "father of strength."
HEBREW EQUIVALENT: Aviaz.

Avichai From the Hebrew, meaning "my father lives."
HEBREW EQUIVALENT: Avichai.

Avicha'yil From the Hebrew, meaning "my father is
strength." HEBREW EQUIVALENT: Avicha'yil.

Avichen From the Hebrew, meaning "father of grace."
HEBREW EQUIVALENT: Avichen.

Avida From the Hebrew, meaning "my father knows."
HEBREW EQUIVALENT: Avida.

Avidan From the Hebrew, meaning "my father is judge."
HEBREW EQUIVALENT: Avidan.

Avideror A variant spelling of Avidror.

Avidor From the Hebrew, meaning "father of a generation."
HEBREW EQUIVALENT: Avidor.

Avidror From the Hebrew, meaning "father of freedom."
HEBREW EQUIVALENT: Avidror.

Aviel From the Hebrew, meaning "my father is God."
HEBREW EQUIVALENT: Aviel.

Aviem From the Hebrew, meaning "grandfather." HEBREW EQUIVALENT: Aviem.

Aviezer From the Hebrew, meaning "God is help, salvation." HEBREW EQUIVALENT: Aviezer.

Avigdor From the Hebrew, meaning "father protector." HEBREW EQUIVALENT: Avigdor.

Avihu From the Hebrew, meaning "he is my father." HEBREW EQUIVALENT: Avihu.

Avimelech From the Hebrew, meaning "my father is the king." HEBREW EQUIVALENT: Avimelech.

Avimi A contraction of *avi immi*, meaning "grandfather." HEBREW EQUIVALENT: Avimi.

Avin The Aramaic form of Av, meaning "father." HEBREW EQUIVALENT: Avin.

Avina From the Aramaic, meaning "father." HEBREW EQUIVALENT: Avina.

Avinadav From the Hebrew, meaning "my father is noble." HEBREW EQUIVALENT: Avinadav.

Avinatan From the Hebrew, meaning "my father's [God's] gift." HEBREW EQUIVALENT: Avinatan.

Avinoam From the Hebrew, meaning "father of delight." HEBREW EQUIVALENT: Avinoam.

Avira From the Aramaic, meaning "air, atmosphere, spirit." HEBREW EQUIVALENT: Avira.

Aviram From the Hebrew, meaning "my father is mighty." HEBREW EQUIVALENT: Aviram.

Aviran From the Hebrew, meaning "father of joy." HEBREW EQUIVALENT: Aviran.

Aviri From the Hebrew, meaning "air, atmosphere." HEBREW EQUIVALENT: Aviri.

Avishai, Avishay From the Hebrew, meaning "father's gift." HEBREW EQUIVALENT: Avishai.

Avital From the Hebrew, meaning "father of dew." HEBREW EQUIVALENT: Avital.

Avitul A variant form of Avital. HEBREW EQUIVALENT: Avitul.

Avitus From the Latin, meaning "bird." HEBREW EQUIVALENT: A'ya.

Avituv From the Hebrew, meaning "father of goodness."
HEBREW EQUIVALENT: Avituv.

Aviur From the Hebrew, meaning "father of fire." HEBREW
EQUIVALENT: Aviur.

Aviv From the Hebrew, meaning "spring, springtime."
HEBREW EQUIVALENT: Aviv.

Avivi From the Hebrew, meaning "springlike, springtime."
HEBREW EQUIVALENT: Avivi.

Aviya From the Hebrew, meaning "God is my father."
HEBREW EQUIVALENT: Aviya.

Avner From the Hebrew, meaning "father's candle." HEBREW
EQUIVALENT: Avner.

Avniel From the Hebrew, meaning "God is my rock."
HEBREW EQUIVALENT: Avniel.

Avraham From the Hebrew, meaning "father of a mighty
nation." HEBREW EQUIVALENT: Avraham.

Avram Avraham's original name. HEBREW EQUIVALENT:
Avram.

Avrohom A variant spelling of Avraham.

Avrom A variant Yiddish form of Avraham.

Avron From the Hebrew, meaning "father of song." HEBREW
EQUIVALENT: Avron.

Avrum A variant Yiddish form of Avraham.

Avrumi A pet form of Avrum.

Avshalom From the Hebrew, meaning "father of peace."
HEBREW EQUIVALENT: Avshalom.

Axel, Axtel Swedish names of Germanic origin, meaning
"divine source of life." HEBREW EQUIVALENT: Amichai.

Ayal From the Hebrew, meaning "ram." HEBREW
EQUIVALENT: A'yal.

Ayali From the Hebrew, meaning "my ram." HEBREW
EQUIVALENT: A'yali.

Az From the Hebrew, meaning "strong." HEBREW
EQUIVALENT: Az.

Azan From the Hebrew, meaning "strength." HEBREW
EQUIVALENT: Azan.

Azarya, Azaryahu From the Hebrew, meaning "the help of God." HEBREW EQUIVALENT: Azarya.

Azaz From the Hebrew, meaning strength. HEBREW EQUIVALENT: Azaz.

Azi From the Hebrew, meaning "strength." HEBREW EQUIVALENT: Azi.

Aziel From the Hebrew, meaning "God is my strength." HEBREW EQUIVALENT: Aziel.

Aziz From the Hebrew, meaning "strength." HEBREW EQUIVALENT: Aziz.

Azriel From the Hebrew, meaning "God is my help." HEBREW EQUIVALENT: Azriel.

Azzy A pet form of Azarya or Azriel.

Baba A variant spelling of Bava.

Baldwin From the Middle High German, meaning "bold friend." HEBREW EQUIVALENT: Bildad.

Banet A short form of Barnett and Benedict.

Bani From the Aramaic, meaning "son" or "build." HEBREW EQUIVALENT: Bani.

Barak From the Hebrew, meaning "flash of light." HEBREW EQUIVALENT: Barak.

Baram From the Aramaic, meaning "son of the nation." HEBREW EQUIVALENT: Baram.

Bard From the Gaelic and Irish, meaning "minstrel" or "poet." HEBREW EQUIVALENT: Amiron.

Bari A variant spelling of Barrie.

Barker From the Old English, meaning "logger of birch trees." HEBREW EQUIVALENT: Bar-Ilan.

Barnaby From the Aramaic, meaning "speech." HEBREW
EQUIVALENT: Amarya.

Barnard The French form of Bernard.

Barnet, Barnett Variant forms of Bernard.

Barney A pet form of Bernard or Barnaby.

Barr, Barre A short form of Bernard and Barnard.

Barret, Barrett A short form of Barnet.

Barri, Barrie Variant spellings of Barry

Barry A Welsh patronymic form of Harry. Also, a pet form
of Baruch. HEBREW EQUIVALENT: Baruch.

Bart A pet form of Barton and Bartholomew.

Barth A pet form of Bartholomew.

Bartholomew From the Greek and Aramaic, meaning "son
of Talmai."

Bartlet, Bartlett Variant forms of Bartholomew.

Barton From the Anglo-Saxon, meaning "barley town."
HEBREW EQUIVALENT: Dagan.

Baruch From the Hebrew, meaning "blessed." HEBREW
EQUIVALENT: Baruch.

Barzilai From the Aramaic, meaning "man of iron." HEBREW
EQUIVALENT: Barzilai.

Basil From the Greek, meaning "royal, kingly." HEBREW
EQUIVALENT: Avimelech.

Bava From the Aramaic, meaning "gate." HEBREW
EQUIVALENT: Bava.

Bazak From the Hebrew, meaning "flash of light." HEBREW
EQUIVALENT: Bazak.

Bear From the German name Baer, meaning "bear." HEBREW
EQUIVALENT: Dov.

Beau From the Latin and French, meaning "pretty,
handsome." HEBREW EQUIVALENT: Adin.

Beck From the Middle English and Old Norse, meaning
"brook." HEBREW EQUIVALENT: Beri.

Bede From the Middle English, meaning "prayer." HEBREW
EQUIVALENT: Paliel.

Bedell From the Old French, meaning "messenger." HEBREW
EQUIVALENT: Malach.

Beebe From the Anglo-Saxon, meaning "one who lives on a bee farm." HEBREW EQUIVALENT: Bustana'i.

Bell From the Latin and French, meaning "beautiful." HEBREW EQUIVALENT: Kalil.

Bellamy From the Latin and French, meaning "beautiful friend." HEBREW EQUIVALENT: Avinoam.

Ben From the Hebrew, meaning "son." HEBREW EQUIVALENT: Ben.

Ben-Ami From the Hebrew, meaning "son of my people." HEBREW EQUIVALENT: Ben-Ami.

Benedict From the Latin, meaning "blessed." HEBREW EQUIVALENT: Baruch.

Benesh The Yiddish form of Benedict.

Ben-Gurion From the Hebrew, meaning "son of the lion." HEBREW EQUIVALENT: Ben-Guryon.

Benish A Yiddish form of Benedict.

Benjamin The Anglicized form of Binyamin.

Bennet, Bennett Variant English forms of the Latin Benedict.

Benor, Ben-Or From the Hebrew, meaning "son of light." HEBREW EQUIVALENT: Benor.

Benroy From the Gaelic and French, meaning "royal mountain." HEBREW EQUIVALENT: Harel.

Benson A variant form of Ben-Tziyon.

Bentley From the Old English, meaning "meadows of grass." HEBREW EQUIVALENT: Yarden.

Benton From the Old English, meaning "Ben's town."

Bentzi A pet form of Ben-Tziyon and Binyamin.

Ben-Tziyon From the Hebrew, meaning "excellence" or "son of Zion." HEBREW EQUIVALENT: Ben-Tziyon.

Benzecry A patronymic form, meaning "son of Zechariah."

Benzi A pet form of Ben Zion.

Ben Zion A variant spelling of Ben-Tziyon.

Ber A Yiddish name from the German name Baer, meaning "bear." HEBREW EQUIVALENT: Dov.

Berg From the German, meaning "mountain." HEBREW EQUIVALENT: Haran.

Bergen From the German, meaning "one who lives on a mountain." HEBREW EQUIVALENT: Aharon.

Berger A variant form of Burgess.

Beril A variant spelling of Beryl.

Berish A variant Yiddish form of Ber.

Berk, Berke Variant spellings of Burk.

Berkeley, Berkley, Berkly From the Anglo-Saxon, meaning "from the birch meadow." HEBREW EQUIVALENT: Bar-Ilan.

Berlin, Berlyn From the German, meaning "boundary line." HEBREW EQUIVALENT: Galil.

Bern, Berna From the German, meaning "bear." HEBREW EQUIVALENT: Dubi.

Bernard From the Old High German, meaning "bold as a bear." HEBREW EQUIVALENT: Barzilai.

Bernd, Berndt Variant forms of Bernard.

Bernhard, Bernhardt Variant German forms of Bernard.

Berni, Bernie Pet forms of Bernard.

Bert, Bertie Pet form of Albert.

Berthold From the German, meaning "bright." HEBREW EQUIVALENT: Barak.

Bertol, Bertold Variant forms of Berthold.

Berton A variant form of Berthold.

Bertram From the Old High German, meaning "bright, illustrious one." HEBREW EQUIVALENT: Bazak.

Bertran A variant form of Bertram.

Bertrand A variant form of Bertram.

Bertrem A variant spelling of Bertram.

Berwin From the Anglo-Saxon, meaning "powerful friend." HEBREW EQUIVALENT: Regem.

Beryl From the Yiddish, meaning "bear." HEBREW EQUIVALENT: Dov.

Betzalel From the Hebrew, meaning "shadow of God," signifying God's protection. HEBREW EQUIVALENT: Betzalel.

Beverley, Beverly From the Old English, meaning "beaver meadow." HEBREW EQUIVALENT: Carmel.

Bezalel A variant spelling of Betzalel.

Bibi A pet form of Binyamin.

Bichri From the Hebrew, meaning "my eldest." HEBREW
EQUIVALENT: Bichri.

Bildad From the Hebrew, meaning "Baal has loved."
HEBREW EQUIVALENT: Bildad.

Bilga, Bilgah From the Hebrew, meaning "joy, cheer."
HEBREW EQUIVALENT: Bilga.

Bilgai From the Arabic and Aramaic meaning "joy,
cheerfulness." HEBREW EQUIVALENT: Bilgai.

Bilguy A variant spelling of Bilgai.

Bil, Bill, Billie, Billy, Billye Pet forms of William.

Bin A pet form of Binyamin.

Binyamin From the Hebrew, meaning "son of my right
hand." HEBREW EQUIVALENT: Binyamin.

Binyomin A variant spelling of Binyamin.

Bird From the Anglo-Saxon, meaning "bird." HEBREW
EQUIVALENT: Tzipor.

Birk A variant form of Barker.

Blaine From the Old English, meaning "the source of a
river." HEBREW EQUIVALENT: Beri.

Blake From the Anglo-Saxon, meaning "to whiten." HEBREW
EQUIVALENT: Lavan.

Blanchard A variant form of Blake.

Boaz From the Hebrew, meaning "strength," or "swiftness."
HEBREW EQUIVALENT: Boaz.

Bo, Bobbie, Bobby Pet forms of Robert.

Bonesh From the Yiddish, meaning "good." HEBREW
EQUIVALENT: Ben-Tovim.

Boni From the Italian, meaning "good."

Boniface From the Latin, meaning "well-doer." HEBREW
EQUIVALENT: Toviel.

Booker From the Anglo-Saxon, meaning "beech tree."
HEBREW EQUIVALENT: Bar-Ilan.

Boone From the Latin and the Old French, meaning
"good." HEBREW EQUIVALENT: Tuviya.

Borg From the Old Norse, meaning "castle." HEBREW
EQUIVALENT: Armon.

Boris From the Russian, meaning "warrior." HEBREW EQUIVALENT: Ben-Cha'yil.

Boruch A variant spelling of Baruch.

Bowen A Celtic patronymic, meaning "son [or descendant] of Owen." HEBREW EQUIVALENT: Ben-Guryon.

Boyd From the Slavic, meaning "fighting warrior." HEBREW EQUIVALENT: Ben-Cha'yil.

Brad A pet form of Braden and Bradley.

Braden From the Old English, meaning "broad, wide." HEBREW EQUIVALENT: Rechavam.

Bradford From the Anglo-Saxon, meaning "broad ford." HEBREW EQUIVALENT: Rechavya.

Bradley From the Old English, meaning "broad lea, meadow." HEBREW EQUIVALENT: Rechavam.

Brady From the Anglo-Saxon, meaning "broad island." HEBREW EQUIVALENT: Rechavya.

Brahm, Bram Short forms of Abram.

Bran From the Irish, meaning "raven." HEBREW EQUIVALENT: Orev.

Branch From the Late Latin, meaning "an extension from the tree trunk." HEBREW EQUIVALENT: Bar-Ilan.

Brand A variant form of Bran.

Brandon A variant form of Brand.

Brandt A variant form of Brand.

Bremel, Breml Yiddish pet forms of Avraham.

Brian From the Celtic and Gaelic, meaning "strength." HEBREW EQUIVALENT: Abir.

Briand From the French, meaning "castle." HEBREW EQUIVALENT: Armoni.

Brock From the Anglo-Saxon meaning "grain dealer." HEBREW EQUIVALENT: Dagan.

Broderick A name compounded from Brad and Richard.

Bromley From the Anglo-Saxon, meaning "meadow." HEBREW EQUIVALENT: Nir.

Brook, Brooke From the Old English, meaning "stream." HEBREW EQUIVALENT: Arnon.

Bruce A Scottish name of French origin, probably meaning "woods, thicket." HEBREW EQUIVALENT: Artzi.

Bruno From the German, meaning "fountain." HEBREW EQUIVALENT: Arnon.

Bry A pet from of Bryan.

Bryan, Bryant Variant forms of Brian.

Bubba From the German, meaning "boy." HEBREW EQUIVALENT: Ben.

Buck From the Anglo-Saxon and German, meaning "male deer." HEBREW EQUIVALENT: Tzevi.

Bucky A pet form of Buck.

Bud, Budd From the Old English, meaning "messenger." HEBREW EQUIVALENT: Calev.

Buddy A pet form of Budd.

Buell A variant spelling of the British *bul*, meaning "bull." HEBREW EQUIVALENT: Arad.

Buki From the Hebrew, meaning "bottle." HEBREW EQUIVALENT: Buki.

Buna From the Hebrew, meaning "knowledge, understanding." HEBREW EQUIVALENT: Buna.

Buni, Bunni From the Hebrew, meaning "built, constructed." HEBREW EQUIVALENT: Buni.

Bunim From the Yiddish, meaning "good." HEBREW EQUIVALENT: Ben-Tov.

Burdette From the Middle English, meaning "small bird." HEBREW EQUIVALENT: Efron.

Burgess From the Middle English and Old French, meaning "shopkeeper [signifying a free man]." HEBREW EQUIVALENT: Avidror.

Burk, Burke Old English forms of the German name Burg, meaning "castle." HEBREW EQUIVALENT: Armon.

Burl, Burle From the Latin, meaning "coarse hair." HEBREW EQUIVALENT: Anuv.

Burleigh From the Old English, meaning "field with burr-covered plants." HEBREW EQUIVALENT: Avgar.

Burley A variant spelling of Burleigh.

Burr A short form of Burleigh.

Burt, Burte Either a form of Burton or from the Anglo-Saxon, meaning "bright, excellent." HEBREW EQUIVALENT: Ben-Tzion.

Burton From the Old English, meaning "town on a hill." HEBREW EQUIVALENT: Harel.

Bustan From the Arabic and Hebrew, meaning "garden." HEBREW EQUIVALENT: Bustan.

Byk From the Polish, meaning "ox." HEBREW EQUIVALENT: Shor.

Byrd From the Anglo-Saxon, meaning "bird." HEBREW EQUIVALENT: Tzipor.

Byron From the Old English, meaning "bear." HEBREW EQUIVALENT: Dov.

BEST BABY NAMES   BEST BABY NAMES

Cal A pet form of Caleb.

Calder From the Celtic, meaning "from the stony river." HEBREW EQUIVALENT: Chamat.

Cale A pet form of Caleb.

Caleb, Calev Anglicized spellings of Kalev.

Calvert An Old English occupational name for a herdsman. HEBREW EQUIVALENT: Maron.

Calvin From the Latin, meaning "bald." HEBREW EQUIVALENT: Korach.

Cameron From the Greek, meaning "a vaulted chamber." HEBREW EQUIVALENT: Aron.

Camillus From the Latin, meaning "attendant" or "messenger." HEBREW EQUIVALENT: Kalev.

Capp A variant form of Chaplin.

Carey From the Welsh or Cornish, meaning "rock island." HEBREW EQUIVALENT: Almog.

Carl A variant form of Charles.

Carlton From the Old English, meaning "Carl's town."

Carmel From the Hebrew, meaning "vineyard," or "garden." HEBREW EQUIVALENT: Carmel.

Carmeli From the Hebrew, meaning "my vineyard." HEBREW EQUIVALENT: Carmeli.

Carmen The Spanish form of Carmel.

Carmiel From the Hebrew, meaning "the Lord is my vineyard." HEBREW EQUIVALENT: Carmiel.

Carmine The Italian form of Carmen.

Carney From the Celtic, meaning "fighter." HEBREW EQUIVALENT: Gavriel.

Carol A variant form of Charles.

Caroll Variant spelling of Carol.

Carrol, Carroll Variant forms of Charles.

Carr From the Scandinavian and Old Norse, meaning "marshy land." HEBREW EQUIVALENT: Beri.

Cary A variant form of Carey.

Case From the Old French, meaning "chest, box." HEBREW EQUIVALENT: Aron.

Casey From the Celtic, meaning "valorous." HEBREW EQUIVALENT: Chason.

Cash A short form of Cassius.

Caspar From the German, meaning "imperial." HEBREW EQUIVALENT: Katriel.

Casper A variant spelling of Caspar.

Cecil From the Latin, meaning "blind." EUPHEMISTIC HEBREW EQUIVALENT: Koresh.

Cedric A Welsh name meaning "bountiful." HEBREW EQUIVALENT: Yitro.

Cerf From the French, meaning "hart, deer." HEBREW EQUIVALENT: Tzevi.

Chad From the Celtic, meaning "warrior." HEBREW EQUIVALENT: Ben-Cha'yil.

Chag From the Hebrew, meaning "holiday." HEBREW EQUIVALENT: Chag.

Chagai From the Aramaic and Hebrew, meaning "my festivals." HEBREW EQUIVALENT: Chagai.

Chagi A variant form of Chagai. HEBREW EQUIVALENT: Chagi.

Chai From the Hebrew, meaning "life." HEBREW EQUIVALENT: Chai.

Chaim A variant spelling of Chayim.

Champ From the Latin *campus*, meaning "field, stadium." Also, from the Middle English meaning "gladiator." HEBREW EQUIVALENT: Mordechai.

Champion A variant form of Champ.

Chanan A variant form of Chanina. HEBREW EQUIVALENT: Chanan.

Chancellor From the Middle English and Old French, meaning "secretary." HEBREW EQUIVALENT: Sofer.

Chandler From the French, meaning "candle maker." HEBREW EQUIVALENT: Avner.

Chanina From the Aramaic, meaning "gracious." HEBREW EQUIVALENT: Chanina.

Chanoch From the Hebrew, meaning "dedicated" or "educated." HEBREW EQUIVALENT: Chanoch.

Chaplin From the Middle English, meaning "chaplain." HEBREW EQUIVALENT: Rav.

Chapman From the Middle English, meaning "trader." HEBREW EQUIVALENT: Amal.

Charles A French form of the Anglo-Saxon, meaning "manly, strong." HEBREW EQUIVALENT: Chizkiyahu.

Charley, Charlie Pet forms of Charles.

Charlton A French-German name, meaning "Charles' town."

Charney From the Slavic, meaning "black." HEBREW EQUIVALENT: Pinchas.

Chase From the Old French and Middle English, meaning "hunt." HEBREW EQUIVALENT: Sheva'ya.

Chauncey, Chauncy Pet forms of Chancellor.

Chavakuk From the Assyrian, meaning "garden plant." HEBREW EQUIVALENT: Chavakuk.

Chaviv From the Hebrew, meaning "beloved." HEBREW EQUIVALENT: Chaviv.

Chavivi From the Hebrew, meaning "my beloved" or "my friend." HEBREW EQUIVALENT: Chavivi.

Chayim, Chayyim, Chayym From the Hebrew, meaning "life." HEBREW EQUIVALENT: Cha'yim.

Chemdat From the Hebrew, meaning "desirable, charming." HEBREW EQUIVALENT: Chemdat.

Chen From the Hebrew, meaning "grace, charm." HEBREW EQUIVALENT: Chein.

Chermon From the Hebrew, meaning "consecrated, sacred." HEBREW EQUIVALENT: Chermon.

Chermoni A variant form of Chermon. HEBREW EQUIVALENT: Chermoni.

Chesky A pet form of Yechezkel (Ezekiel).

Chester From the Latin, meaning "fortress" or "camp." HEBREW EQUIVALENT: Chosa.

Chet A pet form of Chester.

Chevy From the British, meaning "hunt, chase." HEBREW EQUIVALENT: Tzedani.

Chia A variant spelling of Chiya.

Chiel From the Hebrew, meaning "God lives." HEBREW EQUIVALENT: Chi'el.

Chilton From the Anglo-Saxon, meaning "town by the river." HEBREW EQUIVALENT: Chamat.

Chiram From the Hebrew, meaning "lofty, exalted." HEBREW EQUIVALENT: Chiram.

Chirom A variant spelling of Chiram (Hiram).

Chiya A short form of Yechiel.

Chizkiya, Chizkiyahu From the Hebrew, meaning "God is my strength." HEBREW EQUIVALENT: Chizkiya.

Choni From the Hebrew, meaning "gracious." HEBREW EQUIVALENT: Choni.

Chovav A variant form of Chovev. HEBREW EQUIVALENT: Chovav.

Chovev From the Hebrew, meaning "friend" or "lover." HEBREW EQUIVALENT: Chovev.

Chur From the Akkadian, meaning "child." HEBREW
EQUIVALENT: Chur.

Churi A variant form of Chur.

Cicero From the Latin, meaning "orator." HEBREW
EQUIVALENT: Amir.

Cid A Spanish name derived from the Arabic, meaning
"lord, sir." HEBREW EQUIVALENT: Chirom.

Cimon A variant spelling of Simon.

Claiborn, Claiborne Compounded from the German and
French, meaning "boundary marked by clovers." HEBREW
EQUIVALENT: Chavakuk.

Clarence From the Latin, meaning "illustrious." HEBREW
EQUIVALENT: Katriel.

Clark, Clarke From the Old English, meaning "clergyman,
scholar." HEBREW EQUIVALENT: Kalev.

Claud, Claude From the French and Latin, meaning
"lame." EUPHEMISTIC HEBREW EQUIVALENT: Ben-Tzevi.

Claudell A variant form of Claude.

Clay From the German and Indo-European, meaning "to
stick together." HEBREW EQUIVALENT: Levi.

Clayton A variant form of Clay, meaning "town built upon
clay." HEBREW EQUIVALENT: Adam.

Clem A pet form of Clement.

Clement From the Latin, meaning "merciful" or "gracious."
HEBREW EQUIVALENT: Chanan.

Cleo A variant spelling of Clio.

Cleon A variant form of Clio.

Cleve A pet form of Cleveland.

Cleveland From the Old English, meaning "land near a
steep waterfall." HEBREW EQUIVALENT: Afek.

Clever From the Old English, meaning "claw, hand."
HEBREW EQUIVALENT: Chofni.

Cliff, Cliffe From the Old English, meaning "steep, bank."
HEBREW EQUIVALENT: Talmai.

Clifford An English local name meaning "crossing near the
cliff." HEBREW EQUIVALENT: Tzuriel.

Clifton From the Old English, meaning "town near the cliff." HEBREW EQUIVALENT: Tzuriel.

Clint A pet form of Clinton.

Clinton From the Anglo-Saxon, meaning "town on a hill." HEBREW EQUIVALENT: Tilon.

Clio From the Greek, meaning "to praise, to acclaim." HEBREW EQUIVALENT: Shevach.

Clive A variant form of Cliff.

Clovis From the Anglo-Saxon and German, meaning "clover." HEBREW EQUIVALENT: Tzemach.

Clyde From the Welsh, meaning "heard from afar." HEBREW EQUIVALENT: Shemuel.

Clydell A variant form of Clyde.

Colby From the Old English and Danish, meaning "coal town." HEBREW EQUIVALENT: Rishpon.

Cole A pet form of Colby or Coleman.

Coleman From the Latin, meaning "dove." HEBREW EQUIVALENT: Yona.

Colin Usually taken as a pet form of Nicholas, meaning "victory." Or from the Celtic, meaning "cub, whelp." HEBREW EQUIVALENT: Kefir.

Colvin From the Middle English, meaning "coal miner." HEBREW EQUIVALENT: Rishpon.

Conan, Conant From the Celtic, meaning "chief, king." HEBREW EQUIVALENT: Katriel.

Conrad From the Old High German, meaning "able counsellor." HEBREW EQUIVALENT: Haskel.

Corbet, Corbett From the Old French and the Middle English, meaning "raven." HEBREW EQUIVALENT: Orev.

Corbin A variant form of Corbet.

Cord A pet form of Cordell.

Cordell From the Latin and Old French, meaning "cord, rope." HEBREW EQUIVALENT: Petil.

Corey A variant spelling of Cory.

Corliss A variant form of Carl.

Cornelius From the Norman-French, meaning "crow." HEBREW EQUIVALENT: Orev.

Corwin, Corwyn From the Latin, meaning "raven." HEBREW
EQUIVALENT: Orev.
Cory From the Anglo-Saxon, meaning "chosen one."
HEBREW EQUIVALENT: Bachir.
Craig From the Celtic and Gaelic, meaning "from the rocky
mass." HEBREW EQUIVALENT: Avitzur.
Crawford From the Old English, meaning "ford or stream
where the crows flock." HEBREW EQUIVALENT: Peleg.
Curt A variant spelling of Kurt.
Cy A pet form of Cyrus.
Cyril From the Greek, meaning, "lord, lordly." HEBREW
EQUIVALENT: Katriel.
Cyrus From the Persian, meaning "sun, brightness." HEBREW
EQUIVALENT: Koresh.

Dab A pet form of David.
Dabbey, Dabby A pet form of David.
Dabney A pet form of David.
Dado A pet form of David.
Dael From the Hebrew, meaning "knowledge of God."
HEBREW EQUIVALENT: Da'el.
Dag From the Danish and German, meaning "day." Also,
from the Hebrew, meaning "fish." HEBREW EQUIVALENT:
Dag.
Dagan From the Hebrew, meaning "grain." HEBREW
EQUIVALENT: Dagan.
Dagul From the Hebrew, meaning "flag, emblem." HEBREW
EQUIVALENT: Dagul.
Dahn A variant spelling of Dan.
Dahvid A variant spelling of David.

Dale From the Old English and the Old Norse, meaning "valley." HEBREW EQUIVALENT: Gai.

Dalin A variant spelling of Dallin.

Dall A variant form of Dale.

Dallin From the Anglo-Saxon, meaning "from the dale, valley."HEBREW EQUIVALENT: Gai.

Dama From the Hebrew and Aramaic, meaning "to resemble." HEBREW EQUIVALENT: Dama.

Damon From the Anglo-Saxon, meaning "day." HEBREW EQUIVALENT: Yom Tov.

Dan From the Hebrew, meaning "judge." HEBREW EQUIVALENT: Dan.

Dana A variant form of Dan.

Dani A variant form of Dan or Daniel.

Daniel From the Hebrew, meaning "God is my judge." HEBREW EQUIVALENT: Daniel.

Danil, Danile, Danilo Variant forms of Daniel.

Dannie, Danny Pet forms of Daniel.

Dar From the Hebrew, meaning "pearl, mother-of-pearl." HEBREW EQUIVALENT: Dar.

Daren A variant form of Darius.

Darian, Darien Variant forms of Darius.

Darin, Darren Variant forms of Darius.

Darius From the Persian, meaning "king" or "rich." HEBREW EQUIVALENT: Daryavesh.

Darlin From the British, meaning "grove of oak trees." HEBREW EQUIVALENT: Eilon.

Daro A variant form of Darrow.

Darold A variant form of Darrell and Darlin.

Darom From the Hebrew, meaning "south." HEBREW EQUIVALENT: Darom.

Darrel, Darrell From the Anglo-Saxon, meaning "dear, darling." HEBREW EQUIVALENT: Eldad.

Darren From the British, meaning "small, rocky hill." HEBREW EQUIVALENT: Harel.

Darrol, Darroll Variant forms of Darrell.

Darrow From the Old English, meaning "spear." HEBREW EQUIVALENT: Siryon.

Darry A pet form of Darren. Also, from the French, meaning "from Harry."

Darryl A variant form of Darren.

Darwin From the British and Anglo-Saxon, meaning "lover of the sea." HEBREW EQUIVALENT: Dalfon.

Daryl, Daryle Variant spellings of Darrell.

Datan From the Hebrew, meaning "law." HEBREW EQUIVALENT: Datan.

Daoud, Daud The Arabic form of David.

Dave A pet form of David.

Davey A pet form of David.

Davi A pet form of David.

David From the Hebrew, meaning "beloved." HEBREW EQUIVALENT: David.

Davie A pet form of David.

Daviel A variant form of David.

Davis A patronymic form of David, meaning "son of David." HEBREW EQUIVALENT: Ben-David.

Davy A pet form of David.

Davyd A variant spelling of David.

Daw, Dawe From the Old English, meaning "doe." HEBREW EQUIVALENT: Tzevi.

Dawson A patronymic form, meaning "son of David."

Dean, Deane From the Old French, meaning "head, leader." HEBREW EQUIVALENT: Rosh.

Dekel From the Arabic and Hebrew, meaning "palm (date) tree." HEBREW EQUIVALENT: Dekel.

Delano From the Erse, meaning "healthy, dark man." HEBREW EQUIVALENT: Kedar.

Demetrius From the Greek, meaning "lover of the earth." HEBREW EQUIVALENT: Adam.

Denis The French form of the Greek name Dionysius, the god of wine and revelry. HEBREW EQUIVALENT: Anav.

Dennis A variant spelling of Denis.

Deno An Italian form of Dean.

Denys A variant spelling of Denis.

Derek An English form of the Old High German name Hrodrich, meaning "famous." HEBREW EQUIVALENT: Hillel.

Derel A variant form of Darlin.

Deror From the Hebrew, meaning "a bird [swallow]" or "free, freedom." HEBREW EQUIVALENT: Deror.

Derori A variant form of Deror. HEBREW EQUIVALENT: Derori.

Derorli, Deror-Li From the Hebrew, meaning "I am free." HEBREW EQUIVALENT: Derorli.

Derry From the British, meaning "oak tree." HEBREW EQUIVALENT: Alon.

Desi A pet form of Desiderio.

Desiderio From the Latin, meaning "desire." HEBREW EQUIVALENT: Chemdan.

Desmond From the French and Latin, meaning "mankind." HEBREW EQUIVALENT: Adam.

Deuel From the Hebrew, meaning "knowledge of God." HEBREW EQUIVALENT: De'uel.

Devir From the Hebrew, meaning "sanctuary." HEBREW EQUIVALENT: Devir.

Devlin An Irish form of David.

Dewey A Welsh form of David.

Diamond From the Latin and Greek, meaning "precious stone." HEBREW EQUIVALENT: Chamadel.

Dick, Dickey, Dickie, Dicky Pet forms of Richard.

Didi From the Hebrew, meaning "beloved." HEBREW EQUIVALENT: Didi.

Dimitry A variant form of Demetrius.

Dirk An English form of the Old High German name Hrodrich, meaning "famous." HEBREW EQUIVALENT: Yehuda.

Divri From the Hebrew, meaning "orator." HEBREW EQUIVALENT: Divri.

Dixon A patronymic form of Richard, meaning "Richard's [Dick's] son."

Dob A variant form of Robert.

Dodic, Dodick Pet forms of David.

Dodo From the Hebrew, meaning "his beloved" or "his uncle." HEBREW EQUIVALENT: Dodo.

Dodya A pet form of David.

Doeg From the Hebrew, meaning "anxious, concerned." HEBREW EQUIVALENT: Do'eg.

Dolph A short form of Adolph.

Dom A pet form of Dominic.

Dominic, Dominick From the Latin, meaning "pertaining to God." HEBREW EQUIVALENT: De'uel.

Don A pet form of Donald.

Donald From the Scottish, meaning "proud ruler." HEBREW EQUIVALENT: Adoniya.

Donnie, Donny Pet forms of Donald.

Donniel A variant spelling of Daniel.

Dor From the Hebrew, meaning "generation." HEBREW EQUIVALENT: Dor.

Doran From the Hebrew and Greek, meaning "gift." HEBREW EQUIVALENT: Doran.

Dore From the Greek, meaning "gift." HEBREW EQUIVALENT: Doran.

Dori A variant form of Dor, meaning "my generation." HEBREW EQUIVALENT: Dori.

Doron From the Hebrew, meaning "gift, present." HEBREW EQUIVALENT: Doron.

Dorris The masculine form of the feminine Doris.

Dotan From the Hebrew, meaning "law." HEBREW EQUIVALENT: Dotan.

Dothan An Anglicized form of Dotan.

Doug A short form of Douglas.

Douglas From the Gaelic, meaning "black stream." HEBREW EQUIVALENT: Adar.

Dov From the Hebrew, meaning "bear." HEBREW EQUIVALENT: Dov.

Dovev From the Hebrew, meaning "to speak, whisper." HEBREW EQUIVALENT: Dovev.

Dovid A variant spelling of David.

Drew A pet form of Andrew.

Dror A variant form of Deror.

Drori A variant spelling of Derori.

Drory A variant spelling of Derori.

Dru A variant spelling of Drew.

Duane A variant form of Wayne.

Duber A variant form of David.

Dubi From the Hebrew, meaning "my bear." HEBREW EQUIVALENT: Dubi.

Dudi A pet form of David.

Duddy A pet form of David.

Dudley From the Old English, meaning "Dodd's meadow [lea]." HEBREW EQUIVALENT: Admata.

Dudu A pet form of David. HEBREW EQUIVALENT: Dudu.

Duff From the Celtic, meaning "dark, black-faced." HEBREW EQUIVALENT: Kedar.

Duke From the Latin, meaning "leader." HEBREW EQUIVALENT: Aluf.

Duma From the Hebrew, meaning "slience." HEBREW EQUIVALENT: Duma.

Duncan From the Celtic, meaning "warrior with dark skin." HEBREW EQUIVALENT: Chumi.

Dunn, Dunne From the Old English, meaning "brown." HEBREW EQUIVALENT: Chum.

Dunstan From the Old English, meaning "brown, rock quarry." HEBREW EQUIVALENT: Sela.

Dur From the Hebrew, meaning "to heap, pile up" or "to circle." Also, from the Old English, meaning "wild animal, deer." HEBREW EQUIVALENT: Dur.

Durand The French form of the Latin, meaning "enduring." HEBREW EQUIVALENT: Notzer.

Durant, Durante Variant Italian forms of Durand.

Duriel From the Hebrew, meaning "God is my dwelling place." HEBREW EQUIVALENT: Duriel.

Durk A variant spelling of Dirk.

Duryea From the Latin, meaning "enduring, eternal." HEBREW EQUIVALENT: Amiad.

Dustin A variant form of Dunstan.

Dusty A pet form of Dustin.

Dwight From the Anglo-Saxon, meaning "white, fair."
HEBREW EQUIVALENT: Lavan.

Dyck A variant spelling of Dick.

Dyke, Dykes Variant spellings of Dick and Dix.

Dylan From the Welsh, meaning "sea." HEBREW EQUIVALENT:
Moshe.

BEST BABY NAMES BEST BABY NAMES

Earl, Earle From the Middle English, meaning "nobleman,
intelligent." HEBREW EQUIVALENT: Maskil.

Eban A variant form of Even.

Ebin A variant form of Even.

Ebril A Yiddish form of Abraham.

Ed A pet form of Edward.

Edan From the Celtic, meaning "fire, flame." HEBREW
EQUIVALENT: Lapid.

Edd, Eddie Pet forms of Edward.

Eddy From the Middle English, meaning "whirlpool" or
"energetic." HEBREW EQUIVALENT: Arnon.

Eden From the Hebrew, meaning "delight." HEBREW
EQUIVALENT: Eden (Ayden).

Eder From the Hebrew, meaning "herd, flock." HEBREW
EQUIVALENT: Eder (Ayder).

Edgar From the Anglo-Saxon, meaning "happy, blessed
warrior." HEBREW EQUIVALENT: Baruch.

Edison A patronymic form, meaning "son of Ed [Edward]."

Edlow From the Old English, meaning "fruitful hill."
HEBREW EQUIVALENT: Efra'yim.

Edmond From the Anglo-Saxon, meaning "rich, fortunate."
HEBREW EQUIVALENT: Asher.

Edmund A variant spelling of Edmond.

Edri From the Hebrew, meaning "my flock." HEBREW
EQUIVALENT: Edri.

Edric From the Anglo-Saxon, meaning "rich ruler." HEBREW
EQUIVALENT: Elrad.

Edsel From the Anglo-Saxon, meaning "rich, prosperous."
HEBREW EQUIVALENT: Ashir.

Edson A patronymic form, meaning "son of Ed [Edward]."

Edward From the Anglo-Saxon, meaning "blessed, happy
guardian." HEBREW EQUIVALENT: Avigdor.

Edwin From the Anglo-Saxon, meaning "happy, blessed
friend." HEBREW EQUIVALENT: David.

Edy A variant spelling of Eddy.

Effie A pet form of Ephraim.

Effron A variant spelling of Efron.

Efraim A variant spelling of Efra'yim.

Efrat From the Hebrew, meaning "honored, distinguished."
HEBREW EQUIVALENT: Efrat.

Efra'yim From the Hebrew, meaning "fruitful." HEBREW
EQUIVALENT: Efra'yim.

Efrem A variant form of Efra'yim.

Efron From the Hebrew, meaning "bird." HEBREW
EQUIVALENT: Efron.

Efry A variant form of Ephraim.

Egan From the Anglo-Saxon, meaning "formidable, strong."
HEBREW EQUIVALENT: Gibor.

Egon A variant spelling of Egan.

Egoz From the Hebrew, meaning "nut." HEBREW
EQUIVALENT: Egoz.

Egron From the Hebrew, meaning "lexicon." HEBREW
EQUIVALENT: Egron.

Eilon From the Hebrew, meaning "oak tree." HEBREW
EQUIVALENT: Eilon.

Eitan From the Hebrew, meaning "strong, firm,
permanent." HEBREW EQUIVALENT: Eitan.

Elad From the Hebrew, meaning "forever, eternal." HEBREW EQUIVALENT: Elad.

Elan A variant spelling of Ilan.

Elazar From the Hebrew, meaning "God has helped." HEBREW EQUIVALENT: Elazar.

Elbert A variant form of Albert.

Elbie A pet form of Elbert.

Eldad From the Hebrew, meaning "beloved of God." HEBREW EQUIVALENT: Eldad.

Eldar From the Hebrew, meaning "habitation of God." HEBREW EQUIVALENT: Eldar.

Elden From the Anglo-Saxon, meaning "older." HEBREW EQUIVALENT: Kedem.

Elder From the Old English, meaning "old, older."

Eleazar A variant spelling of Elazar.

Elex A variant form of Alex.

Elford From the Old English, meaning "the old river crossing." HEBREW EQUIVALENT: Beri.

Elgin From the the Old English, meaning "true nobility." HEBREW EQUIVALENT: Yisrael.

Eli From the Hebrew, meaning "ascend" or "uplift." HEBREW EQUIVALENT: Eli.

Elia A variant form of Elijah.

Eliad From the Hebrew, meaning "my God is eternal." HEBREW EQUIVALENT: Eliad.

Eliah A variant form of Eliyahu.

Eliahu A variant form of Eliyahu.

Elias The Greek form of Elijah.

Eliata From the Aramaic, meaning "my God has come." HEBREW EQUIVALENT: Eliata.

Eliav From the Hebrew, meaning "my God is [my] Father." HEBREW EQUIVALENT: Eliav.

Eliaz From the Hebrew, meaning "my God is strong." HEBREW EQUIVALENT: Eliaz.

Elidad From the Hebrew, meaning "my God is a friend." HEBREW EQUIVALENT: Elidad.

Elie A pet form of Eliyahu.

Eliezer A variant form of Elazar. From the Hebrew, meaning "my God has helped." HEBREW EQUIVALENT: Eliezer.

Elihu A variant form of Eliyahu. HEBREW EQUIVALENT: Elihu.

Elijah The Anglicized form of Eliyahu.

Elika A variant form of Elyakim.

Elio A Spanish form of Elijah.

Elior From the Hebrew, meaning "my God is light." HEBREW EQUIVALENT: Elior.

Eliot A variant form of Elijah.

Eliram From the Hebrew, meaning "my God is mighty." HEBREW EQUIVALENT: Eliram.

Eliraz From the Hebrew, meaning "my God is joy." HEBREW EQUIVALENT: Eliraz.

Elisha From the Hebrew, meaning "my God is salvation." HEBREW EQUIVALENT: Elisha.

Elison A variant spelling of Ellison.

Eliya A short form of Eliyahu.

Eliyahu From the Hebrew, meaning "the Lord is my God." HEBREW EQUIVALENT: Eliyahu.

Elkan A pet form of Elkanah.

Elkana, Elkanah From the Hebrew, meaning "God has acquired." HEBREW EQUIVALENT: Elkana.

Elkin A variant spelling of Elkan.

Ellery From the Old English, meaning "alder tree." HEBREW EQUIVALENT: Ilan.

Elliot, Elliott A variant spelling of Eliot.

Ellis A variant form of Elisha.

Ellison A patronymic form, meaning "son of Elijah."

Elly A pet form of Elijah.

Elmer From the Old English, meaning "noble, famous." HEBREW EQUIVALENT: Mehalalel.

Elmo A variant form of Elmer.

Elmor, Elmore Variant forms of Elmer.

Elnatan From the Hebrew, meaning "gift of God." HEBREW EQUIVALENT: Elnatan.

Elon From the Hebrew, meaning "oak tree." HEBREW EQUIVALENT: Eilon.

Elrad From the Hebrew, meaning "God is the ruler." HEBREW EQUIVALENT: Elrad.

Elroy From the Latin, meaning "royal, king." HEBREW EQUIVALENT: Malkiel.

Elsen A patronymic form, meaning "son of Elias."

Elvin From the Anglo-Saxon, meaning "godly friend." HEBREW EQUIVALENT: Eldad.

Elwin, Elwyn Variant forms of Elvin.

Ely A pet form of Eliyahu.

Elyakim From the Hebrew, meaning "God will establish." HEBREW EQUIVALENT: Elyakim.

Elyakum A variant form of Elyakim. HEBREW EQUIVALENT: Elyakum.

Emanuel From the Hebrew, meaning "God is with us." HEBREW EQUIVALENT: Imanuel.

Emerson A patronymic form, meaning "son of Emery."

Emery From the Old High German, meaning "industrious." HEBREW EQUIVALENT: Mahir.

Emil From the Latin, meaning "industrious." HEBREW EQUIVALENT: Yaziz.

Emile A French form of Emil.

Emmanuel A variant spelling of Emanuel.

Emmet, Emmett From the Hebrew, meaning, "truth." HEBREW EQUIVALENT: Emmet.

Emory A variant spelling of Emery.

Ennis A short form of Denis.

Enoch An Anglicized form of the Hebrew Chanoch, meaning "educated" or "dedicated." HEBREW EQUIVALENT: Chanoch.

Enosh From the Hebrew, meaning "man." HEBREW EQUIVALENT: Enosh.

Ephraim A variant spelling of Efra'yim.

Er From the Hebrew, meaning "awake." HEBREW EQUIVALENT: Er.

Eran From the Hebrew, meaning "industrious." HEBREW EQUIVALENT: Eran.

Erel From the Hebrew, meaning "I will see God." HEBREW EQUIVALENT: Erel.

Erez From the Hebrew, meaning "cedar tree." HEBREW EQUIVALENT: Erez.

Eri From the Hebrew, meaning "my guardian." HEBREW EQUIVALENT: Eri.

Eric, Erich From the Old Norse, meaning "honorable ruler." HEBREW EQUIVALENT: Eliram.

Erik A variant spelling of Eric.

Ernest From the Old High German, meaning "earnest, sincere." HEBREW EQUIVALENT: Amitai.

Ernie A pet form of Ernest.

Erno A Hungarian form of Ernest.

Ernst A variant form of Ernest.

Errol From the Latin, meaning "wanderer." HEBREW EQUIVALENT: Gershom.

Erv A variant spelling of Irv (Irving).

Erve A short form of Ervin.

Ervin A German form of Irvin.

Erwin A variant form of Ervin.

Eryk A variant speeling of Eric.

Eryle A variant spelling of Errol.

Eshel From the Hebrew, meaning "[tamarisk] tree." HEBREW EQUIVALENT: Eshel.

Eshkol From the Hebrew, meaning "cluster of grapes." HEBREW EQUIVALENT: Eshkol.

Esmond From the Anglo-Saxon, meaning "gracious protector." HEBREW EQUIVALENT: Chasun.

Esmund A variant spelling of Esmond.

Etan A variant spelling of Eitan.

Ethan An Anglicized spelling of Eitan.

Eugen A variant form of Eugene.

Eugene From the Greek, meaning "well-born, of noble descent." HEBREW EQUIVALENT: Yehoram.

Evan A Welsh form of John, meaning "gracious." HEBREW
EQUIVALENT: Yochanan.

Evander A variant form of Evan.

Evans A patronymic form of Evan.

Even From the Hebrew, meaning "stone." HEBREW
EQUIVALENT: Even.

Everett, Everette From the Norse, meaning "warrior."
HEBREW EQUIVALENT: Avicha'yil.

Evril A Yiddish form of Avraham.

Evron From the Hebrew, meaning "overflowing anger."
HEBREW EQUIVALENT: Evron.

Ewen A variant form of Evan, the Welsh form of John.

Eyal A variant spelling of A'yal.

Eytan A variant spelling of Eitan.

Ezekiel From the Hebrew, meaning "God will strengthen."
HEBREW EQUIVALENT: Yechezkel.

Ezer From the Hebrew, meaning "help." HEBREW
EQUIVALENT: Ezer.

Ezra From the Hebrew, meaning "help." HEBREW
EQUIVALENT: Ezra.

Ezri From the Hebrew, meaning "my help." HEBREW
EQUIVALENT: Ezri.

Ezriel A variant form of Azriel

BEST BABY NAMES   BEST BABY NAMES

Fabian A variant form of Fabius.

Fabius From the Latin, meaning "bean farmer." HEBREW
EQUIVALENT: Adam.

Farleigh, Fairley, Farley From the Anglo-Saxon, meaning
"beautiful meadow." HEBREW EQUIVALENT: Shifron.

Farrel, Farrell From the Celtic, meaning "valorous one." HEBREW EQUIVALENT: Abir.

Feibush A variant form of Feivel.

Feivel The Yiddish form of Phoebus, from the Greek, meaning "bright one." HEBREW EQUIVALENT: Avner.

Feiwel A variant spelling of Feivel.

Felix From the Latin, meaning "happy, fortunate, prosperous." HEBREW EQUIVALENT: Yitzchak.

Ferd, Ferde A short form of Ferdinand.

Ferdie A pet form of Ferd.

Ferdinand From the German, meaning "courageous." HEBREW EQUIVALENT: Abir.

Ferdy A pet form of Ferd.

Fergus From the Irish and Gaelic, meaning "manly." HEBREW EQUIVALENT: Ben-Gever.

Ferrin A variant form of Ferris.

Ferris From the Latin, meaning "iron." HEBREW EQUIVALENT: Barzilai.

Fish From the German, meaning "fish." HEBREW EQUIVALENT: Dag.

Fishel A Yiddish pet form of Fish.

Fishke A Yiddish pet form of Fish.

Fishkin A Slavic form of Fish.

Fishlin A pet form of Fish.

Fisk, Fiske From the Scandinavian, meaning "fish." HEBREW EQUIVALENT: Dag .

Floren, Florence, Florentz, Florenz From the Latin, meaning "blooming." HEBREW EQUIVALENT: Tzemach.

Floyd A corrupt form of Lloyd.

Forest, Forrest From the Latin, meaning "woods." HEBREW EQUIVALENT: Ya'ar.

Forester An Old French occupational name, meaning "one in charge of a forest." HEBREW EQUIVALENT: Yaari.

Fox From the German, meaning "fox." HEBREW EQUIVALENT: Shual.

Francis From the Middle English, meaning "a free man." HEBREW EQUIVALENT: Deror.

Frank A pet form of Francis and Franklin.

Frankie A pet form of Frank.

Franklin From the Old English, meaning "freeholder."
    HEBREW EQUIVALENT: Konen.

Franklyn A variant spelling of Franklin.

Franz The German form of Francis.

Fred, Freddie, Freddy Pet forms of Frederick.

Frederic A variant spelling of Frederick.

Frederick From the Latin and Old High German, meaning
    "peaceful ruler." HEBREW EQUIVALENT: Melech.

Frederic, Fredrick Variant spellings of Frederick.

Freed A variant form of Freeman.

Freeman From the Anglo-Saxon, meaning "one born free."
    HEBREW EQUIVALENT: Dror-Li.

Fremont From the French, meaning "freedom mountain."
    HEBREW EQUIVALENT: Harel.

Frits A variant spelling of Fritz.

Fritz A German form of Frederick.

Froim, Froime Yiddish pet forms of Ephraim.

From, Fromel, Frommel Yiddish forms of Avraham
    (Abraham).

Fyvush A Yiddish name akin to Feivel.

Gab A pet for of Gabriel.

Gabai From the Hebrew, meaning "communal official."
    HEBREW EQUIVALENT: Gabai.

Gabby A pet form of Gabriel.

Gabe A pet form of Gabriel.

Gabi A pet form of Gabriel.

Gabriel From the Hebrew, meaning "God is my strength." HEBREW EQUIVALENT: Gavriel.

Gad From the Hebrew and Arabic, meaning "fortunate, lucky" or "warrior." HEBREW EQUIVALENT: Gad.

Gadi, Gaddi Variant forms of Gad.

Gadiel From the Hebrew, meaning "God is my good fortune." HEBREW EQUIVALENT: Gadiel.

Gafni From the Hebrew, meaning "my vineyard." HEBREW EQUIVALENT: Gafni.

Gai From the Hebrew, meaning "valley." HEBREW EQUIVALENT: Gai.

Gal From the Hebrew, meaning "wave" or "heap, mound." HEBREW EQUIVALENT: Gal.

Gali From the Hebrew, meaning "my wave" or "my hill." HEBREW EQUIVALENT: Gali.

Galia A variant form of Galya.

Galil From the Hebrew, meaning "a rolled sheet." HEBREW EQUIVALENT: Galil.

Galmud From the Hebrew, meaning "lonely." HEBREW EQUIVALENT: Galmud.

Galya From the Hebrew, meaning "wave of God." HEBREW EQUIVALENT: Galya.

Gamal From the Arabic and Hebrew, meaning "camel." HEBREW EQUIVALENT: Gamal.

Gamaliel A variant spelling of Gamliel.

Gamliel From the Hebrew, meaning "God is my reward." HEBREW EQUIVALENT: Gamliel.

Gan From the Hebrew, meaning "garden." HEBREW EQUIVALENT: Gan.

Gani From the Hebrew, meaning "my garden." HEBREW EQUIVALENT: Gani.

Garden From the Old High German and Danish, meaning "enclosure, garden." HEBREW EQUIVALENT: Gan.

Gardener A variant form of Garden.

Garfield From the Old English, meaning "promontory." HEBREW EQUIVALENT: Artzi.

Garner From the Latin, meaning "granary." HEBREW
EQUIVALENT: Goren.

Garnet, Garnett From the Latin, meaning "grain." Also, a
"red jewel." HEBREW EQUIVALENT: Admon.

Garon From the Hebrew, meaning "threshing floor [for
grain]." HEBREW EQUIVALENT: Garon.

Garret, Garrett From the Old French, meaning "to guard."
HEBREW EQUIVALENT: Shemarya.

Garth From the Old English, meaning "garden, enclosed
field." HEBREW EQUIVALENT: Ginat.

Garvey From the Anglo-Saxon, meaning "warrior." HEBREW
EQUIVALENT: Gibor.

Gary, Garry Variant forms of Gerard and Gerald.

Gavan A variant spelling of Gavin.

Gavin From the Welsh, meaning "little hawk." HEBREW
EQUIVALENT: Gozal.

Gavirol A Sephardic form of Gavriel.

Gavri A variant form of Gavriel.

Gavriel From the Hebrew, meaning "God is my strenth."
HEBREW EQUIVALENT: Gavriel.

Gedalia, Gedaliah Variant spellings of Gedalya.

Gedalya From the Hebrew, meaning "God is great." HEBREW
EQUIVALENT: Gedalya.

Gedalyahu A variant form of Gedalya. HEBREW EQUIVALENT:
Gedalyahu.

Gedi From the Hebrew, meaning "goat." HEBREW
EQUIVALENT: Gedi.

Gefania, Gefaniah Variant spellings of Gefanya.

Gefanya From the Hebrew, meaning "vineyard of the Lord."
HEBREW EQUIVALENT: Gefanya.

Gefen From the Hebrew, meaning "vine." HEBREW
EQUIVALENT: Gefen.

Gene A pet form of Eugene.

Geoff A pet form of Geoffrey.

Geoffrey From the Anglo-Saxon, meaning "gift of peace."
HEBREW EQUIVALENT: Avshalom.

George From the Greek, meaning "farmer." HEBREW
EQUIVALENT: Choresh.

Gerald An Old French and German form of Gerard.

Gerard From the Anglo-Saxon, meaning "spearbearer,
warrior." HEBREW EQUIVALENT: Gavriel.

Gerhard, Gerhardt, Gerhart Variant forms of Gerard.

Gerome From the Greek, meaning "sacred name." HEBREW
EQUIVALENT: Shem-Tov.

Gerre A variant spelling of Gerry.

Gerry A pet form of Gerome.

Gershom From the Hebrew, meaning "stranger." HEBREW
EQUIVALENT: Gershom.

Gershon A variant form of Gershom. HEBREW EQUIVALENT:
Gershon.

Gerson A variant form of Gershon.

Getzel A Yiddish pet form of the German name Gottfried.

Geva From the Hebrew, meaning "hill." HEBREW
EQUIVALENT: Geva.

Gib A pet form of Gilbert.

Gibor, Gibbor From the Hebrew, meaning "strong person."
HEBREW EQUIVALENT: Gibor.

Gideon A variant spelling of Gidon.

Gidi A pet form of Gidon.

Gidon From the Hebrew, meaning either "maimed" or
"mighty warrior." HEBREW EQUIVALENT: Gidon.

Gidoni A variant form of Gidon. HEBREW EQUIVALENT:
Gidoni.

Gifford From the Middle English, meaning "worthy gift."
HEBREW EQUIVALENT: Avishai.

Gil From the Hebrew, meaning "joy." HEBREW EQUIVALENT:
Gil.

Gilad From the Hebrew, meaning "mound [hill] of
testimony." HEBREW EQUIVALENT: Gilad.

Giladi A variant form of Gilad, meaning "man from Gilad
[Gilead]." HEBREW EQUIVALENT: Giladi.

Gilbert From the Anglo-Saxon, meaning "bright promise."
HEBREW EQUIVALENT: Barak.

Gildor From the Hebrew, meaning "generation of joy."
HEBREW EQUIVALENT: Gildor.

Gilead A variant form of Gilad.

Giles From the Greek, meaning "goatskin." HEBREW
EQUIVALENT: Efer.

Gili From the Hebrew, meaning "my joy." HEBREW
EQUIVALENT: Gili.

Gill A variant spelling of Gil.

Gilli A variant spelling of Gili.

Gilmore From the Celtic, meaning "valley near the sea."
HEBREW EQUIVALENT: Avigal.

Gimpel A Yiddish form of the German Gumprecht,
meaning "bright." HEBREW EQUIVALENT: Ori.

Ginat From the Hebrew, meaning "garden." HEBREW
EQUIVALENT: Ginat.

Ginson A variant spelling of Ginton.

Ginton From the Hebrew, meaning "garden, orchard."
HEBREW EQUIVALENT: Ginton.

Giora From the Hebrew, meaning "strong." HEBREW
EQUIVALENT: Giora.

Girard A variant spelling of Gerard.

Gitai From the Aramaic, meaning "one who presses grapes."
HEBREW EQUIVALENT: Gitai.

Giti A variant form of Gitai. HEBREW EQUIVALENT: Giti.

Giva From the Aramaic and Hebrew, meaning "hill."
HEBREW EQUIVALENT: Giv'a.

Givol From the Hebrew, meaning "budding, blooming."
HEBREW EQUIVALENT: Givol.

Givon From the Hebrew, meaning "hill, heights." HEBREW
EQUIVALENT: Givon.

Glen, Glenn From the Celtic, meaning "glen, secluded
mountain valley." HEBREW EQUIVALENT: Gai.

Goddard From the Old English, meaning "good in counsel."
HEBREW EQUIVALENT: Navon.

Godfrey A variant form of Gottfried.

Godwin From the Anglo-Saxon, meaning "friend of God."
HEBREW EQUIVALENT: Yedidya.

Goel From the Hebrew, meaning "redeemer." HEBREW EQUIVALENT: Go'el.

Golan From the Hebrew, meaning "refuge." HEBREW EQUIVALENT: Golan.

Goliath From the Hebrew, meaning "exiled one, stranger." HEBREW EQUIVALENT: Golyat.

Goral From the Hebrew, meaning "lot, lottery." HEBREW EQUIVALENT: Goral.

Goran From the British, meaning "cathedral." HEBREW EQUIVALENT: Devir.

Gordon From the Gaelic, meaning "hero, strongman." HEBREW EQUIVALENT: Gavriel.

Gore A short form of either Goran or Gordon.

Goren From the Hebrew, meaning "threshing floor." HEBREW EQUIVALENT: Goren.

Gorman From the British, meaning "member of a choir." HEBREW EQUIVALENT: Amiron.

Gottfried From the German, meaning "peace of God." HEBREW EQUIVALENT: Shelemya.

Gozal From the Hebrew, meaning "young bird." HEBREW EQUIVALENT: Gozal.

Graham From the Old English, meaning "gray, dwelling place." HEBREW EQUIVALENT: Avgar.

Granger From the Old French, meaning "farm steward." HEBREW EQUIVALENT: Shimshai.

Grant From the Old French, meaning "to grant, bequeath." HEBREW EQUIVALENT: Doron.

Gray From the Old English, meaning "to shine." HEBREW EQUIVALENT: Me'ir.

Greeley, Greely Abbreviated forms of the Anglo-Saxon *greenlea*, meaning "green meadow." HEBREW EQUIVALENT: Yogev.

Greg, Gregg From the Anglo-Saxon, meaning "to shine." HEBREW EQUIVALENT: Zerach.

Gregory From the Greek, meaning "vigilent watchman." HEBREW EQUIVALENT: Avigdor.

Griffin From the Welsh, meaning "strong in faith." HEBREW EQUIVALENT: Amitai.

Griffith A Welsh form of Griffin.

Grover From the Anglo-Saxon, meaning "one who grows trees." HEBREW EQUIVALENT: Oren.

Guni From the Hebrew, meaning "reddish black." HEBREW EQUIVALENT: Guni.

Gunther From the Old German, meaning "war" or "warrior." HEBREW EQUIVALENT: Gidon.

Gur From the Hebrew, meaning "young lion." HEBREW EQUIVALENT: Gur.

Gur-Ari A variant form of Gur-Arye. HEBREW EQUIVALENT: Gur-Ari.

Gur-Arye, Gur-Aryeh From the Hebrew, meaning "young lion, cub." HEBREW EQUIVALENT: Gur-Aryei.

Guri From the Hebrew, meaning "my young lion." HEBREW EQUIVALENT: Guri.

Guria A variant spelling of Gurya.

Guriel From the Hebrew, meaning "God is my lion" or "God is my refuge." HEBREW EQUIVALENT: Guriel.

Gurion The popular spelling of Guryon.

Gurya An Aramaic and Hebrew form of Gur.

Guryon From the Hebrew, meaning "lion." HEBREW EQUIVALENT: Guryon.

Gus A pet form of Gustavus.

Gustaf The Swedish form of Gustavus.

Gustav, Gustave German forms of Gustavus.

Gustavus From the German and Swedish, meaning "the staff [weapon] of the Goths." HEBREW EQUIVALENT: Gad.

Guthrie From the Celtic, meaning "war serpent" or "war hero." HEBREW EQUIVALENT: Gavriel.

Guy A variant spelling of Gai, meaning "valley." HEBREW EQUIVALENT: Gai.

Gyles A variant spelling of Giles.

Habakuk, Habakkuk From the Hebrew, meaning "to embrace." HEBREW EQUIVALENT: Chavakuk.

Habib A variant spelling of Chaviv.

Habibi A variant spelling of Chavivi.

Hada A variant form of Hadar.

Hadad From the Hebrew, meaning "echo." HEBREW EQUIVALENT: Hadad.

Hadar From the Hebrew, meaning "beautiful, ornamented." HEBREW EQUIVALENT: Hadar.

Hadrian From the Greek, meaning "rich." HEBREW EQUIVALENT: Ashir.

Hadriel From the Hebrew, meaning "splendor of the Lord." HEBREW EQUIVALENT: Hadriel.

Hag A variant spelling of Chag.

Hagai, Haggai Variant spellings of Chagai.

Hagi A variant spelling of Chagi.

Hai A variant form and spelling of Chai.

Haim A variant spelling of Chaim.

Hal A pet form of Harold or Haley.

Hale A pet form of Haley.

Haley From the Old English, meaning "healthy." HEBREW EQUIVALENT: Refael.

Hallel From the Hebrew, meaning "praise." HEBREW EQUIVALENT: Hallel.

Halley, Hallie Variant spellings of Haley.

Ham The Anglicized form of Cham.

Hamilton A variant form of Hamlet and Hamlin.

Hamish A variant form of the Gaelic name Seumas, a form of James.

Hamlet From the Old German, meaning "home." HEBREW EQUIVALENT: Lotan.

Hamlin From the Old English, meaning "a brook near home." HEBREW EQUIVALENT: Avi'yam.

Hanan A variant spelling of Chanan.

Hanina A variant spelling of Chanina.

Hanoch A variant spelling of Chanoch.

Hans A short form of the German name Johannes (John).

Hansel A Bavarian form of Hans.

Hansen A variant spelling of Hanson.

Hanson A Bavarian form of Hans.

Harel From the Hebrew, meaning "mountain of God." HEBREW EQUIVALENT: Harel.

Harlan From the Old English, meaning "warrior." HEBREW EQUIVALENT: Gavriel.

Harley From the Old English, meaning "field of plants." HEBREW EQUIVALENT: Chavakuk.

Harlin A variant spelling of Harlan.

Harlow From the Old Norse, meaning "army leader." HEBREW EQUIVALENT: Gevaryahu.

Harman From the Anglo-Saxon, meaning "soldier." HEBREW EQUIVALENT: Mishmar.

Harmon From the Greek, meaning "peace, harmony." HEBREW EQUIVALENT: Avshalom.

Harold From the Old English, meaning "warrior." HEBREW EQUIVALENT: Gevarya.

Harris, Harrison Patronymic forms of Harry, meaning "Harry's son."

Harry From the Middle English, a variant form of Henry.

Hart, Harte From the Middle English, meaning "deer, stag." HEBREW EQUIVALENT: A'yal.

Hartley From the Old English, meaning "field in which the deer roam." HEBREW EQUIVALENT: Tzevi.

Harvey From the Celtic, meaning "progressive, liberal, flourishing." HEBREW EQUIVALENT: Meron.

Haskel, Haskell From the Hebrew, meaning "wise, wisdom." HEBREW EQUIVALENT: Ish-Sechel.

Havelock From the Anglo-Saxon, meaning "dwelling near the lake." HEBREW EQUIVALENT: Yesheivav.

Haviv A variant spelling of Chaviv.

Hayden From the Anglo-Saxon, meaning "hay field, pasture land." HEBREW EQUIVALENT: Yagev.

Haym A variant spelling of Chaim.

Hayyim, Hayym Variant spellings of Chayim.

Hector From the Greek, meaning "anchor, protector." HEBREW EQUIVALENT: Chetzron.

Hed From the Hebrew, meaning "echo." HEBREW EQUIVALENT: Hed.

Hedley From the Old English, meaning "covered meadow." HEBREW EQUIVALENT: Gidron.

Heinrich The German form of Henry.

Helem From the Hebrew, meaning "hammer." HEBREW EQUIVALENT: Helem.

Heller An Old High German form of the Latin, meaning "sun." HEBREW EQUIVALENT: Shimshon.

Heman From the Hebrew, meaning "faithful." HEBREW EQUIVALENT: Heman.

Henri The French form of Henry.

Henry From the Anglo-Saxon, meaning "ruler of the home, rich lord." HEBREW EQUIVALENT: Adoniya.

Herbert From the Old High German, meaning "excellent ruler." HEBREW EQUIVALENT: Avraham.

Hercules From the Greek, meaning "glory." HEBREW EQUIVALENT: Hadar.

Herman, Hermann From the Old High German, meaning "soldier." HEBREW EQUIVALENT: Gera.

Hermon The Anglicized form of Chermon.

Hermoni The Anglicized form of Chermoni.

Hersch, Herschel Variant spellings of Hersh and Hershel.

Hersh From the Yiddish, meaning "deer." HEBREW EQUIVALENT: Efron.

Hershel A pet form of Hersh.

Hertz A pet form of Hersh.

Hertzel, Hertzl Variant form spellings of Herzl.

Herz A variant spelling of Hertz.

Hertzke A pet form of Herzl.

Herzl A variant spelling of Hertzel.

Heschel A variant form of Hershel.

Hesh A Yiddish pet form of Hersh.

Heshel A variant spelling of Heschel.

Heske A pet form of Heskel.

Heskel A variant form of Haskel.

Hesketh Probably a variant form of Hezekia.

Heskiah A variant spelling of Hezekia.

Hevel From the Hebrew, meaning "breath, vapor." HEBREW EQUIVALENT: Hevel.

Heywood From the Old English, meaning "hay field." HEBREW EQUIVALENT: Efa.

Hezekia, Hezekiah Variant spellings of Chizkiya.

Hi, High A variant form of Hiram and Hyman.

Hiel A variant spelling of Chiel.

Hila From the Aramaic and Hebrew, meaning "praise." HEBREW EQUIVALENT: Hila.

Hilary From the Greek and Latin, meaning "cheerful." HEBREW EQUIVALENT: Yagil.

Hili A pet form of Hillel.

Hill From the Anglo-Saxon, meaning "hill, high place." HEBREW EQUIVALENT: Harel.

Hillard A variant form of Hill.

Hillary A variant form of Hilary.

Hillel From the Hebrew, meaning "praised, famous." HEBREW EQUIVALENT: Hillel.

Hilliard A variant form of Hill.

Hiram A variant spelling of Chiram.

Hirsch A variant spelling of Hersh.

Hirsh, Hirshel Variant spellings of Hersh and Hershel.

Hob A variant Middle English form of Rob and Robert.

Hobart From the Danish, meaning "Bart's hill."

Hobert A variant form of Hobart.

Hobs A variant form of Hob, meaning "son of Hob."

Hod From the Hebrew, meaning "splendor, vigor." HEBREW EQUIVALENT: Hod.

Hodia, Hodiah Variant spellings of Hodiya.

Hodiya From the Hebrew, meaning "God is my splendor."
HEBREW EQUIVALENT: Hodiya.

Holden From the Old English *haldan*, meaning "to tend
sheep." HEBREW EQUIVALENT: Maron.

Hollis A variant form of Haley.

Holm From the Old Norse, meaning "island." HEBREW
EQUIVALENT: Aviyam.

Holmes A variant form of Holm.

Holt From the Old English and the German, meaning
"wood, wooded area." HEBREW EQUIVALENT: Ya'ar.

Hon From the Hebrew, meaning "wealth." HEBREW
EQUIVALENT: Hone.

Honi A variant spelling of Choni.

Honor, Honore From the Middle English and the Latin,
meaning "dignity, esteem." HEBREW EQUIVALENT: Hadar.

Hopkins A pet form of Hob and Hobs, forms of Robert.

Horace From the Greek, meaning "to see, behold." HEBREW
EQUIVALENT: Ro'eh.

Horatio The Italian form of Horace.

Horton From the Latin, meaning "garden." HEBREW
EQUIVALENT: Bustan.

Hosea The Anglicized form of Hoshe'a.

Hoshe'a From the Hebrew, meaning "salvation." HEBREW
EQUIVALENT: Hosheia.

Howard From the Anglo-Saxon, meaning "watchman,
protector." HEBREW EQUIVALENT: Avigdor.

Howe From the Anglo-Saxon, meaning "hill." HEBREW
EQUIVALENT: Aharon.

Howel, Howell From the Old English, meaning "well on the
hill." HEBREW EQUIVALENT: Be'er.

Howie A pet form of Howard.

Hubert A variant form of Herbert.

Huey A pet form of Hubert.

Hugh A pet form of Hubert.

Hugo A pet form of Hubert.

Humphrey, Humphry From the Old German, meaning
"man of peace," HEBREW EQUIVALENT: Meshulam.

Hur The Anglicized form of Chur.

Hy A pct form of Hyland and Hyman.

Hyland From the Anglo-Saxon, meaning "one who lives on high land." Akin to Hyman.

Hyman From the Anglo-Saxon, meaning "one who lives in a high place." HEBREW EQUIVALENT: Aharon.

Ian The Scottish form of John.

Idan From the Aramaic, meaning "time, era." HEBREW EQUIVALENT: Idan.

Idi A variant form of Ido.

Ido, Iddo From the Hebrew and Aramaic, meaning "to rise up [like a cloud]" or "to reckon time." HEBREW EQUIVALENT: Ido.

Idra From the Aramaic, meaning "granary." HEBREW EQUIVALENT: Idra.

Igor From the Scandinavian, meaning "hero." HEBREW EQUIVALENT: Abir.

Ike A pet form of Isaac.

Iki A pet form of Isaac.

Ila From the Aramaic, meaning "exalted," and the Arabic, meaning "noble cause." HEBREW EQUIVALENT: Ila.

Ila'i From the Hebrew and Aramaic, meaning "superior." HEBREW EQUIVALENT: Ila'i.

Ilan From the Hebrew, meaning "tree." HEBREW EQUIVALENT: Ilan.

Ili, Ilie A variant form of Ila. HEBREW EQUIVALENT: Ili.

Ilija A variant Slavic form of Elijah.

Ilya A variant spelling of Ilija.

Imanuel, Immanuel From the Hebrew, meaning "God is with us." HEBREW EQUIVALENT: Imanuel.

Imri, Imrie From the Hebrew, meaning "my utterance." HEBREW EQUIVALENT: Imri.

Ingmar From the Old English, meaning "meadow near the sea." HEBREW EQUIVALENT: Avigal.

Ir From the Hebrew, meaning "city, town." HEBREW EQUIVALENT: Ir.

Ira From the Hebrew and Arabic, meaning "to escape [by being swift]." HEBREW EQUIVALENT: Ira.

Iran A variant form of Ira.

Iri A variant form of Ira.

Irvin From the Gaelic, meaning "beautiful, handsome, fair." HEBREW EQUIVALENT: Shefer.

Irvine A variant form of Irvin.

Irving A variant form of Irvin.

Irwin, Irwyn Variant spellings of Irvin.

Is A short form of Isaiah.

Isa, Issa Short forms of Isaiah and Isaac.

Isaac From the Hebrew, meaning "he will laugh." HEBREW EQUIVALENT: Yitzchak.

Isador, Isadore Variant spellings of Isidor.

Isaiah From the Hebrew, meaning "God is salvation." HEBREW EQUIVALENT: Yesha'ya and Yesha'yahu.

Isak A variant spelling of Isaac.

Iser A variant spelling of Isser.

Ish From the Hebrew, meaning "man." HEBREW EQUIVALENT: Ish.

Ishmel From the Hebrew, meaning "God will hear." HEBREW EQUIVALENT: Yishmael.

Ish-Shalom From the Hebrew, meaning "man of peace." HEBREW EQUIVALENT: Ish-Shalom.

Ish-Tov From the Hebrew, meaning "good man." HEBREW EQUIVALENT: Ish-Tov.

Isi A variant spelling of Issi.

Isidor, Isidore From the Greek, meaning "gift of Isis." HEBREW EQUIVALENT: Avishai.

Isidoro The Spanish form of Isidor.

Ismar A variant form of Itamar.

Israel The Anglicized form of the Hebrew, meaning "prince of God" or "wrestled with God." HEBREW EQUIVALENT: Yisrael.

Issachar From the Hebrew, meaning "there is a reward." HEBREW EQUIVALENT: Yisachar.

Isser A Yiddish form of Yisrael (Israel).

Issi A pet form of Isser and Isaac.

Itai From the Hebrew, meaning "God is with me." HEBREW EQUIVALENT: Itai.

Itamar From the Hebrew, meaning "island of palms." HEBREW EQUIVALENT: Itamar.

Itche A Yiddish form of Isaac.

Itiel From the Hebrew, meaning "God is with me." HEBREW EQUIVALENT: Itiel.

Ittai A variant spelling of Itai.

Ittamar A variant spelling of Itamar.

Itzig, Itzik Yiddish forms of Yitzchak (Isaac).

Ivan The Russian form of John.

Ivri From the Hebrew, meaning "Hebrew." HEBREW EQUIVALENT: Ivri.

Iz A pet form of Isidor.

Izzie, Izzy Pet forms of Isidor.

Jac A short from of Jack.

Jack A pet form of Jacob. A nickname for John.

Jackie A pet form of Jack.

Jackson A patronymic form, meaning "son of Jack" or "son of Jacob."

Jacob From the Hebrew, meaning "held by the heel, supplanted, or protected." HEBREW EQUIVALENT: Ya'akov.

Jacobo A Spanish form of Jacob.

Jacque, Jacques French forms of Jacob.

Jaime, Jaimie Pet forms of James.

Jake A pet form of Jacob.

Jakob A variant spelling of Jacob.

James The English form of the Hebrew name Jacob.

Jamin A short form of Benjamin.

Jan A form of John. Also, a pet form of James.

Janus From the Latin, meaning "gate, passageway" or "opening, beginning." HEBREW EQUIVALENT: Rosh.

Japhet, Japheth Variant spellings of Yefet.

Jardine From the Anglo-Saxon and French, meaning "garden." HEBREW EQUIVALENT: Gan.

Jared A variant spelling of Yared.

Jaron A variant spelling of Yaron.

Jarvis From the Old English, meaning "battle spear" or "conqueror." HEBREW EQUIVALENT: Gevarya.

Jascha A Russian form of James and Jacob.

Jason From the Greek, meaning "healer." HEBREW EQUIVALENT: Asa.

Jaspar, Jasper From the Greek, meaning "precious stone." HEBREW EQUIVALENT: Sapir.

Jay From the Old French and Latin, referring to a bird in the crow family. HEBREW EQUIVALENT: Efron.

Jean The French form of John.

Jed From the Arabic, meaning "hand." Also a pet form of Jedediah. HEBREW EQUIVALENT: Yeda'ya.

Jedediah A variant form of Yedidya.

Jef, Jeff Short forms of Jeffrey and Geoffrey.

Jeffers A patronymic form, meaning "son of Jeffrey."

Jefferson A patronymic form, meaning "son of Jeffers."

Jeffery, Jefferey Variant spellings of Geoffrey.

Jeffrey A variant spelling of Geoffrey.

Jeffry A variant spelling of Geoffrey.

Jehiel A variant spelling of Yechiel.

Jehoiakim A variant spelling of Yehoyakim.

Jekuthiel, Jekutiel Variant forms of Yekutiel.

Jephthah, Jephtah Variant spellings of Yiftach.

Jerald A variant spelling of Gerald.

Jere A variant spelling of Jerry.

Jered A variant spelling of Yered.

Jeremiah From the Hebrew, meaning "God will uplift [the spirit]." HEBREW EQUIVALENT: Yirmeyahu.

Jeremias The Greek form of Jeremiah.

Jeremy A pet form of Jeremiah.

Jerold A variant spelling of Gerald.

Jerome A variant spelling of Gerome, meaning "holy person" or "sacred name." HEBREW EQUIVALENT: Zakai.

Jerrald, Jerrold Variant spellings of Jerold.

Jerri A variant spelling of Jerry.

Jerry A pet form of Jerold, Jerome, and Jeremiah.

Jess A short form of Jesse.

Jesse From the Hebrew, meaning "wealthy" or "gift." HEBREW EQUIVALENT: Yishai.

Jethro From the Hebrew, meaning "abundance, riches." HEBREW EQUIVALENT: Yitro.

Jim Pet form of James.

Jimbo A pet form of James, a short form of Jimboy.

Jimm, Jimmie, Jimmy Pet forms of James.

Joab A variant spelling of Yoav.

Job From the Hebrew, meaning "hated, oppressed." HEBREW EQUIVALENT: Iyov.

Joce A variant form of Joseph.

Jochanan A variant spelling of Yochanan.

Jody A pet form of Joseph.

Joe, Joey Pet forms of Joseph.

Joel From the Hebrew, meaning "God is willing." HEBREW EQUIVALENT: Yo'el.

Johanan A variant spelling of Yochanan.

Johannes A Latin form of John.

John The Anglicized form of Yochanan, meaning "God is gracious." HEBREW EQUIVALENT: Yochanan.

Johnnie, Johnny Pet forms of John.

Jojo A pet form of Joseph.

Jon A pet form of John or Jonathan.

Jona, Jonah From the Hebrew, meaning "dove." HEBREW EQUIVALENT: Yona.

Jonas The Greek and Latin form of Jonah.

Jonathan From the Hebrew, meaning God has given" or "gift of God." HEBREW EQUIVALENT: Yehonatan.

Jonji A pet form of Jonathan.

Jon-Jon A pet form of Jonathan.

Jonni, Jonnie, Jonny Pet forms of Jonathan and John.

Jordan From the Hebrew, meaning "descent." HEBREW EQUIVALENT: Yarden.

Jordy A pet form of Jordan.

Jori, Jory Pet forms of Jordan.

Jose An Aramaic form of Joseph.

Joseph From the Hebrew, meaning "He [God] will add, increase." HEBREW EQUIVALENT: Yosef.

Josephus The Latin form of Joseph. HEBREW EQUIVALENT: Yosifus.

Josh A pet form of Joshua.

Joshua From the Hebrew, meaning "the Lord is my salvation." HEBREW EQUIVALENT: Yehoshua.

Josiah From the Hebrew, meaning "fire of the Lord." HEBREW EQUIVALENT: Yoshiyahu.

Jotham A variant spelling of Yotam.

Jud A variant spelling of Judd.

Judah From the Hebrew, meaning "praise." HEBREW EQUIVALENT: Yehuda.

Judas The Latin form of Judah.

Judd A variant form of Judah.

Judel A Yiddish form of Judah.

Judson A patronymic form of Judah, meaning "Judah's [or Judd's] son."

Jule, Jules Variant forms of Julian or Julius.

Julian From the Greek, meaning "soft-haired, mossy-bearded," symbolizing youth. HEBREW EQUIVALENT: Elino'ar.

Julius A variant form of Julian.

Junior From the Latin, meaning "young." HEBREW EQUIVALENT: Aviv.

Junius From the Latin, meaning "young lion." HEBREW EQUIVALENT: Ari.

Justin A variant form of Justus.

Justus From the Latin, meaning "just, honest." HEBREW EQUIVALENT: Yashar.

Kadi From the Hebrew, meaning "my pitcher." HEBREW EQUIVALENT: Kadi.

Kadish, Kaddish From the Hebrew, meaning "sanctification." HEBREW EQUIVALENT: Kadish.

Kadmiel From the Hebrew, meaning "the Ancient One is my God." HEBREW EQUIVALENT: Kadmiel.

Kadosh From the Hebrew, meaning "holy, holy one." HEBREW EQUIVALENT: Kadosh.

Kailil A variant form of Kalil.

Kal A short form of Kalman.

Kalev From the Hebrew, meaning "dog" or "heart." HEBREW EQUIVALENT: Kalev.

Kalil From the Greek, meaning "beautiful." Also, from the Hebrew, meaning "crown, wreath." HEBREW EQUIVALENT: Kalil.

Kalman A short form of Kalonymos.

Kanai From the Hebrew, meaning "zealous." HEBREW EQUIVALENT: Kana'i.

Kane A variant form of Keene.

Kani A pet form of Kaniel.

Kaniel From the Hebrew, meaning "reed [support]." HEBREW EQUIVALENT: Kaniel.

Kareem From the Arabic, meaning "noble, exalted." HEBREW EQUIVALENT: Adonikam.

Karel A variant from of Carol.

Karim A variant spelling of Kareem.

Karin From the Arabic, meaning "horn." HEBREW EQUIVALENT: Karin.

Karl A variant spelling of Carl.

Karmel From the Hebrew, meaning "vineyard." HEBREW EQUIVALENT: Karmel.

Karmeli From the Hebrew, meaning "my vineyard." HEBREW EQUIVALENT: Karmeli.

Karna From the Aramaic, meaning "horn." HEBREW EQUIVALENT: Karna.

Karni From the Hebrew, meaning "my horn." HEBREW EQUIVALENT: Karni.

Karniel From the Hebrew, meaning "God is my horn." HEBREW EQUIVALENT: Karniel.

Kaski A Yiddish pet form of Yechezkel.

Karol, Karole Variant spellings of Carol.

Kasriel A variant spelling of Katriel.

Kati A short form of Katriel. HEBREW EQUIVALENT: Kati.

Katriel From the Hebrew, meaning "God is my crown." HEBREW EQUIVALENT: Katriel.

Katzin From the Hebrew, meaning "rich lord." HEBREW EQUIVALENT: Katzin.

Kaufman, Kaufmann From the German, meaning "buyer." HEBREW EQUIVALENT: Elkana.

Kay From the Greek, meaning "rejoicing," or from the Anglo-Saxon, meaning "warden of a fortified place." HEBREW EQUIVALENT: Akiva.

Kedem From the Hebrew, meaning "east." HEBREW EQUIVALENT: Kedem.

Keenan A variant form of Keene.

Keene From the Old English, meaning "wise, learned."
HEBREW EQUIVALENT: Buna.

Kefir From the Hebrew, meaning "lion cub." HEBREW
EQUIVALENT: Kefir.

Keith From the Old Gaelic, meaning "wood, woody area."
HEBREW EQUIVALENT: Ya'ar.

Kelsey A variant form of Kelson.

Kelson From the Middle Dutch, meaning "boat." HEBREW
EQUIVALENT: Sira.

Kelvin, Kelwin, Kelwyn From the Anglo-Saxon, meaning
"lover of ships." HEBREW EQUIVALENT: Narkis.

Ken A pet form of Kenneth.

Kendal, Kendall From the Celtic, meaning "ruler of the
valley." HEBREW EQUIVALENT: Emek.

Kendrick From the Anglo-Saxon, meaning "royal." HEBREW
EQUIVALENT: Katriel.

Kenen From the Old English and German, meaning "to
know." HEBREW EQUIVALENT: Yavin.

Kenneth From the Celtic and Scottish, meaning "beautiful,
handsome." HEBREW EQUIVALENT: Kalil.

Kennie A pet form of Kenneth.

Kenny A pet form of Kenneth.

Kent A variant form of Kenneth.

Kerby A variant spelling of Kirby.

Kerem From the Hebrew, meaning "vineyard." HEBREW
EQUIVALENT: Kerem.

Keren From the Hebrew, meaning "horn." HEBREW
EQUIVALENT: Keren.

Kermit From the Dutch, meaning "church." HEBREW
EQUIVALENT: Kadosh.

Kern From the Old Irish, meaning "band of soldiers."
HEBREW EQUIVALENT: Nimrod.

Kerr From the Norse, meaning "marshland." HEBREW
EQUIVALENT: Beri.

Kessem From the Hebrew, meaning "fortune telling."
HEBREW EQUIVALENT: Kessem.

Keter From the Hebrew, meaning "crown." HEBREW EQUIVALENT: Keter.

Kevin From the Gaelic, meaning "handsome, beautiful." HEBREW EQUIVALENT: Kalil.

Kibby From the British, meaning "cottage by the water." HEBREW EQUIVALENT: Aviyam.

Kidd From the British, meaning "strong." HEBREW EQUIVALENT: Chizkiya.

Kile A variant spelling of Kyle.

Kin A pet form of Kingsley and Kingston.

King From the Anglo-Saxon, meaning "ruler." HEBREW EQUIVALENT: Melech.

Kingsley From the Anglo-Saxon, meaning "from the king's meadow." HEBREW EQUIVALENT: Carmel.

Kingston From the Old English, meaning "king's town." HEBREW EQUIVALENT: Melech.

Kinori From the Hebrew, meaning "my lyre, my harp." HEBREW EQUIVALENT: Kinori.

Kinsey From the British, meaning "royal." HEBREW EQUIVALENT: Elrad.

Kirby From the British, meaning "cottage by the water." HEBREW EQUIVALENT: Avi'yam.

Kirk From the Old Norse and Old English, meaning "church." HEBREW EQUIVALENT: Kadosh.

Kitron From the Hebrew, meaning "crown." HEBREW EQUIVALENT: Kitron.

Kiva A pet form of Akiva.

Kive A pet form of Akiva and Yaakov.

Kivi A pet form of Akiva and Yaakov.

Kochbiel From the Hebrew, referring to the "angel who governs the stars." HEBREW EQUIVALENT: Kochbiel.

Konrad A variant spelling of Conrad.

Koppel A Yiddish form of Yaakov.

Korach From the Hebrew, meaning "bald." HEBREW EQUIVALENT: Korach.

Korah A variant spelling of Korach.

Kovi A pet form of Yaakov.

Kurt A pet form of Konrad.

Kus A short form of Yekusiel (Yekutiel).

Kyle A Gaelic form of the Old English, meaning "hill where the cattle graze." HEBREW EQUIVALENT: Talmai.

L

Laban A variant spelling of Lavan.

Label A pet form of the Yiddish name Leib, meaning "lion." HEBREW EQUIVALENT: Ariel.

Lamar, Lamarr From the Latin and French, meaning "of the sea." HEBREW EQUIVALENT: Avi'yam.

Lambert From the German and French, meaning "brightness of the land." HEBREW EQUIVALENT: Avner.

Lamed From the Hebrew, meaning "learning." HEBREW EQUIVALENT: Lamed.

Lance From the Latin, meaning "servant, spear-carrier." HEBREW EQUIVALENT: Patiel.

Lancelot A variant form of Lance.

Lane From the Old English, meaning "to move ahead," hence a path. HEBREW EQUIVALENT: Nativ.

Lang From the German, meaning "long, tall." HEBREW EQUIVALENT: Aricha.

Lapid From the Hebrew, meaning "flame, torch." HEBREW EQUIVALENT: Lapid.

Lapidos A variant form of Lapidot.

Lapidot From the Hebrew, meaning "flame, torch." HEBREW EQUIVALENT: Lapidot.

Larry A pet form of Laurence.

Lars A Swedish pet form of Laurence.

Laurence From the Latin, meaning "laurel, crown." HEBREW EQUIVALENT: Kalil.

Lavan From the Hebrew, meaning "white." HEBREW EQUIVALENT: Lavan.

Lavi From the Hebrew, meaning "lion." HEBREW EQUIVALENT: Lavi.

Lawrence A variant spelling of Laurence.

Lazar A Yiddish form of Elazar.

Lazarus A Greek form of Elazar.

Lebush A variant spelling of Leibush.

Lee A pet form of Leo, Leon, Leonard, or Leslie. Also, from the Anglo-Saxon, meaning "meadow." HEBREW EQUIVALENT: Lavi.

Leeser A Yiddish form of Eliezer.

Leib A Yiddish form of the German name Loeb, meaning "lion." HEBREW EQUIVALENT: Arel.

Leibel A pet form of Leib.

Leibush A variant form of Leib.

Leif An Old Norse form of Lief.

Leigh A variant spelling of Lee.

Len A pet form of Leonard.

Lenn A variant spelling of Len.

Lennard, Lennart Variant forms of Leonard.

Lennie, Lenny A pet form of Leonard.

Leo From the Latin, meaning "lion" or "the lion's nature." HEBREW EQUIVALENT: Aryei.

Leon A Greek form of Leo.

Leonard A French form of the Old High German, meaning "strong as a lion." HEBREW EQUIVALENT: Ariel.

Leopold From the Old High German and the Old English, meaning "defender of people." HEBREW EQUIVALENT: Avigdor.

Leor, Le-or A variant spelling of Lior.

Leron, Lerone A variant spelling of Liron.

LeRoy A French form of the Latin, meaning "the king, royalty." HEBREW EQUIVALENT: Elimelech.

Les A pet form of Leslie and Lester.

Leser A variant spelling of Lesser.

Leshem From the Hebrew, meaning "precious stone."
HEBREW EQUIVALENT: Leshem.

Lesley A variant spelling of Leslie.

Leslie From the Anglo-Saxon, meaning "meadowlands."
HEBREW EQUIVALENT: Karmel.

Lesser A Yiddish form of Eliezer.

Lester Originally Leicester, a place-name in England. From
the Latin and the Old English, meaning "camp, protected
area." HEBREW EQUIVALENT: Lot.

Lev From the Hebrew, meaning "heart." HEBREW
EQUIVALENT: Lev.

Levanon From the Hebrew, meaning "white" or "moon,
month." HEBREW EQUIVALENT: Levanon.

Levi From the Hebrew, meaning "joined to" or "attendant
upon." HEBREW EQUIVALENT: Levi.

Levitas A variant form of Levi.

Lew A pet form of Lewis.

Lewes A variant spelling of Lewis.

Lewi The Hawaiian form of Levi.

Lewis An English form of the French name Louis.

Lezer A Yiddish form of Eliezer.

Li From the Hebrew, meaning "me" or "to me." HEBREW
EQUIVALENT: Li.

Liba A variant spelling of Lieber.

Lieb A short form of Lieber.

Lieber A Yiddish form of the German, meaning "beloved."
HEBREW EQUIVALENT: David.

Lief From the Middle English, meaning "beloved, dear."
HEBREW EQUIVALENT: Bildad.

Liezer A short form of Eliezer.

Limon From the Hebrew, meaning "lemon." HEBREW
EQUIVALENT: Limon.

Lincoln From the Old English meaning "camp near the
stream." HEBREW EQUIVALENT: Peleg.

Lindsay A variant form of Lindsey.

Lindsey From the Old English, meaning "linden trees near
the water [sea]." HEBREW EQUIVALENT: Ilan.

Lindsy A variant spelling of Lindsey.
Link From the Old English, meaning "enclosure." HEBREW EQUIVALENT: Lotan.
Lion A variant spelling of Leon.
Li-On From the Hebrew, meaning "I have strength." HEBREW EQUIVALENT: Li-On (Li'on).
Lionel A variant form of Lion.
Lior, Li-Or From the Hebrew, meaning "my light" or "I see." HEBREW EQUIVALENT: Lior.
Lipman, Lipmann A Yiddish form of the German name Liebman, meaning "lover of man." HEBREW EQUIVALENT: Eldad.
Liron, Li-Ron From the Hebrew, meaning "song is mine." HEBREW EQUIVALENT: Liron.
Livni From the Hebrew, meaning "white" or "frankincense [because of its white color]." HEBREW EQUIVALENT: Livni.
Llewellyn From the Welsh, meaning "in the likeness of a lion." HEBREW EQUIVALENT: Lavi.
Lloyd From the Celtic or Welsh, meaning "grey or brown" or "dark-complexioned person." HEBREW EQUIVALENT: Tziltai.
Loeb From the German, meaning "lion." HEBREW EQUIVALENT: Aryei.
Loel A variant spelling of Lowell.
Lon, Lonnie, Lonny Pet forms of Alphonso.
Lorence A variant spelling of Laurence.
Lorn, Lorne Variant forms of Laurence.
Lorry A pet form of Laurence.
Lot From the Hebrew, meaning "envelop, protect." HEBREW EQUIVALENT: Lot.
Lotan From the Hebrew, meaning "envelop, protect." HEBREW EQUIVALENT: Lotan.
Lothar, Lother, Lothur From the Anglo-Saxon, meaning "renowned warrior" or "hero of the people." HEBREW EQUIVALENT: Naftali.
Louis From the Old French, meaning "famous in battle." HEBREW EQUIVALENT: Avicha'yil.

Lovell A variant form of Lowell.

Lowe A variant form of the German name Loeb.

Lowell From the Old English, meaning "beloved." HEBREW EQUIVALENT: Eldad.

Loy A pet form of Loyal.

Loyal From the Old French and Latin, meaning "faithful, true." HEBREW EQUIVALENT: Amitai.

Luca A variant form of Lucas or Lucius.

Lucas A variant form of Lucius.

Lucian A variant form of Lucius.

Lucius From the Latin, meaning "light." HEBREW EQUIVALENT: Lior.

Lucky From the Middle English, meaning "good fortune." HEBREW EQUIVALENT: Mazal.

Ludwig A German form of Louis.

Luke The English form of Lucius.

Lupo From the Latin, meaning "wolf." HEBREW EQUIVALENT: Ze'ev.

Lupus A variant form of Lupo.

Luz From the Hebrew, meaning "almond tree." HEBREW EQUIVALENT: Luz.

Lyall A variant form of Lyle.

Lyell A variant form of Lyle.

Lyle A French form of the Latin, meaning "from the island." HEBREW EQUIVALENT: Peleg.

Lynn From the Old English and Welsh, meaning "cataract, lake, brook." HEBREW EQUIVALENT: Yuval.

Lyon The French form of Lion.

Lyonell A variant form of Lyon.

Lyron A variant spelling of Liron.

Mac From the Gaelic, meaning "son of." HEBREW EQUIVALENT: Ben.

Macabee, Maccabee From the Hebrew, meaning "hammer." HEBREW EQUIVALENT: Makabi.

Mace An English form of the Old French, meaning "club, hammer."

Macey A variant form of Mace.

Mack A variant spelling of Mac.

Mackey A variant form of Mack.

Macy A variant spelling of Macey.

Maer A variant spelling of Meir.

Magen From the Hebrew, meaning "protector." HEBREW EQUIVALENT: Magen.

Magnus From the Latin, meaning "great." HEBREW EQUIVALENT: Gedalya.

Maher From the Hebrew, meaning "quick, industrious, expert." HEBREW EQUIVALENT: Maher.

Mahir From the Hebrew, meaning "quick, industrious." HEBREW EQUIVALENT: Mahir.

Maimon From the Arabic, meaning "luck, good fortune." HEBREW EQUIVALENT: Maimon.

Maimun A variant spelling of Maimon.

Major From the Latin, meaning "great." Akin to Magnus.

Makabi A variant spelling of Macabee.

Maks A variant spelling of Max.

Malachai A variant spelling of Malachi.

Malachi From the Hebrew, meaning "my messenger" or "my servant." HEBREW EQUIVALENT: Malachi.

Malachy A variant form of Malachi.

Malbin From the Hebrew, meaning "to whiten." HEBREW EQUIVALENT: Malbin.

Malcam A variant spelling of Malkam.

Malcolm From the Arabic, meaning "dove." HEBREW EQUIVALENT: Yona.

Malkam From the Hebrew, meaning "God is their King." HEBREW EQUIVALENT: Malkam.

Malki From the Hebrew, meaning "my king." HEBREW EQUIVALENT: Malki.

Malon From the Hebrew, meaning "lodge, inn." HEBREW EQUIVALENT: Malon.

Malvin A variant spelling of Melvin.

Manashi A variant spelling of Menashi.

Manasseh An Anglicized form of Menashe.

Mandel From the Old French and the Middle Latin, meaning "almond." HEBREW EQUIVALENT: Shaked.

Mandy A pet form of Manfred.

Manford From the Anglo-Saxon, meaning "small bridge over a brook." HEBREW EQUIVALENT: Arnon.

Manfred From the German, meaning "man of peace." HEBREW EQUIVALENT: Shalom.

Mani A pet form of Emanuel, Manasseh, Manfred, and Manuel.

Manin A variant form of Mann.

Manis A variant form of Mann.

Manish A Yiddish form of Mann.

Manley, Manly From the Old English, meaning "protected field." HEBREW EQUIVALENT: Shimron.

Mann From the German, meaning "man." HEBREW EQUIVALENT: Adam.

Mannes, Mannis Variant Yiddish forms of Mann.

Manni A variant spelling of Mani and Manny.

Manny, Mannye Pet forms of Emanuel, Manasseh, Manfred, and Manuel.

Manu A pet form of Manuel.

Manuel A short form of Emanuel.

Manus A variant form of Magnus.

Maon From the Hebrew, meaning "dwelling." HEBREW EQUIVALENT: Ma'on.

Maor From the Hebrew, meaning "light." HEBREW EQUIVALENT: Ma'or.

Maoz From the Hebrew, meaning "strength" or "fortress." HEBREW EQUIVALENT: Ma'oz.

Mar From the Aramaic, meaning "master" or "lord." HEBREW EQUIVALENT: Mar.

Marc A short form of Marcus.

Marcel A French pet form of Marcus.

Marcelo, Marcello Pet forms of Marcus.

March A variant form of Marcus.

Marchall A variant spelling of Marshall.

Marcos A variant form of Marcus.

Marcus From the Latin name Mars, meaning "warlike." HEBREW EQUIVALENT: Mordechai.

Marcy A variant form of Marcus.

Marek A Polish form of Marcus.

Mari A pet form of Marius.

Marin From the Latin, meaning "small harbor." HEBREW EQUIVALENT: Moshe.

Mario A variant form of Marian or Marcus.

Maris From the Old English and French, meaning "sea, lake." HEBREW EQUIVALENT: Moshe.

Marius A variant form of Marcus.

Mark A variant form of Marcus.

Marlin From the Latin, Old English, and French, meaning "sea." HEBREW EQUIVALENT: Moshe.

Malkosh From the Hebrew, meaning "rain." HEBREW EQUIVALENT: Malkosh.

Marlo A variant form of Marlin.

Marlow, Marlowe A variant form of Marlin.

Marne From the Latin and French, meaning "sea." HEBREW EQUIVALENT: Moshe.

Marnin From the Hebrew, meaning "one who sings." HEBREW EQUIVALENT: Marnin.

Marom From the Hebrew, meaning "lofty, exalted." HEBREW EQUIVALENT: Marom.

Maron From the Hebrew, meaning "flock of sheep." HEBREW EQUIVALENT: Maron.

Marshal, Marshall From the Old English, meaning "an officer in charge of military matters." HEBREW EQUIVALENT: Ben-Cha'yil.

Marshe variant form of Marcus and Marshal.

Martin A French form of the Latin name Martinus. Akin to Marcus. HEBREW EQUIVALENT: Makabi.

Marvin From the Old English, meaning "friend of the sea." HEBREW EQUIVALENT: Moshe.

Marwin A variant form of Marvin.

Masad From the Hebrew, meaning "foundation, support." HEBREW EQUIVALENT: Masad.

Mashiach From the Hebrew, meaning "anointed one." HEBREW EQUIVALENT: Mashiach.

Maskil From the Hebrew, meaning "enlightened, educated." HEBREW EQUIVALENT: Maskil.

Mason From the Anglo-Saxon, meaning "mason, worker in stone." HEBREW EQUIVALENT: Shamir.

Mat A pet form of Matthew.

Matan From the Hebrew, meaning "gift." HEBREW EQUIVALENT: Matan.

Matania, Mataniah Variant spellings of Matanya.

Matanya, Matanyahu From the Hebrew, meaning "gift of God." HEBREW EQUIVALENT: Matanya.

Mateo A Spanish form of Matthew.

Mati A pet form of Matanya. HEBREW EQUIVALENT: Mati.

Matia, Matiah Variant spellings of Matya.

Matitya, Matityahu From the Hebrew, meaning "gift of God." HEBREW EQUIVALENT: Matitya.

Matmon From the Hebrew, meaning "treasure, wealth." HEBREW EQUIVALENT: Matmon.

Matok From the Hebrew, meaning "sweet." HEBREW EQUIVALENT: Matok.

Matri From the Hebrew, meaning "my rain." HEBREW EQUIVALENT: Matri.

Matt A pet form of Matthew.

Mattathias From the Greek, meaning "gift of God." HEBREW EQUIVALENT: Matityahu.

Matthew A variant form of Mattathias.

Mattie, Matty, Mattye Pet forms of Matthew.

Maurey A pet form of Maurice.

Maurice From the Middle English, meaning "moorish, dark-skinned." HEBREW EQUIVALENT: Cham.

Maurie A pet form of Maurice.

Maury A pet form of Maurice

Max A short form of Maximilian.

Maximilian From the Latin, meaning "great" or "famous." HEBREW EQUIVALENT: Mehulal.

Maxwell An English form of Maximilian.

Mayer A variant spelling of Meir.

Maynard From the Old High German, meaning "powerful, strong." HEBREW EQUIVALENT: Amotz.

Mazal From the Hebrew, meaning "star" or "luck." HEBREW EQUIVALENT: Mazal.

Mazal-Tov From the Hebrew, meaning "good star, lucky star." HEBREW EQUIVALENT: Mazal-Tov.

Medad From the Hebrew, meaning "measurement." HEBREW EQUIVALENT: Meidad.

Meged From the Hebrew, meaning "goodness, sweetness, exellence." HEBREW EQUIVALENT: Meged.

Meir From the Hebrew, meaning "one who brightens or shines." HEBREW EQUIVALENT: Me'ir.

Meiri A variant form of Meir.

Mel, Mell Pet forms of Melvin.

Melchior A variant form of the Latin name Melchita. Derived from the Hebrew *melech*, meaning "king." HEBREW EQUIVALENT: Melech.

Melech From the Hebrew, meaning "king." HEBREW EQUIVALENT: Melech.

Melton A variant form of Milton.

Melville From the Old English, meaning "village near the mill." HEBREW EQUIVALENT: Kimchi.

Melvin From the Anglo-Saxon, meaning "friendly toiler" or "famous friend." HEBREW EQUIVALENT: Amel.

Melvyn A variant spelling of Melvin.

Menachem From the Hebrew, meaning "comforter." HEBREW EQUIVALENT: Menachem.

Menahem A variant spelling of Menachem.

Menashe From the Hebrew, meaning "causing to forget." HEBREW EQUIVALENT: Menashe.

Menashi A variant form of Menashe. HEBREW EQUIVALENT: Menashi.

Mendel, Mendelle A Yiddish name derived from Menachem.

Mendl A variant spelling of Mendel.

Meredith From the Anglo-Saxon, meaning "sea dew" or "sea defender." HEBREW EQUIVALENT: Avi'yam.

Merom From the Hebrew, meaning "heights." HEBREW EQUIVALENT: Merom.

Meron From the Hebrew, meaning "sheep." HEBREW EQUIVALENT: Meron.

Merrill From the Old English, meaning "sea, pool, river." HEBREW EQUIVALENT: Avi'yam.

Merton From the Anglo-Saxon, meaning "from the farm by the sea." HEBREW EQUIVALENT: Avi'yam.

Mervin A Welsh form of Marvin.

Mervyn A variant spelling of Mervin.

Merwin, Merwyn Variant forms of Marvin.

Meshi From the Hebrew, meaning "silk." HEBREW EQUIVALENT: Meshi.

Meyer A variant spelling of Meir.

Mica, Micah Anglicized forms of Micha.

Micha From the Hebrew, meaning "Who is like God?" HEBREW EQUIVALENT: Micha.

Michael From the Hebrew, meaning "Who is like God?" HEBREW EQUIVALENT: Michael.

Michal A short form of Michael.

Michel A variant form of Michael.

Mickey, Mickie, Micky Pet forms of Michael.

Mika A variant spelling of Micah.

Mike, Mikel Pet forms of Michael.

Mikhail A Russian form of Michael.

Miki A pet form of Michael.

Miles From the Greek and Latin, meaning "warrior, soldier." HEBREW EQUIVALENT: Mordechai.

Milton From the Old English, meaning "mill town." HEBREW EQUIVALENT: Shadmon.

Misha A Russian form of Michael.

Mishael From the Hebrew, meaning "borrowed." HEBREW EQUIVALENT: Mishael.

Mitch A pet form of Mitchell.

Mitchel, Mitchell Variant forms of Michael.

Mo, Moe A pet form of Morris.

Moise, Moises French forms of Moses.

Monroe From the Celtic, meaning "red marsh." HEBREW EQUIVALENT: Moshe.

Montague The French form of the Latin, meaning "from the pointed mountain." HEBREW EQUIVALENT: Amir.

Monte A pet form of Montague and Montgomery.

Montgomery The English variant of the French name Montague.

Monty A variant spelling of Monte. Also a short form of Montague and Montgomery.

Mor From the Hebrew, referring to myrrh, a type of spice. HEBREW EQUIVALENT: Mor.

Mordecai The Anglicized form of Mordechai.

Mordechai From the Persian and Babylonian, meaning "warrior, warlike." HEBREW EQUIVALENT: Mordechai.

Mordy A pet form of Mordechai.

Moreg From the Hebrew, meaning "grain thresher." HEBREW EQUIVALENT: Moreg.

Morenu From the Hebrew, meaning "our teacher." HEBREW EQUIVALENT: Morenu.

Morey A pet form of Maurice.

Morgan From the Celtic, meaning "one who lives near the sea." HEBREW EQUIVALENT: Avi'yam.

Mori, Morie From the Hebrew, meaning "my teacher."
HEBREW EQUIVALENT: Mori.

Moritz A variant form of Maurice.

Morrey A variant spelling of Morey.

Morrie A variant spelling of Morey.

Morris A variant form of Maurice. Also, from the Gaelic,
meaning "great warrior." HEBREW EQUIVALENT: Mordechai.

Morrison A patronymic form, meaning "son of Morris."

Morry A variant spelling of Morey.

Morse A variant spelling of Maurice.

Mortimer From the Anglo-French, meaning "one who lives
near the sea." HEBREW EQUIVALENT: Moshe.

Morton From the Old English, meaning "town near the sea."
HEBREW EQUIVALENT: Ma'ayan.

Mosad, Mossad From the Hebrew, meaning "establishment."
HEBREW EQUIVALENT: Mosad.

Mose A pet form of Moses.

Moses The Anglicized form of Moshe.

Mosha From the Hebrew, meaning "salvation." HEBREW
EQUIVALENT: Mosha.

Moshe From the Hebrew, meaning "drawn out [of the
water]." HEBREW EQUIVALENT: Moshe.

Moss An English variant form of Moses.

Motel A Yiddish pet form of Mordechai.

Moti, Motti Nicknames for Mordechai. HEBREW EQUIVALENT:
Moti.

Moy, Moyse Variant English forms of Moses.

Muki A pet form of Meir.

Murray From the Celtic and Welsh, meaning "sea" or
"seaman." HEBREW EQUIVALENT: Moshe.

Mychal A variant spelling of Michael.

Myer A variant spelling of Mayer.

Myles A variant spelling of Miles.

Myron From the Greek, meaning "fragrant, sweet, pleasant." HEBREW EQUIVALENT: Achino'am.

Myrton A variant spelling of Merton.

Naam From the Hebrew, meaning "sweet, pleasant." HEBREW EQUIVALENT: Na'am.

Naaman From the Hebrew, meaning "sweet, beautiful, pleasant, good." HEBREW EQUIVALENT: Na'aman.

Nachman From the Hebrew, meaning "comforter." HEBREW EQUIVALENT: Nachman.

Nachmani From the Hebrew, meaning "comfort." HEBREW EQUIVALENT: Nachmani.

Nachum From the Hebrew, meaning "comfort." HEBREW EQUIVALENT: Nachum.

Nadav From the Hebrew, meaning "generous, noble." HEBREW EQUIVALENT: Nadav.

Nadiv From the Hebrew, meaning "princely, generous." HEBREW EQUIVALENT: Nadiv.

Naf A pet form of Naftali.

Naftali, Naftalie From the Hebrew, meaning "to wrestle" or "to be crafty." HEBREW EQUIVALENT: Naftali.

Nagara From the Aramaic, meaning "carpenter." HEBREW EQUIVALENT: Nagara.

Nagid From the Hebrew, meaning "ruler, prince." HEBREW EQUIVALENT: Nagid.

Nagiv From the Hebrew, meaning "pertaining to the south." HEBREW EQUIVALENT: Nagiv.

Nahir A variant form of Nahor. HEBREW EQUIVALENT: Nahir.

Nahor From the Aramaic, meaning "light." HEBREW EQUIVALENT: Nahor.

Nahum A variant spelling of Nachum.

Naim From the Hebrew, meaning "pleasant." HEBREW EQUIVALENT: Na'im.

Namer From the Hebrew, meaning "leopard." HEBREW EQUIVALENT: Namer.

Namir From the Hebrew, meaning "leopard." HEBREW EQUIVALENT: Namir.

Nanod From the Hebrew, meaning "wanderer." HEBREW EQUIVALENT: Nanod.

Naom A variant form of Naaman. HEBREW EQUIVALENT: Na'om.

Naor From the Hebrew, meaning "light" or "enlightened." HEBREW EQUIVALENT: Na'or.

Naphtali, Naphthali Variant spellings of Naftali.

Nasi From the Hebrew, meaning "prince, leader." HEBREW EQUIVALENT: Nasi.

Nason A variant form of Natan.

Natan From the Hebrew, meaning "gift." HEBREW EQUIVALENT: Natan.

Nate A pet form of Nathan.

Nathan A variant spelling of Natan.

Nathanel, Nathaniel Variant spellings of Netanel.

Nativ From the Hebrew, meaning "path, road." HEBREW EQUIVALENT: Nativ.

Navon From the Hebrew, meaning "wise." HEBREW EQUIVALENT: Navon.

Neal, Neale From the Middle English and the Gaelic, meaning "dark-complexioned." HEBREW EQUIVALENT: Pinchas.

Nechemia, Nechemiah Variant spellings of Nechemya.

Nechemya From the Hebrew, meaning "comforted by the Lord." HEBREW EQUIVALENT: Nechemya.

Ned A pet form of Edmond and Edward.

Neddy A pet form of Edmond and Edward.

Negev From the Hebrew, meaning "south, southerly." HEBREW EQUIVALENT: Negev.

Nehemiah, Nehemiah Variant spellings of Nechemya.

Neil A variant spelling of Neal.

Neilson A patronymic form of Neil, meaning "son of Neil."

Nelson A patronymic form of Neal, meaning "son of Neal."

Nemuel From the Hebrew, meaning "ant." HEBREW EQUIVALENT: Nemuel.

Ner From the Hebrew, meaning "light." HEBREW EQUIVALENT: Ner.

Neri From the Hebrew, meaning "my light." HEBREW EQUIVALENT: Neri.

Nerli, Ner-Li From the Hebrew, meaning "I have [a] light." HEBREW EQUIVALENT: Nerli.

Nes, Ness From the Hebrew, meaning "miracle." HEBREW EQUIVALENT: Nes.

Nesher From the Hebrew, meaning "eagle." HEBREW EQUIVALENT: Nesher.

Neta From the Hebrew, meaning "sapling." HEBREW EQUIVALENT: Neta.

Netanel From the Hebrew, meaning "gift of God." HEBREW EQUIVALENT: Netanel.

Netaniel A variant form of Netanel. HEBREW EQUIVALENT: Netaniel.

Netanya From the Hebrew, meaning "gift of God." HEBREW EQUIVALENT: Netanya.

Netanyahu A variant form of Netanya.

Nethanel A variant spelling of Netanel.

Nethaniel A variant spelling of Netanel.

Nevil, Nevile, Nevill, Neville From the French, meaning "new town." HEBREW EQUIVALENT: Zevulun.

Newbold From the Old English, meaning "new town [beside the tree]." Akin to Newton.

Newman From the Anglo-Saxon, meaning "new man." HEBREW EQUIVALENT: Adam.

Newton From the Old English, meaning "from the new farmstead" or "new town." HEBREW EQUIVALENT: Shadmon.

Nicholas From the Greek, meaning "victory of the people." HEBREW EQUIVALENT: Netzach.

Nicolas A variant spelling of Nicholas.

Nidri From the Hebrew, meaning "my oath." HEBREW EQUIVALENT: Nidri.

Niel A variant Norse form of Nicholas.

Nike A pet form of Nicholas.

Niles A patronymic form of Neal, meaning "son of Neal."

Nili An acronym of the Hebrew words for "the glory [or eternity] of Israel will not lie" (I Samuel 15:29). HEBREW EQUIVALENT: Nili.

Nils A patronymic form of Neal, meaning "son of Neal."

Nimrod From the Hebrew, meaning "man of might," or "hunter." HEBREW EQUIVALENT: Nimrod.

Nir From the Hebrew, meaning "to plough, to cultivate a field." HEBREW EQUIVALENT: Nir.

Nirel, Nir-El From the Hebrew, meaning "cultivated field of the Lord." HEBREW EQUIVALENT: Nirel.

Niria, Niriah Variant spellings of Niriya.

Niriel A variant form of Nirel. HEBREW EQUIVALENT: Niriel.

Niriya From the Hebrew, meaning "cultivated field of the Lord." HEBREW EQUIVALENT: Niriya.

Nirya A variant form of Niriya. HEBREW EQUIVALENT: Nirya.

Nisan, Nissan From the Hebrew, meaning "banner, emblem" or "miracle." HEBREW EQUIVALENT: Nissan.

Nissi A variant form of Nisim. HEBREW EQUIVALENT: Nissi.

Nisim, Nissim From the Hebrew, meaning "miracles." HEBREW EQUIVALENT: Nisim.

Nitzan From the Hebrew, meaning "sapling." HEBREW EQUIVALENT: Nitzan.

Niv From the Aramaic and Arabic, meaning "speech, expression." HEBREW EQUIVALENT: Niv.

Noach From the Hebrew, meaning "rest, quiet, peace." HEBREW EQUIVALENT: No'ach.

Noah The Anglicized form of Noach.

Noam From the Hebrew, meaning "sweetness" or "friendship." HEBREW EQUIVALENT: No'am.

Noaz From the Hebrew, meaning "daring, bold." HEBREW EQUIVALENT: No'az.

Noble From the Latin, meaning "well-known, famous." HEBREW EQUIVALENT: Noda.

Noda From the Hebrew, meaning "famous, well-known." HEBREW EQUIVALENT: Noda.

Noel A Christian name referring to the birth of Jesus.

Nof From the Hebrew, meaning "beautiful landscape." HEBREW EQUIVALENT: Nof.

Noga From the Hebrew, meaning "light, bright." HEBREW EQUIVALENT: Noga.

Nolan From the Celtic, meaning "noble" or "famous." HEBREW EQUIVALENT: Noda.

Noland A variant form of Nolan.

Norbert From the German, meaning "divine brightness." HEBREW EQUIVALENT: Avner.

Norman From the Anglo-Saxon, meaning "man from the north." HEBREW EQUIVALENT: Tzefanyahu.

Normann A variant spelling of Norman.

Norris From the Anglo-Saxon, meaning "the dwelling place of a man from the north." HEBREW EQUIVALENT: Tzefanyahu.

North From the Anglo-Saxon, meaning "man from the north." HEBREW EQUIVALENT: Tzefanya.

Norton From the Anglo-Saxon, meaning "town in the north." HEBREW EQUIVALENT: Tzefanya.

Norwood From the Old English, meaning "woods in the north." HEBREW EQUIVALENT: Tzefanyahu.

Nosson A variant form of Natan.

Noy From the Hebrew, meaning "beauty." HEBREW EQUIVALENT: Noy.

Nun From the Hebrew, meaning "fish." HEBREW EQUIVALENT: Nun.

Nur From the Hebrew and Aramaic, meaning "fire, light." HEBREW EQUIVALENT: Nur.

Nuri From the Hebrew and Aramaic, meaning "my fire, my light." HEBREW EQUIVALENT: Nuri.

Nuria, Nuriah Variant spellings of Nuriya.

Nuriel From the Aramaic and Hebrew, meaning "fire of the Lord." HEBREW EQUIVALENT: Nuriel.

Nuriya From the Aramaic and Hebrew, meaning "fire of the Lord." HEBREW EQUIVALENT: Nuriya.

Nurya A variant form of Nuriya. HEBREW EQUIVALENT: Nurya.

Nyle A variant Irish form of Neal.

Oakleigh A variant spelling of Oakley.

Oakley From the Old English, meaning "field of oak trees." HEBREW EQUIVALENT: Alon.

Obadiah The Anglicized form of Ovadya.

Obe A pet form of Obadiah.

Oded From the Hebrew, meaning "to restore." HEBREW EQUIVALENT: Oded.

Odik A pet form of Oded.

Odo From the Old German and the Old English, meaning "rich." HEBREW EQUIVALENT: Yitro.

Ofar From the Hebrew, meaning "young deer." HEBREW EQUIVALENT: Ofar.

Ofer From the Hebrew, meaning "young mountain goat" or "young deer." HEBREW EQUIVALENT: Ofer.

Ofra From the Hebrew, meaning "young mountain goat" or "young deer." HEBREW EQUIVALENT: Ofra.

Ofri From the Hebrew, meaning "my deer." HEBREW EQUIVALENT: Ofri.

Og From the Hebrew, meaning "giant." HEBREW EQUIVALENT: Og.

Ogen From the Hebrew, meaning "to chain, anchor." HEBREW EQUIVALENT: Ogen.

Ohev From the Hebrew, meaning "lover." HEBREW EQUIVALENT: Oheiv.

Olaf From the Norse and Danish, meaning "ancestor." HEBREW EQUIVALENT: Kadmiel.

Oleg From the Norse, meaning "holy." HEBREW EQUIVALENT: Kadosh.

Olin From the Middle English, meaning "holy." HEBREW EQUIVALENT: Kadosh.

Oliver From the Latin, meaning "man of peace." HEBREW EQUIVALENT: Avshalom.

Olivier The French form of Oliver.

Ollie A pet form of Oliver.

Omen From the Hebrew, meaning "faithful." HEBREW EQUIVALENT: Omen.

Omer From the Hebrew, meaning "sheaf." HEBREW EQUIVALENT: Omer.

Ometz From the Hebrew, meaning "strength." HEBREW EQUIVALENT: Ometz.

Omri From the Hebrew, meaning "my sheaf." HEBREW EQUIVALENT: Omri.

Opher A variant spelling of Ofer.

Orde From the Old English, meaning "beginning." HEBREW EQUIVALENT: Rishon.

Oren From the Hebrew, meaning "a pine tree." HEBREW EQUIVALENT: Oren.

Orev From the Hebrew, meaning "raven." HEBREW EQUIVALENT: Oreiv.

Ori From the Hebrew, meaning "my light." HEBREW EQUIVALENT: Ori.

Orin, Orrin Variant forms of Oren.

Orland A variant form of Roland.

Orlando A variant form of Orland.

Oron From the Hebrew, meaning "light." HEBREW EQUIVALENT: Oron.

Orson From the Latin, meaning "bear." HEBREW EQUIVALENT: Dov.

Orval A variant form of Orville.

Orville From the French, meaning "golden city." HEBREW EQUIVALENT: Ofar.

Osbert From the Anglo-Saxon and German, meaning "famous [bright] god." HEBREW EQUIVALENT: Bahir.

Oscar, Oskar From the Anglo-Saxon, meaning "divine spear" or "divine strength." HEBREW EQUIVALENT: Gavriel.

Oshri From the Hebrew, meaning "my good fortune." HEBREW EQUIVALENT: Oshri.

Osman From the Anglo-Saxon, meaning "servant of God" or "protected by God." HEBREW EQUIVALENT: Avimelech.

Osmand A variant form of Osman.

Osmond A variant spelling of Osmand.

Osmund A variant spelling of Osmond.

Ossie A pet form of Oscar or Oswald.

Oswald From the Old English, meaning "god of the forest" or "house steward." HEBREW EQUIVALENT: Ovadya.

Otis From the Greek, meaning "one who hears well." HEBREW EQUIVALENT: Oz.

Otniel From the Hebrew, meaning "God is my strength." HEBREW EQUIVALENT: Otniel.

Otto From the Old High German, meaning "prosperous, wealthy." HEBREW EQUIVALENT: Hotir.

Otzar From the Hebrew, meaning "treasure." HEBREW EQUIVALENT: Otzar.

Ovadya From the Hebrew, meaning "servant of God." HEBREW EQUIVALENT: Ovadya.

Ovadyahu A variant form of Ovadya. HEBREW EQUIVALENT: Ovadyahu.

Owen From the Latin, meaning "well-born," or from the Welsh, meaning "young warrior." HEBREW EQUIVALENT: Ish-Hod.

Oz From the Hebrew, meaning "strength." HEBREW EQUIVALENT: Oz.

Ozar A variant spelling of Otzar.

Ozer From the Hebrew, meaning "strength" or "helper." HEBREW EQUIVALENT: Ozer.

Ozni From the Hebrew, meaning "my ear" or "my hearing." HEBREW EQUIVALENT: Ozni.

Ozzi, Ozzy A pet form of Oswald.

Ozri From the Hebrew, meaning "my helper." HEBREW EQUIVALENT: Ozri.

Paddy A pet form of Patrick.

Page From the Italian, meaning "servant." HEBREW EQUIVALENT: Ovadya.

Palmer From the Middle English, meaning "pilgrim who carries a palm leaf." HEBREW EQUIVALENT: Itamar.

Palti From the Hebrew, meaning "my deliverance." HEBREW EQUIVALENT: Palti.

Paltiel From the Hebrew, meaning "God is my savior." HEBREW EQUIVALENT: Paltiel.

Parker An occupational name, meaning "one who tends a park." HEBREW EQUIVALENT: Carmi.

Parnell A variant form of Peter.

Pat A pet form of Patrick.

Patrick From the Latin, meaning "one of noble descent." HEBREW EQUIVALENT: Chirom.

Paul From the Latin, meaning "small." HEBREW EQUIVALENT: Katan.

Pauley A variant form of Paul.

Paxton From the Latin, meaning "town of peace." HEBREW EQUIVALENT: Avshalom.

Payton The Scottish form of Patrick.

Paz From the Hebrew, meaning "golden, sparkling." HEBREW EQUIVALENT: Paz.

Pazi From the Hebrew, meaning "my gold." HEBREW EQUIVALENT: Pazi.

Pedro A Spanish and Portuguese form of Peter.

Pele, Peleh From the Hebrew, meaning "miracle." HEBREW EQUIVALENT: Peleh.

Peli A variant form of Pele. HEBREW EQUIVALENT: Peli.

Peniel A variant form of Penuel.

Penini From the Hebrew, meaning "pearl" or "precious stone." HEBREW EQUIVALENT: Penini.

Penuel From the Hebrew, meaning "face of God" or "sight of God." HEBREW EQUIVALENT: Penuel.

Per A Swedish form of Peter. Akin to the English Piers.

Peretz From the Hebrew, meaning "burst open." HEBREW EQUIVALENT: Peretz.

Perez A variant spelling of Peretz.

Perry The French form of Peter.

Pesach From the Hebrew, meaning "to pass over." HEBREW EQUIVALENT: Pesach.

Pete A pet form of Peter.

Peter From the Greek and the Latin, meaning "rock." HEBREW EQUIVALENT: Avitzur.

Phelps A variant form of Philip.

Philip A variant spelling of Phillip.

Phillip From the Greek, meaning "lover of horses." HEBREW EQUIVALENT: Peresh.

Phillipe A French form of Phillip.

Phillipp A Scottish form of Phillip.

Philo From the Greek, meaning "loving." HEBREW EQUIVALENT: Ahuv.

Phineas The Anglicized form of Pinchas.

Phoebus In Greek mythology, the god of light and sun. HEBREW EQUIVALENT: Bahir.

Pierce A variant form of Peter.

Pierre A French form of Peter.

Piers An English variant form of Peter.

Pinchas From the Egyptian, meaning "dark-complexioned." HEBREW EQUIVALENT: Pinchas.

Pinchos A variant spelling of Pinchas.

Pincus A variant form of Pinchas.

Pinhas A variant spelling of Pinchas.

Pini A pet form of Pinchas.

Pinkas A variant form of Pinchas.

Pinkus A variant form of Pincus.

Pip A pet form of Philip.

Placid   From the Latin, meaning "to be tranquil, at peace."
HEBREW EQUIVALENT: Shalom.

Pol   From the Hebrew, meaning "bean." HEBREW
EQUIVALENT: Pol.

Poul   A variant spelling of Paul.

Prentice   From the Middle English, meaning "beginner,
learner." HEBREW EQUIVALENT: Petachya.

Prentiss   A variant spelling of Prentice.

Preston   An Old English name, meaning "priest's town."
HEBREW EQUIVALENT: Devir.

Price   From the Middle English and Old French, meaning
"price, value." HEBREW EQUIVALENT: Machir.

BEST BABY NAMES   Q–R   BEST BABY NAMES

Quentin   From the Latin, meaning "fifth." There are no
Hebrew equivalents.

Quenton   A variant spelling of Quentin.

Quincy   A variant form of Quentin.

Quinn   A variant form of Quentin.

Raam   From the Hebrew, meaning "thunder, noise." HEBREW
EQUIVALENT: Ra'am.

Raamya   From the Hebrew, meaning "God's thunder."
HEBREW EQUIVALENT: Ra'amya.

Raanan   From the Hebrew, meaning "fresh, luxuriant,
beautiful." HEBREW EQUIVALENT: Ra'anan.

Rabi   From the Hebrew, meaning "my teacher." HEBREW
EQUIVALENT: Rabi.

Rachaman   From the Hebrew, meaning "compassionate One
[God]." HEBREW EQUIVALENT: Rachaman.

Rachamin   From the Hebrew, meaning "compassion, mercy."
HEBREW EQUIVALENT: Rachamim.

Rafa From the Hebrew, meaning "heal." HEBREW
EQUIVALENT: Rafa.

Rafael A Spanish form of Refael.

Raff A pet form of Refael.

Rafi A pet form of Refael and its variant forms.

Raleigh From the Old English, meaning "deer meadow."
HEBREW EQUIVALENT: Efer.

Ralph From the Old Norse and Anglo-Saxon, meaning
"fearless advisor." HEBREW EQUIVALENT: Aleksonder.

Ram From the Hebrew, meaning "high, exalted, mighty."
HEBREW EQUIVALENT: Ram.

Rami A variant form of Ram. HEBREW EQUIVALENT: Rami.

Ramon A Spanish form of Raymond.

Ramsay A variant spelling of Ramsey.

Ramsey From the Old English, meaning "ram's island."
HEBREW EQUIVALENT: Zimri.

Ran From the Hebrew, meaning "joy" or "song." HEBREW
EQUIVALENT: Ran.

Ranan A variant spelling of Raanan.

Randal, Randall From the Anglo-Saxon, meaning "superior
protection." HEBREW EQUIVALENT: Shemarya.

Randell A variant spelling of Randall.

Randi A variant spelling of Randy.

Randolph From the Anglo-Saxon, meaning "good counsel."
HEBREW EQUIVALENT: Azarya.

Randy A pet form of Randal or Randolph.

Ranen From the Hebrew, meaning "to sing, to be joyous."
HEBREW EQUIVALENT: Ranen.

Rani From the Hebrew, meaning "my joy" or "my song."
HEBREW EQUIVALENT: Rani.

Ranon A variant form of Ranen. HEBREW EQUIVALENT:
Ranon.

Raoul A French form of Ralph and Randolph.

Raph A pet form of Raphael.

Raphael A variant spelling of Refael.

Raul A variant spelling of Raoul.

Rav From the Hebrew, meaning "teacher." HEBREW EQUIVALENT: Rav.

Rava A variant form of Rav.

Raven From the Old English, meaning "raven." HEBREW EQUIVALENT: Oreiv.

Ravi A variant form of Rabi.

Ravid From the Hebrew, meaning "ornament, jewelry." HEBREW EQUIVALENT: Ravid.

Raviv From the Hebrew, meaning "rain" or "dew." HEBREW EQUIVALENT: Raviv.

Ray From the Old English, meaning "stream" or from the Celtic, meaning "grace." HEBREW EQUIVALENT: Arnon.

Raya From the Hebrew, meaning "friend." HEBREW EQUIVALENT: Ray'a.

Raymond From the Old French, meaning "mighty protector," or from the German, meaning "quiet, peaceful." HEBREW EQUIVALENT: Magen.

Raymund A variant spelling of Raymond.

Raz From the Aramaic, meaning "secret." HEBREW EQUIVALENT: Raz.

Razi, Razzi From the Hebrew, meaning "my secret." HEBREW EQUIVALENT: Razi.

Raziel From the Aramaic, meaning "God is my secret." HEBREW EQUIVALENT: Raziel.

Read, Reade From the Old English, meaning "reed." HEBREW EQUIVALENT: Kaniel.

Redd A variant form of Read.

Reece A Welsh form of the Old English, meaning "stream." HEBREW EQUIVALENT: Arnon.

Reed A variant spelling of Read.

Reese A variant spelling of Reece.

Refael From the Hebrew, meaning "God has healed." HEBREW EQUIVALENT: Refa'el.

Refi A pet form of Refael.

Regem From the Hebrew, meaning "to stone." Also, from the Arabic, meaning "friend." HEBREW EQUIVALENT: Regem.

Reg, Reggie Pet forms of Reginald.

Reginald From the Old High German, meaning "wise, judicious" or "powerful ruler." HEBREW EQUIVALENT: Razin.

Reid A variant spelling of Read.

Reinhard, Reinhart Variant forms of Reynard.

Reinhold A German form of Reginald.

Remez From the Hebrew, meaning "sign" or "signal." HEBREW EQUIVALENT: Remez.

Rene A French name from the Latin, meaning "to be reborn, renew." HEBREW EQUIVALENT: Cha'yim.

Renen From the Hebrew, meaning "song." HEBREW EQUIVALENT: Renen.

Rennie A pet form of Reginald.

Reo A variant form of the Old English *rae*, meaning "stream." HEBREW EQUIVALENT: Arnan.

Rephael A variant spelling of Refael.

Rephi A variant spelling of Refi.

Reshef From the Hebrew, meaning "spark" or "flame." HEBREW EQUIVALENT: Resef.

Reuben, Reubin Variant forms of Reuven.

Reuel From the Hebrew, meaning "friend of God." HEBREW EQUIVALENT: Re'uel.

Reuven From the Hebrew, meaning "behold, a son." HEBREW EQUIVALENT: Re'uven.

Revital From the Hebrew, meaning "much dew." HEBREW EQUIVALENT: Revital.

Rex From the Latin, meaning "king." HEBREW EQUIVALENT: Melech.

Reynard From the Old High German, meaning "rich in good counsel." HEBREW EQUIVALENT: Buna.

Reynold A variant French form of Reginald.

Rhett From the Old English, meaning "small stream." HEBREW EQUIVALENT: Arnon.

Ricardo, Riccardo Spanish and Italian forms of Richard.

Ricci A pet form of Richard.

Ricco A pet form of Richard.

Rich, Richie Pet forms of Richard.

Richard A French form of the Old High German Reynard, meaning "powerful, rich ruler" or "valiant rider." HEBREW EQUIVALENT: Gavriel.

Richardo A Spanish form of Richard.

Rici, Ricci Pet forms of Richard.

Richie A pet form of Richard.

Ricki, Rickie, Ricky Pet forms of Richard.

Rimon, Rimmon From the Hebrew, meaning "pomegranate." HEBREW EQUIVALENT: Rimon.

Rip From the Latin, meaning "river bank." HEBREW EQUIVALENT: Arnon.

Rishon From the Hebrew, meaning "first." HEBREW EQUIVALENT: Rishon.

Rob A pet form of Robert.

Robard, Robart Variant French forms of Robert.

Robert From the Anglo-Saxon, meaning "bright, wise counsel." HEBREW EQUIVALENT: Zerach.

Robin A pet form of Robert popular in France.

Robson A patronymic form, meaning "son of Rob [Robert]."

Robyn A variant spelling of Robin.

Rocco A pet form of Richard or Rockne.

Rock A short form of Rockne.

Rockne From the Old English, meaning "rock." HEBREW EQUIVALENT: Tzuri.

Rockwell From the Old English, meaning "the well near the rock." HEBREW EQUIVALENT: Tzur.

Rocky A pet form of Rockne and Rockwell.

Rod, Rodd From the British, meaning "open, cleared land." HEBREW EQUIVALENT: Regev.

Roddy A pet form of Rod or Rodman.

Roderic, Roderick From the Old High German, meaning "famous ruler." HEBREW EQUIVALENT: Melech.

Rodger A variant spelling of Roger.

Rodgers A patronymic form of Roger.

Rodney From the Old English, meaning "cleared land near the water" or "one who carries a leveling rod, a surveyor." HEBREW EQUIVALENT: Artzi.

Rofi A pet form of Refael.

Roger From the Old French and the Anglo-Saxon, meaning "famous, noble warrior" or "honorable man." HEBREW EQUIVALENT: Efrat.

Rohn From the Greek, meaning "rose." HEBREW EQUIVALENT: Vered.

Roland A French form of the Old High German, meaning "fame of the land." HEBREW EQUIVALENT: Artza.

Rolando An Italian and Portuguese form of Roland.

Rolf, Rolfe Pet forms of Rudolph.

Rolland A variant spelling of Roland.

Rollen, Rollin Variant forms of Roland.

Rom From the Hebrew, meaning "heights." HEBREW EQUIVALENT: Rom.

Roman From Middle English and Old French, meaning "a romantic novel." HEBREW EQUIVALENT: Roman.

Romem A variant form of Rom. HEBREW EQUIVALENT: Romem.

Romi, Romie From the Hebrew, meaning "heights" or "nobility." HEBREW EQUIVALENT: Romi.

Ron From the Hebrew, meaning "joy" or "song." HEBREW EQUIVALENT: Ron.

Ronald The Scottish form of Reginald.

Ronel From the Hebrew, meaning "song of the Lord" or "joy of the Lord." HEBREW EQUIVALENT: Ronel.

Ronen From the Hebrew, meaning "song" or "joy." HEBREW EQUIVALENT: Ronen.

Roni A pet form of Ronald.

Ronli, Ron-Li From the Hebrew, meaning "song is mine." HEBREW EQUIVALENT: Ronli.

Ronnie, Ronny Pet forms of Ronald.

Rory An Irish form of Roderick.

Roscoe A variant form of Ross.

Ross From the Anglo-Saxon, meaning "woods, meadows." HEBREW EQUIVALENT: Artza.

Rowe A short form of Rowland.

Rowland A variant form of Roland.

Rowle A variant form of Ralph.

Roy From the Old French, meaning "king." HEBREW EQUIVALENT: Katriel.

Royal From the Middle English and the Latin, meaning "king." HEBREW EQUIVALENT: Avimelech.

Roye A variant spelling of Roy.

Rube A pet form of Reuben.

Ruben A variant form of Reuben.

Rubens A patronymic form of Reuben, meaning "son of Reuben."

Rubin A variant spelling of Reuben.

Ruby A pet form of Reuben.

Rudd From the Anglo-Saxon, meaning "red." HEBREW EQUIVALENT: Admon.

Rudolph A variant form of Randolph and Ralph.

Rueben A variant spelling of Reuben.

Ruel A variant spelling of Reuel.

Rufus From the Latin, meaning "red, red-haired." HEBREW EQUIVALENT: Tzochar.

Rupert A variant English, French, and German form of Robert.

Russ A pet form of Russell.

Russel, Russell French forms of the Latin, meaning "rusty-haired." Also, from the Anglo-Saxon, meaning "horse." HEBREW EQUIVALENT: Peresh.

Ruvane A variant spelling of Reuven.

Ruvik A pet form of Reuven.

BEST BABY NAMES   BEST BABY NAMES

Saad From the Aramaic, meaning "support." HEBREW EQUIVALENT: Sa'ad.

Saadi From the Hebrew, meaning "my support." HEBREW EQUIVALENT: Sa'adi.

Saadia, Saadiah Variant spellings of Saadya.

Saadli A variant form of Saadi. HEBREW EQUIVALENT: Sa'adli.

Saadya From the Hebrew, meaning "God is my support." HEBREW EQUIVALENT: Saadya.

Saba A variant form of Sava.

Sabra From the Aramaic, meaning "cactus" or "prickly pear." HEBREW EQUIVALENT: Sabar. Tzabar is an alternate form.

Sacha A Russian pet form of Alexander.

Sachar A short form of Yisachar (Issachar). HEBREW EQUIVALENT: Sachar.

Sadir From the Aramaic, meaning "order." HEBREW EQUIVALENT: Sadir.

Sagi From the Aramaic and Hebrew, meaning "sufficient" or "strong, mighty." HEBREW EQUIVALENT: Sagi.

Sagiv From the Aramaic and Hebrew, meaning "tall, noble" or "strong, mighty." HEBREW EQUIVALENT: Sagiv.

Sagy A variant spelling of Sagi.

Sal From the Latin, meaning "salt," or from the Old English, meaning "willow." Also, a pet form of Salvador. HEBREW EQUIVALENT: Ilan.

Salem The English form of the Hebrew *shalom*, meaning "peace." HEBREW EQUIVALENT: Shalem.

Sali, Salli From the Hebrew, meaning "my basket." Also, a pet form of Yisrael. HEBREW EQUIVALENT: Sali.

Salil From the Hebrew, meaning "path." HEBREW EQUIVALENT: Salil.

Salim From the Arabic, meaning "peace." HEBREW EQUIVALENT: Shalom.

Salman A variant spelling of Salmon.

Salmon From the Aramaic, meaning "garment," or a variant form of Solomon. HEBREW EQUIVALENT: Shalmon.

Salo A short form of Saloman.

Saloman, Salomon Variant forms of Solomon.

Salu From the Aramaic, meaning "basket." HEBREW EQUIVALENT: Salu.

Salvador, Salvatore From the Latin, meaning "to be saved."
HEBREW EQUIVALENT: Hoshei'a.

Sam A pet form of Samuel.

Samal From the Aramaic, meaning "sign, symbol." Also,
from the modern Hebrew, meaning "sergeant." HEBREW
EQUIVALENT: Samal.

Samm A variant spelling of Sam.

Sammy A pet form of Samuel.

Sampson A variant spelling of Samson.

Samson From the Hebrew, meaning "sun." HEBREW
EQUIVALENT: Shimshon.

Samuel From the Hebrew, meaning "His name is God" or
"God has dedicated." HEBREW EQUIVALENT: Shemuel.

Samy A pet form of Samuel.

Sander A short form of Alexander.

Sanders A patronymic form of Sander.

Sandor A variant spelling of Sander, a pet form of
Alexander.

Sandy A pet form of Alexander and Sanford.

Sanford From the Old English, meaning "sandy river
crossing" or "peaceful counsel." HEBREW EQUIVALENT:
Shalom.

Sapir From the Greek, meaning "precious stone." HEBREW
EQUIVALENT: Sapir.

Sar From the Hebrew, meaning "prince." HEBREW
EQUIVALENT: Sar.

Sarid From the Hebrew, meaning "remnant." HEBREW
EQUIVALENT: Sarid.

Sasha A Russian pet form of Alexander.

Saul From the Hebrew, meaning "borrowed." The
Anglicized form of Shaul.

Saunders A variant spelling of Sanders.

Sav A variant form of Sava.

Sava From the Aramaic, meaning "grandfather" or "old
man." HEBREW EQUIVALENT: Sava.

Savyon The Hebrew name of a plant. HEBREW EQUIVALENT:
Savyon.

Sawyer From the Middle English, meaning "one who saws wood." HEBREW EQUIVALENT: Nagara.

Sayer From the Old German, meaning "victory of the people." HEBREW EQUIVALENT: Shua.

Scott The Late Latin form for "Scotchman," meaning "tattoed one." HEBREW EQUIVALENT: Sofer.

Scottie, Scotty Pet forms of Scott.

Sean A popular Gaelic form of John.

Seff A Yiddish form of Zev (Ze'ev).

Sefi A pet form of Yosef (Joseph).

Segel From the Hebrew, meaning "treasure." HEBREW EQUIVALENT: Segel.

Segev From the Hebrew, meaning "glory, majesty, exalted." HEBREW EQUIVALENT: Segev.

Seguv From the Hebrew, meaning "exalted." HEBREW EQUIVALENT: Seguv.

Selby A variant form of Shelby.

Selden, Seldon From the Middle English, meaning "rare," connoting an article of value. HEBREW EQUIVALENT: Leshem.

Seled From the Hebrew, meaning "leap for joy" or "praise." HEBREW EQUIVALENT: Seled.

Selig A Yiddish name, from the German and Old English, meaning "blessed, holy." HEBREW EQUIVALENT: Asher.

Selwyn From the Anglo-Saxon, meaning "holy place" or "friend at court." HEBREW EQUIVALENT: Bildad.

Semel From the Hebrew, meaning "sign, symbol." HEBREW EQUIVALENT: Semel.

Sender A Yiddish form of Sander, a form of Alexander.

Senior From the Latin, meaning "elder." Shneur is a Yiddish variant form. HEBREW EQUIVALENT: Zaken.

Serge From the Old French and the Latin, meaning "serve." HEBREW EQUIVALENT: Ovadya.

Seth The Anglicized form of Shet, the son of Adam.

Seton From the Anglo-Saxon, meaning "town near the sea." HEBREW EQUIVALENT: Avi'yam.

Seward From the Anglo-Saxon, meaning "defender of the sea coast." HEBREW EQUIVALENT: Shemer.

Sewell From the Old English, meaning "well near the sea." HEBREW EQUIVALENT: Moshe.

Seymore A variant spelling of Seymour.

Seymour From the Old English, meaning "marshy land near the sea." HEBREW EQUIVALENT: Arnon.

Shaanan From the Hebrew, meaning "peaceful." HEBREW EQUIVALENT: Sha'anan.

Shabbetai, Shabetai Variant forms of Shabtai.

Shabbtai, Shabtai From the Hebrew and Aramaic, meaning "rest, sabbath." HEBREW EQUIVALENT: Shabtai.

Shabtiel A variant form of Shabtai. HEBREW EQUIVALENT: Shabtiel.

Shachar From the Hebrew, meaning "morning." HEBREW EQUIVALENT: Shachar.

Shael A pet form of Mishael.

Shahar A variant spelling of Shachar.

Shai From the Hebrew and Aramaic, meaning "gift." Also, a pet form of Yesha'ya (Isaiah). HEBREW EQUIVALENT: Shai.

Shaked From the Hebrew, meaning "almond tree." HEBREW EQUIVALENT: Shaked.

Shalem From the Hebrew, meaning "whole." HEBREW EQUIVALENT: Shalem.

Shalev From the Hebrew, meaning "peaceful." HEBREW EQUIVALENT: Shalev.

Shalman From the Assyrian, meaning "to be complete" or "to be rewarded." HEBREW EQUIVALENT: Shalman.

Shalom From the Hebrew, meaning "peace." HEBREW EQUIVALENT: Shalom.

Shalum, Shallum From the Hebrew, meaning "whole, complete peace." HEBREW EQUIVALENT: Shalum.

Shalvi A variant form of Shalev. HEBREW EQUIVALENT: Shalvi.

Shamir From the Aramaic and Hebrew, meaning "diamond" or "flint." HEBREW EQUIVALENT: Shamir.

Shami, Shammai From the Hebrew and Aramaic, meaning "name." HEBREW EQUIVALENT: Shamai.

Shanan A variant spelling of Shaanan.

Shane A variant form of Sean used prominently in Ireland.

Shanon A variant spelling of Shanan.

Shaul From the Hebrew, meaning "borrowed." HEBREW EQUIVALENT: Shaul.

Shapir From the Aramaic, meaning "beautiful." HEBREW EQUIVALENT: Shapir.

Sharp, Sharpe From the Old English, meaning "clever, perceptive." HEBREW EQUIVALENT: Navon.

Shatil From the Hebrew, meaning "plant." HEBREW EQUIVALENT: Shatil.

Shatul A variant form of Shatil. HEBREW EQUIVALENT: Shatul.

Shaul From the Hebrew, meaning "asked" or "borrowed." HEBREW EQUIVALENT: Sha'ul.

Shaun, Shawn Variant spellings of Sean.

Shay A variant spelling of Shai.

Shaya, Shaye Short forms of Yesha'ya (Isaiah). HEBREW EQUIVALENT: Sha'ya.

Shea, Sheah Variant spellings of Shia.

Shebsel, Shebsil Variant forms of Shepsel and Shepsil.

Sheeya A variant spelling of Shia.

Shefer From the Hebrew, meaning "pleasant, beautiful." HEBREW EQUIVALENT: Shefer.

Shelby From the Anglo-Saxon, meaning "sheltered town." HEBREW EQUIVALENT: Shimron.

Sheldon From the Old English, meaning "shepherd's hut on a hill" or "protected hill." HEBREW EQUIVALENT: Shemarya.

Sheli From the Hebrew, meaning "mine, belonging to me." HEBREW EQUIVALENT: Sheli.

Shelley From the Old English, meaning "island of shells." HEBREW EQUIVALENT: Peleg.

Shelly A variant spelling of Shelley.

Shelomi A variant spelling of Shlomi.

Shelomo A variant spelling of Shlomo.

Shem From the Hebrew, meaning "name." HEBREW EQUIVALENT: Shem.

Shemaria, Shemariah Variant spellings of Shemarya.

Shemarya From the Hebrew, meaning "protection of God." HEBREW EQUIVALENT: Shemarya.

Shemaryahu A variant form of Shemarya. HEBREW EQUIVALENT: Shemaryahu.

Shemer From the Hebrew, meaning "to guard, watch" or "preserve." HEBREW EQUIVALENT: Shemer.

Shemuel A variant spelling of Shmuel.

Shepard From the Anglo-Saxon, meaning "shepherd." HEBREW EQUIVALENT: Ro'i.

Shepherd From the Old English, meaning "one who tends sheep, protector." HEBREW EQUIVALENT: Shermaryahu.

Shepley From the Old English, meaning "sheep meadow." HEBREW EQUIVALENT: Zimri.

Sheppard A variant spelling of Shepherd.

Shepsel, Shepsil From the Yiddish, meaning "sheep." HEBREW EQUIVALENT: Talya.

Sheraga From the Aramaic, meaning "light." HEBREW EQUIVALENT: Sheraga.

Sherira From the Aramaic, meaning "strong." HEBREW EQUIVALENT: Sherira.

Sherman From the Old English, meaning "servant [or resident] of the shire [district]" or "one who shears [sheep]." HEBREW EQUIVALENT: Ovadya.

Sherry A pet form of Sherman.

Sherwin From the Anglo-Saxon, meaning "one who shears the wind." Also, from the Old English, meaning "shining friend." HEBREW EQUIVALENT: Amitai.

Sherwood From the Anglo-Saxon, meaning "forest, wooded area." HEBREW EQUIVALENT: Ya'ar.

Shet From the Hebrew, meaning "garment" or "appointed." Also from the Syriac, meaning "appearance." HEBREW EQUIVALENT: Shet.

Shia, Shiah Short forms of Yesha'ya (Isaiah). HEBREW EQUIVALENT: Shia.

Shifron From the Hebrew, meaning "pleasant." HEBREW EQUIVALENT: Shifron.

Shimi From the Hebrew, meaning "my name" or "reputation." HEBREW EQUIVALENT: Shimi.

Shimmel A Yiddish form of Shimon.

Shimon From the Hebrew, meaning "to hear, to be heard" or "reputation." HEBREW EQUIVALENT: Shimon.

Shimri From the Hebrew, meaning "my guard." HEBREW EQUIVALENT: Shimri.

Shimshon From the Hebrew, meaning "sun." HEBREW EQUIVALENT: Shimshon.

Shipley A variant form of Shepley.

Shiron From the Hebrew, meaning "song, songfest." HEBREW EQUIVALENT: Shiron.

Shiya A variant spelling of Shia.

Shlomi From the Hebrew, meaning "my peace." HEBREW EQUIVALENT: Shlomi.

Shlomo From the Hebrew, meaning "his peace." HEBREW EQUIVALENT: Shlomo.

Shmuel From the Hebrew, meaning "His name is God." HEBREW EQUIVALENT: Shmuel.

Shneur A Yiddish form of Senior.

Sholom A variant spelling of Shalom.

Shor From the Hebrew, meaning "ox." HEBREW EQUIVALENT: Shor.

Shosh A pet form of Shoshan.

Shoshan From the Hebrew, meaning "lily." HEBREW EQUIVALENT: Shoshan.

Shoul A variant spelling of Shaul.

Shraga A Yiddish form of Sheraga.

Shushan From the Hebrew, menaing "lily." HEBREW EQUIVALENT: Shushan.

Si A pet form of Seymour, Simon, and Simeon.

Sidney A contracted form of Dionysius, the Greek god of wine, drama, and fruitfulness. HEBREW EQUIVALENT: Efra'yim.

Siegfried From the German, meaning "victorious peace." HEBREW EQUIVALENT: Shlomo.

Siegmond, Siegmund From the German, meaning "victory" and "protection." HEBREW EQUIVALENT: Shemarya.

Sigi A pet form of Sigmond.

Sigmond, Sigmund Variant spellings of Siegmond and Siegmund.

Silvester A variant spelling of Sylvester.

Simcha From the Hebrew, meaning "joy." HEBREW EQUIVA-LENT: Simcha.

Simeon An Anglicized form of Shimon.

Simha A variant spelling of Simcha.

Simi, Simie, Simmie Pet forms of Simeon and Simon.

Simon A Greek form of Shimon.

Simpson A patronymic form, meaning "son of Simon."

Sinai The Hebrew name of the mountain on which Moses received the Ten Commandments. HEBREW EQUIVALENT: Seenai.

Sinclair From the Latin, meaning "shining" or "sanctified." HEBREW EQUIVALENT: Zerach.

Sisi From the Hebrew, meaning "my joy." HEBREW EQUIVALENT: Sisi.

Sivan The third month of the Jewish year. HEBREW EQUIVALENT: Sivan.

Sloan From the Celtic, meaning "warrior." HEBREW EQUIVALENT: Gad, Gadiel.

Sodi From the Hebrew, meaning "my secret." HEBREW EQUIVALENT: Sodi.

Sol From the Latin, meaning "sun." HEBREW EQUIVALENT: Shimshon.

Solomon From the Hebrew, meaning "peace." HEBREW EQUIVALENT: Shlomo.

Sonny A popular nickname, meaning "son" or "boy." HEBREW EQUIVALENT: Ben.

Spencer From the Anglo-Saxon, meaning "steward, administrator, guardian." HEBREW EQUIVALENT: Shemaryahu.

Stacey, Stacy From the Latin, meaning "firmly established." HEBREW EQUIVALENT: Elyakim.

Stan A pet form of Stanley.

Stanford From the Old English, meaning "from the stone [or paved] ford." HEBREW EQUIVALENT: Avniel.

Stanley From the Old English, meaning "from the stony field." HEBREW EQUIVALENT: Avniel.

Stefan A variant spelling of the German Stephan.

Stefano An Italian form of Stefan.

Stephan A German form of Stephen.

Stephen From the Greek, meaning "crown." HEBREW EQUIVALENT: Katriel.

Stevan A variant form of Stephen.

Steven A variant form of Stephen.

Stewart From the Anglo-Saxon, meaning "guardian, keeper of the estate." HEBREW EQUIVALENT: Avigdor.

Stone From the Old English, meaning "stone, rock." HEBREW EQUIVALENT: Even.

Stu A pet form of Stuart.

Stuart A variant form of Stewart.

Suf From the Hebrew, meaning "the edge," or "end." HEBREW EQUIVALENT: Suf.

Sumner From the French and Latin, meaning "one who summons a messenger." HEBREW EQUIVALENT: Malachi.

Sy A pet form of Seymour and Sylvan.

Sydney A variant spelling of Sidney.

Sylvan From the Latin, meaning "forest, woods." HEBREW EQUIVALENT: Ya'ar.

Sylvester A variant form of Silvan.

Syshe From the Yiddish, meaning "sweet." HEBREW EQUIVALENT: Avinoam.

 BEST BABY NAMES BEST BABY NAMES

Tab A pet form of David.

Tabai, Tabbai From the Aramaic, meaning "good." HEBREW EQUIVALENT: Tabai.

Tad A pet form of Thadeus.

Tahl A variant spelling of Tal.

Tal From the Hebrew, meaning "dew." HEBREW EQUIVALENT: Tal.

Tali A variant form of Tal. HEBREW EQUIVALENT: Tali.

Tal-Shachar From the Hebrew, meaning "morning dew." HEBREW EQUIVALENT: Tal-Shachar.

Talia, Taliah Variant spellings of Talya.

Talmai From the Aramaic, meaning "mound" or "hill." HEBREW EQUIVALENT: Talmai.

Talmi From the Hebrew, meaning "hill, mound." HEBREW EQUIVALENT: Talmi.

Talmon From the Aramaic, meaning "to oppress, injure." HEBREW EQUIVALENT: Talmon .

Tal-Or From the Hebrew, meaning "dew of the light [morning]." HEBREW EQUIVALENT: Tal-Or.

Talya From the Aramaic, meaning "young lamb." HEBREW EQUIVALENT: Talya.

Tam From the Hebrew, meaning "complete, whole" or "honest." HEBREW EQUIVALENT: Tam.

Tami A variant form of Tam. HEBREW EQUIVALENT: Tami.

Tamir From the Hebrew, meaning "tall, stately [like the palm tree]." HEBREW EQUIVALENT: Tamir.

Tamur A variant form of Tamir. HEBREW EQUIVALENT: Tamur.

Tanchum From the Hebrew, meaning "comfort, consolation." HEBREW EQUIVALENT: Tanchum.

Tanhum A variant spelling of Tanchum.

Tate From the Old English, meaning "tenth, tithing" or "to be cheerful." HEBREW EQUIVALENT: Yachdiel.

Tavi From the Aramaic, meaning "good." HEBREW EQUIVALENT: Tavi.

Taylor Originally a surname, from the Late Latin, meaning "to split, cut." HEBREW EQUIVALENT: Gidon.

Ted, Teddy Pet forms of Theodor.

Tel A variant form of Telem. HEBREW EQUIVALENT: Tel.

Telem From the Hebrew, meaning "mound" or "furrow." HEBREW EQUIVALENT: Telem.

116

Tema, Temah From the Hebrew and Aramaic, meaning "astonishment, wonder." HEBREW EQUIVALENT: Tema.

Teman From the Hebrew, meaning "right side," denoting the south. HEBREW EQUIVALENT: Teiman.

Temani A variant form of Teman. HEBREW EQUIVALENT: Teimani.

Tene, Teneh From the Hebrew, meaning "basket." HEBREW EQUIVALENT: Teneh.

Terence, Terrance, Terrence From the Latin, meaning "tender, good, gracious." HEBREW EQUIVALENT: Tuviya.

Terri, Terry A pet form of Terence.

Tewel, Tewele Yiddish forms of David.

Thaddeus, Thadeus From the Greek, meaning "gift of God." HEBREW EQUIVALENT: Natan.

Than From the Greek, meaning "death." EUPHEMISTIC HEBREW EQUIVALENT: Chai.

Thane A Danish form of Than.

Theo A pet form of Theobald and Theodore.

Theobald, Theobold From the Old German, meaning "brave people." HEBREW EQUIVALENT: Abir.

Theodor, Theodore From the Greek, meaning "divine gift." HEBREW EQUIVALENT: Matanya.

Thomas From the Hebrew and Aramaic, meaning "twin." Also, from the Phoenician, meaning "sun god." HEBREW EQUIVALENT: Te'om.

Tibon, Tibbon Variant spellings of Tivon.

Tiger From the Greek, Latin, and Old French, meaning "tiger." HEBREW EQUIVALENT: Namer.

Tikva From the Hebrew, meaning "hope." HEBREW EQUIVALENT: Tikva.

Tim A pet form of Timothy.

Timo A short form of Timothy.

Timothy From the Greek, meaning "to honor [or fear] God." HEBREW EQUIVALENT: Mokir.

Timur From the Hebrew, meaning "tall, stately" or "to rise up." HEBREW EQUIVALENT: Timur.

Tip A nickname for Thomas.

Tiv From the Hebrew and Aramaic, meaning "good, goodness." HEBREW EQUIVALENT: Tiv.

Tivon From the Hebrew, meaning "natural." HEBREW EQUIVALENT: Tivon.

Tobiah A variant form of Tuviya.

Tobias The Greek form of Tobiah.

Tod From the Old English, meaning "thicket." Also, from the Scottish and Norse, meaning "fox." HEBREW EQUIVALENT: Shu'al.

Toda, Todah From the Hebrew, meaning "thanks, thankfulness." HEBREW EQUIVALENT: Toda.

Todd A variant spelling of Tod.

Todros From the Greek, meaning "gift." Akin to Theodore.

Tolya A variant form of Anatoly (Anatol).

Tom A pet form of Thomas.

Tomer A variant form of Tamar.

Tommy A pet form of Thomas.

Toni, Tony Pet forms of Anthony.

Tov From the Hebrew, meaning "good." HEBREW EQUIVALENT: Tov.

Tovi A variant form of Tov, meaning "my good." HEBREW EQUIVALENT: Tovi.

Tovia, Toviah Variant spellings of Toviya.

Toviel From the Hebrew, meaning "my God is goodness." HEBREW EQUIVALENT: Toviel.

Toviya From the Hebrew, meaning "goodness of God." HEBREW EQUIVALENT: Toviya.

Tracey, Tracy From the Old French, meaning "path" or "road." HEBREW EQUIVALENT: Nativ.

Trygve From the British, meaning "town by the water." HEBREW EQUIVALENT: Afek.

Tuvia, Tuviah Variant spellings of Tuviya.

Tuviya From the Hebrew, meaning "God is good," or "the goodness of God." HEBREW EQUIVALENT: Tuviya.

Tuviyahu A variant form of Tuviya. HEBREW EQUIVALENT: Tuviyahu.

Tyron, Tyrone From the Greek, meaning "lord, ruler." Also, from the Latin, meaning "young soldier." HEBREW EQUIVALENT: Melech.

Tzachi A pet form of Yitzchak.

Tzari From the Hebrew, meaning the name of a plant used in biblical times for healing purposes. HEBREW EQUIVALENT: Tzari.

Tzayad From the Hebrew, meaning "hunter." HEBREW EQUIVALENT: Tza'yad.

Tzefanya From the Hebrew, meaning "God has treasured." HEBREW EQUIVALENT: Tzefanya.

Tzefanyahu A variant form of Tzefanya. HEBREW EQUIVALENT: Tzefanyahu.

Tzevi From the Hebrew, meaning "deer, gazelle." HEBREW EQUIVALENT: Tzevi.

Tzi From the Hebrew, meaning "ship" or "navy." HEBREW EQUIVALENT: Tzi.

Tzofi From the Hebrew, meaning "scout, guard, protector." HEBREW EQUIVALENT: Tzofi.

Tzuriel From the Hebrew, meaning "God is my rock." HEBREW EQUIVALENT: Tzuriel.

Tzvee A variant spelling of Tzevi.

Tzvi A variant spelling of Tzevi.

BEST BABY NAMES BEST BABY NAMES

Uel A short form of Samuel.

Uri From the Hebrew, meaning "my flame" or "my light." HEBREW EQUIVALENT: Uri.

Uria, Uriah Variant spellings of Uriya.

Uriel From the Hebrew, meaning "God is my light" or "God is my flame." HEBREW EQUIVALENT: Uriel.

Uriya From the Hebrew, meaning "God is my flame." HEBREW EQUIVALENT: Uriya.

Uza From the Hebrew, meaning "strength." HEBREW EQUIVALENT: Uza.

Uzi From the Hebrew, meaning "my strength." HEBREW EQUIVALENT: Uzi.

Uziel From the Hebrew, meaning "God is my strength." HEBREW EQUIVALENT: Uziel.

Uziya From the Hebrew, meaning "God is my strength." HEBREW EQUIVALENT: Uziya.

Uzza A variant spelling of Uza.

Uzzi A variant spelling of Uzi.

Uzziah A variant spelling of Uziya.

Vail From the Latin, meaning "valley." HEBREW EQUIVALENT: Gai.

Val A French form of Vail.

Vale A variant spelling of Vail.

Valentine From the Latin, meaning "strong, valorous." HEBREW EQUIVALENT: Amotz.

Vaughan, Vaughn From the Celtic, meaning "small." HEBREW EQUIVALENT: Tzuar.

Velvel A pet form of the Yiddish Volf.

Vered From the Hebrew, meaning "rose." HEBREW EQUIVALENT: Vered.

Vern From the British, meaning "alder tree." Also, a pet form of Vernon. HEBREW EQUIVALENT: Ilan.

Vernon From the Latin, meaning "belonging to spring, springtime." HEBREW EQUIVALENT: Aviv.

Vic, Vickie Pet forms of Victor.

Victor From the Latin, meaning "victor, conqueror." HEBREW
  EQUIVALENT: Gavriel.

Vida A variant form of Vitas.

Vince A pet form of Vincent.

Vincent From the Latin, meaning "victor, conqueror."
  HEBREW EQUIVALENT: Netzach.

Vitas From the Latin, meaning "life." HEBREW EQUIVALENT:
  Avichai.

Volf A Yiddish form of Wolf.

BEST BABY NAMES   BEST BABY NAMES

Wal A short form of Wallace and Walter.

Walbert From the Old English, meaning "secure fortifica-
  tion." HEBREW EQUIVALENT: Tzelafchad.

Walker From the Greek, meaning "to roll up," and from the
  Old English, meaning "to journey." HEBREW EQUIVALENT:
  Shuach.

Wallace From the Anglo-French and the Middle English,
  meaning "foreigner, stranger." HEBREW EQUIVALENT:
  Gershom.

Wallie, Wally Pet forms of Walter and Wallace.

Walt A short from of Walter.

Walter From the Old English, meaning "woods" or "master
  of the woods." HEBREW EQUIVALENT: Yaar.

Ward From the Old English, meaning "to guard, guardian."
  HEBREW EQUIVALENT: Shomer.

Warner A variant form of Warren.

Warren From the Middle English and the Old French,
  meaning "to protect, preserve" or "enclosure, park."
  HEBREW EQUIVALENT: Karmel.

Wayne From the British, meaning "meadow." HEBREW
  EQUIVALENT: Artzi.

Wendel, Wendell From the Old English, meaning "wanderer, stranger." HEBREW EQUIVALENT: Gershom.

Werner A variant form of Warren.

Wesley From the Old English, meaning "west meadow." HEBREW EQUIVALENT: Sharon.

Whitney From the Old English, meaning "land near the water" or "white palace." HEBREW EQUIVALENT: Armon.

Wilber, Wilbert Variant forms of Walbert.

Wilfred, Wilfrid, Wilfried From the Old English, meaning "hope for peace." HEBREW EQUIVALENT: Shalev.

Wilhelm The German form of William.

Will A pet form of William.

Willard From the Old English, meaning "yard of willow trees." HEBREW EQUIVALENT: Alon.

Willi A pet form of William.

William A variant form of the Old French Willaume and the Old High German Willehelm, meaning "resolute protector." HEBREW EQUIVALENT: Magen.

Willie A pet form of William.

Willis A patronymic form, meaning "son of William."

Willoughby From the Old English, meaning "place by the willows." Akin to Willard.

Willy A pet form of William.

Wilmar, Wilmer, Willmer From the Old English, meaning "willows near the sea." Akin to Willard.

Wilt A pet form of Walt (Walter).

Wilton From the Old English, meaning "from the farmstead by the spring." HEBREW EQUIVALENT: Peleg.

Win A short form of Winston.

Winston From the Old English, meaning "victory town" or "a friend firm as a stone." HEBREW EQUIVALENT: Avniel.

Winthrop From the Old English, meaning "victory at the crossroads" or "friendly village." HEBREW EQUIVALENT: Regem.

Wolf, Wolfe From the Anglo-Saxon, meaning "wolf." HEBREW EQUIVALENT: Ze'eiv.

Wood, Woods From the Anglo-Saxon, meaning "from the wooded area." HEBREW EQUIVALENT: Artza.

Woodie A pet form of Woodrow.

Woodrow From the Anglo-Saxon, meaning "wooded hedge." HEBREW EQUIVALENT: Yaari.

Woody A pet form of Woodrow.

Wyn, Wynn From the British, meaning "white, fair." HEBREW EQUIVALENT: Livni.

BEST BABY NAMES BEST BABY NAMES

Xavier From the Latin, meaning "savior," or from the Arabic, meaning "bright." HEBREW EQUIVALENT: Bahir.

Xeno From the Greek, meaning "sign, symbol." HEBREW EQUIVALENT: Nisan.

BEST BABY NAMES BEST BABY NAMES

Yaacov A variant spelling of Yaakov.

Yaakov From the Hebrew, meaning "supplanted" or "held by the heel." HEBREW EQUIVALENT: Yaakov.

Yaar, Yaari From the Hebrew, meaning "forest" and "my forest." HEBREW EQUIVALENT: Yaar and Yaari.

Yadid From the Hebrew, meaning "beloved, friend." HEBREW EQUIVALENT: Yadid.

Yadin A variant form of Yadon. HEBREW EQUIVALENT: Yadin.

Yadon From the Hebrew, meaning "he will judge." HEBREW EQUIVALENT: Yadon.

Yadua From the Hebrew, meaning "celebrity" or "that which is known." HEBREW EQUIVALENT: Yadua.

Yael From the Hebrew, meaning "mountain goat." HEBREW EQUIVALENT: Ya'el.

Yafet A variant form of Yefet. HEBREW EQUIVALENT: Yafet.

Yagel A variant form of Yagil.

Yagil From the Hebrew, meaning "to rejoice." HEBREW EQUIVALENT: Yagil.

Yair From the Hebrew, meaning "to light up" or "to enlighten." HEBREW EQUIVALENT: Ya'ir.

Yakar From the Hebrew, meaning "precious, dear, beloved, honorable." HEBREW EQUIVALENT: Yakar.

Yaki A pet form of Yaakov.

Yakim A short form of Yehoyakim (Jehoiakim). HEBREW EQUIVALENT: Yakim.

Yakir A variant form of Yakar. HEBREW EQUIVALENT: Yakir.

Yale From the Anglo-Saxon, meaning "one who yields [pays]." HEBREW EQUIVALENT: Efra'yim.

Yam From the Hebrew, meaning "sea." HEBREW EQUIVALENT: Yam.

Yamin From the Hebrew, meaning "right, right-handed." HEBREW EQUIVALENT: Yamin.

Yancy A variant form of the Danish Jon (John).

Yaniv From the Hebrew, meaning "to speak." HEBREW EQUIVALENT: Yaniv.

Yankel A Yiddish form of Yaakov (Jacob).

Yarchiel From the Hebrew, referring to the "angel who rules the months." HEBREW EQUIVALENT: Yarchiel.

Yarden From the Hebrew, meaning "to flow down, descent." HEBREW EQUIVALENT: Yarden.

Yardeni A variant form of Yarden. HEBREW EQUIVALENT: Yardeni.

Yared From the Hebrew, meaning "descend, descendant." HEBREW EQUIVALENT: Yared.

Yariv From the Hebrew, meaning "he will quarrel, contend." HEBREW EQUIVALENT: Yariv.

Yarkon From the Hebrew, meaning "green." HEBREW EQUIVALENT: Yarkon.

Yarom From the Hebrew, meaning "he will raise up." HEBREW EQUIVALENT: Yarom.

Yaron From the Hebrew, meaning "he will sing, cry out." HEBREW EQUIVALENT: Yaron.

Yashar A variant form of Yesher. HEBREW EQUIVALENT: Yashar.

Yavin From the Hebrew, meaning "one who is intelligent." HEBREW EQUIVALENT: Yavin.

Yavne'el From the Hebrew, meaning "God builds." HEBREW EQUIVALENT: Yavne'el.

Yavniel A variant form of Yavne'el. HEBREW EQUIVALENT: Yavniel.

Yaziz From the Assyrian and Hebrew, meaning "to move, to rise up" or "to be agitated, angry." HEBREW EQUIVALENT: Yaziz.

Yechezkel From the Hebrew, meaning "God is my strength." HEBREW EQUIVALENT: Yechezkel.

Yechiel From the Hebrew, meaning "May God live." HEBREW EQUIVALENT: Yechiel.

Yechieli A variant form of Yechiel. HEBREW EQUIVALENT: Yechieli.

Yedid A variant form of Yadid.

Yedidya From the Hebrew, meaning "friend of God" or "beloved of God." HEBREW EQUIVALENT: Yedidya.

Yediel From the Hebrew, meaning "knowledge of the Lord." HEBREW EQUIVALENT: Yediel.

Yefet From the Hebrew, meaning "beautiful," or from the Aramaic, meaning "abundant, spacious." HEBREW EQUIVALENT: Yefet.

Yehiel A variant spelling of Yechiel.

Yehieli A variant spelling of Yechieli.

Yehochan A variant form of Yochanan.

Yehonatan From the Hebrew, meaning "God has given" or "gift of God." HEBREW EQUIVALENT: Yehonatan.

Yehoram From the Hebrew, meaning "God is exalted."
HEBREW EQUIVALENT: Yehoram.

Yehoshua From the Hebrew, meaning "God is salvation."
HEBREW EQUIVALENT: Yehoshua.

Yehoyakim From the Hebrew, meaning "God will establish." HEBREW EQUIVALENT: Yehoyakim.

Yehuda, Yehudah From the Hebrew, meaning "praise."
HEBREW EQUIVALENT: Yehuda.

Yehudi A variant form of Yehuda.

Yekusiel The Ashkenazic form of Yekutiel.

Yekutiel From the Hebrew, meaning "God will nourish."
HEBREW EQUIVALENT: Yekutiel.

Yemin From the Hebrew, meaning "right, right-handed."
HEBREW EQUIVALENT: Yemin.

Yered From the Hebrew, meaning "descend." HEBREW
EQUIVALENT: Yered.

Yermi A pet form of Yirmeyahu (Jeremiah).

Yerucham From the Hebrew, meaning "compassionate."
HEBREW EQUIVALENT: Yerucham.

Yeruham A variant spelling of Yerucham.

Yeshaya From the Hebrew, meaning "God is salvation."
HEBREW EQUIVALENT: Yesha'ya.

Yeshayahu A variant form of Yesha'ya. HEBREW EQUIVALENT:
Yesha'yahu.

Yesher From the Hebrew, meaning "upright, honest."
HEBREW EQUIVALENT: Yesher.

Yeshurun From the Hebrew, meaning "upright." HEBREW
EQUIVALENT: Yeshurun.

Yiftach From the Hebrew, meaning "he will open." HEBREW
EQUIVALENT: Yiftach.

Yigael A variant form of Yigal.

Yigal From the Hebrew, meaning "he will redeem." HEBREW
EQUIVALENT: Yigal.

Yigdal From the Hebrew, meaning "he will grow" or "he
will be exalted." HEBREW EQUIVALENT: Yigdal.

Yirmeya From the Hebrew, meaning "God will raise up."
HEBREW EQUIVALENT: Yirmeya.

Yirmeyahu A variant form of Yirmeya. HEBREW EQUIVALENT: Yirmeyahu.

Yishai From the Hebrew, meaning "gift." HEBREW EQUIVALENT: Yishai.

Yishi From the Hebrew, meaning "my deliverer, savior." HEBREW EQUIVALENT: Yishi.

Yishmael From the Hebrew, meaning "God will hear." HEBREW EQUIVALENT: Yishmael.

Yisrael From the Hebrew, meaning "prince of God" or "to contend, fight." HEBREW EQUIVALENT: Yisrael.

Yisroel A variant spelling of Yisrael.

Yissochar A variant spelling of Issachar.

Yitz A pet form of Yitzchak.

Yitzchak From the Hebrew, meaning "he will laugh." HEBREW EQUIVALENT: Yitzchak.

Yitzchok A variant spelling of Yitzchak.

Yitzhak A variant spelling of Yitzchak.

Yitzi A pet form of Yitzchak.

Yizhak A variant spelling of Yitzchak.

Yizhar From the Hebrew, meaning "pure oil." HEBREW EQUIVALENT: Yitzhar.

Yoav From the Hebrew, meaning "God is father" or "God is willing." HEBREW EQUIVALENT: Yo'av.

Yochanan A short form of Yehochanan. HEBREW EQUIVALENT: Yochanan.

Yoel From the Hebrew, meaning "God is willing" or "the Lord is God." HEBREW EQUIVALENT: Yo'el.

Yohanan A variant spelling of Yochanan.

Yon A variant form of Yona or Yonatan.

Yona, Yonah From the Hebrew, meaning "dove." HEBREW EQUIVALENT: Yona.

Yonassan A Hebrew form of Jonathan.

Yonat A pet form of Yonatan. HEBREW EQUIVALENT: Yonat.

Yonatan The Hebrew form of Jonathan.

Yoni A pet form of Yonatan.

Yora From the Hebrew, meaning "to teach" or "to shoot." HEBREW EQUIVALENT: Yora.

Yoram From the Hebrew, meaning "God is exalted."
HEBREW EQUIVALENT: Yoram.

Yoran From the Hebrew, meaning "to sing." HEBREW
EQUIVALENT: Yoran.

Yos A Yiddish pet form of Yosef.

Yosef From the Hebrew, meaning "God will add, increase."
HEBREW EQUIVALENT: Yosef.

Yosel, Yossel Pet forms of Yosef.

Yosi, Yossi Pet forms of Yosef.

Yotam From the Hebrew, meaning "God is perfect." HEBREW
EQUIVALENT: Yotam.

Yotav From the Hebrew, meaning "good." HEBREW
EQUIVALENT: Yotav.

Yuda A variant form of Yehuda.

Yudan From the Hebrew, meaning "will be judged."
HEBREW EQUIVALENT: Yudan.

Yuki A pet form of Yaakov.

Yuri A pet form of Uriah.

Yuval From the Hebrew, meaning "a stream." HEBREW
EQUIVALENT: Yuval.

BEST BABY NAMES   BEST BABY NAMES

Zacharia, Zachariah Anglicized forms of Zecharya.

Zachary A variant form of Zecharya.

Zak A pet form of Yitzchak and Zecharya.

Zakai, Zakkai From the Aramaic and Hebrew, meaning
"pure, clean, innocent." HEBREW EQUIVALENT: Zakai.

Zalkin Yiddish pet forms of Solomon.

Zalki A pet form of Zalkin.

Zalman, Zalmen, Zalmon Yiddish short forms of Solomon.

Zamir From the Hebrew, meaning "song, singing." HEBREW
EQUIVALENT: Zamir.

Zan From the Hebrew, meaning "nourish, sustain." HEBREW EQUIVALENT: Zan.

Zander A variant spelling of Sander.

Zane A variant form of Zan.

Zanvil A Yiddish form of Shemuel.

Zavad From the Hebrew, meaning "gift, portion, dowry." HEBREW EQUIVALENT: Zavad.

Zavdi A variant form of Zavad. HEBREW EQUIVALENT: Zavdi.

Zavdiel A variant form of Zavad. From the Hebrew, meaning "God is my gift." HEBREW EQUIVALENT: Zavdiel.

Zavil A variant form of Zanvil.

Zayde, Zaydeh From the Yiddish, meaning "grandfather." HEBREW EQUIVALENT: Aviav.

Zaydel A pet form of Zayde.

Zeb A pet form of Zebulun.

Zebulon, Zebulun Variant spellings of Zevulun.

Zecharia, Zechariah Variant spellings of Zecharya.

Zecharya From the Hebrew, meaning "memory" or "remembrance of the Lord." HEBREW EQUIVALENT: Zecharya.

Zecharyahu A variant form of Zecharya.

Zedekiah From the Hebrew, meaning "God is righteousness." HEBREW EQUIVALENT: Tzidkiya.

Ze'ev From the Hebrew, meaning "wolf." HEBREW EQUIVALENT: Ze'ev.

Zefania, Zefaniah Anglicized forms of the Hebrew, meaning "God has treasured." HEBREW EQUIVALENT: Tzefanya.

Zehavi From the Hebrew, meaning "gold." HEBREW EQUIVALENT: Zehavi.

Zeide, Zeideh Variant spellings of Zayde and Zaydeh.

Zeidel A variant spelling of Zaydel.

Zeira From the Aramaic, meaning "small, junior." HEBREW EQUIVALENT: Ze'ira.

Zeke A pet form of Zecharia.

Zelig A variant form of Selig.

Zemel From the Yiddish, meaning "bread." HEBREW EQUIVALENT: Lachma.

Best Baby Names

Zemer From the Hebrew, meaning "song." HEBREW EQUIVALENT: Zemer.

Zemira, Zemirah From the Hebrew, meaning "song" or "melody." HEBREW EQUIVALENT: Zemira.

Zeno A variant spelling of Xeno.

Zeph A short form of Zephaniah.

Zephania, Zephaniah Variant spellings of Zefania.

Zer From the Hebrew, meaning "wreath" or "crown." HEBREW EQUIVALENT: Zer.

Zera From the Hebrew, meaning "seed." HEBREW EQUIVALENT: Zera.

Zerachya From the Hebrew, meaning "light of the Lord." HEBREW EQUIVALENT: Zerachya.

Zerem From the Hebrew, meaning "stream." HEBREW EQUIVALENT: Zerem.

Zero A French and Italian form of the Arabic, meaning "cipher." HEBREW EQUIVALENT: Sofer.

Zetan From the Hebrew, meaning "olive tree." HEBREW EQUIVALENT: Zetan.

Zev A variant spelling of Ze'ev.

Zevadia, Zevadiah Variant spellings of Zevadya.

Zevadya From the Hebrew, meaning "God has bestowed." HEBREW EQUIVALENT: Zevadya.

Zevi From the Hebrew, meaning "deer." HEBREW EQUIVALENT: Tzevi.

Zeviel From the Hebrew, meaning "gazelle of the Lord." HEBREW EQUIVALENT: Tzeviel.

Zevulun From the Hebrew, meaning "to exalt" or "lofty house." HEBREW EQUIVALENT: Zevulun.

Zichrini From the Hebrew, meaning "remembrance." HEBREW EQUIVALENT: Zichrini.

Zik A Yiddish pet form of Itzik (Isaac).

Zimra From the Hebrew and Aramaic, meaning "song, tune." HEBREW EQUIVALENT: Zimra.

Zimran A variant form of Zimri. HEBREW EQUIVALENT: Zimran.

Zimri From the Hebrew, meaning "mountain-sheep" or "goat." HEBREW EQUIVALENT: Zimri.

Zindel A variant spelling of Zundel.

Zion From the Hebrew, meaning "a sign" or "excellent." HEBREW EQUIVALENT: Tziyon.

Ziv From the Hebrew, meaning "shine, brilliance" or "gazelle." HEBREW EQUIVALENT: Ziv.

Zohar From the Hebrew, meaning "light, brilliance." HEBREW EQUIVALENT: Zohar.

Zundel, Zundle From the Yiddish, meaning "son, sonny." HEBREW EQUIVALENT: Binyamin.

Zusman, Zussman Yiddish forms of the German, meaning "sweet man." HEBREW EQUIVALENT: No'am.

Zvi A variant spelling of Zevi.

Zvika A pet form of Zevi.

Zvulun A variant spelling of Zevulun.

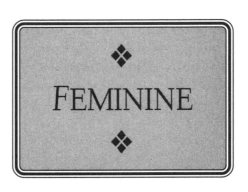

FEMININE

Abbe A pet form of Abigail.

Abbey A pet form of Abigail.

Abbie A pet form of Abigail.

Abby A variant spelling of Abbey.

Abela From the Latin, meaning "beautiful." HEBREW EQUIVA-LENT: Achino'am.

Abibi A variant spelling of Avivi.

Abibit A variant spelling of Avivit.

Abiela, Abiella Variant spellings of Aviela.

Abigail The Anglicized form of Aviga'yil.

Abira From the Hebrew, meaning "strong." HEBREW EQUIVA-LENT: Abira.

Abiri From the Hebrew, meaning "my powerful one" or "my strength." HEBREW EQUIVALENT: Abiri.

Abital A variant spelling of Avital.

Ada, Adah From the Hebrew, meaning "adorned, beautiful." Also, from the Latin and German, meaning "of noble birth." HEBREW EQUIVALENT: Ada.

Adaline A pet form of Adelaide.

Adama From the Hebrew, meaning "earth." HEBREW EQUIVALENT: Adama.

Adamina A feminine pet form of Adama.

Adda A variant spelling of Ada.

Addie A pet form of Adelaide.

Adela A variant form of Adelaide.

Adelaide A French form of the German name Adelheid, meaning "of noble birth." HEBREW EQUIVALENT: Adina.

Adele A variant form of Adelaide.

Adelia A variant form of Adelaide.

Adelina A pet form of Adele and Adelaide.

Adeline A pet form of Adelaide.

Adella A variant form of Adelaide.

Adelle A variant form of Adelaide.

Adena From the Hebrew and Greek, meaning "noble" or "delicate." HEBREW EQUIVALENT: Adina.

Aderet From the Hebrew, meaning "a cape." HEBREW EQUIVALENT: Aderet.

Adi From the Hebrew, meaning "ornament." HEBREW EQUIVALENT: Adi.

Adie A variant spelling of Adi.

Adiel From the Hebrew, meaning "ornament of the Lord." HEBREW EQUIVALENT: Adiel.

Adiela, Adiella A variant form of Adiel. HEBREW EQUIVALENT: Adiela.

Adina, Adinah Variant spellings of Adena.

Adira From the Hebrew, meaning "mighty, strong." HEBREW EQUIVALENT: Adira.

Adiva From the Hebrew and Arabic, meaning "gracious, pleasant." HEBREW EQUIVALENT: Adiva.

Adiya From the Hebrew, meaning "God's treasure, God's ornament." HEBREW EQUIVALENT: Adiya.

Adoniya From the Hebrew, meaning "my Lord is God." HEBREW EQUIVALENT: Adoniya.

Adora From the Latin, meaning "one who is adored or loved." HEBREW EQUIVALENT: Ahada.

Adorna From the Anglo-Saxon, meaning "to adorn." HEBREW EQUIVALENT: Adiel.

Adria, Adrian From the Greek, meaning "rich." HEBREW EQUIVALENT: Ashira.

Adriana A variant form of Adrian.

Adriane A variant spelling of Adrian.

Adrienne A variant spelling of Adrian.

Adva From the Aramaic, meaning "wave, ripple." HEBREW EQUIVALENT: Adva.

Afra A variant spelling of Ofra.

Agala From the Hebrew, meaning "wagon." HEBREW EQUIVALENT: Agala.

Agatha From the Greek, meaning "good." HEBREW EQUIVALENT: Bat-Tziyon.

Agnes From the Greek and Latin, meaning "lamb." HEBREW EQUIVALENT: Talya.

Aharona A feminine form of Aharon (Aaron), meaning "mountain." HEBREW EQUIVALENT: Aharona.

Aharonit A feminine form of Aharon. HEBREW EQUIVALENT: Aharonit.

Ahava, Ahavah From the Hebrew, meaning "love." HEBREW EQUIVALENT: Ahava.

Ahavat From the Hebrew, meaning "love." HEBREW EQUIVALENT: Ahavat.

Ahavia, Ahavya Variant forms of Ahuviya. HEBREW EQUIVALENT: Ahavya.

Ahuda, Ahudah From the Hebrew, meaning "adored." HEBREW EQUIVALENT: Ahuda.

Ahuva, Ahuvah From the Hebrew, meaning "beloved." HEBREW EQUIVALENT: Ahuva.

Ahuvia, Ahuviah Variant forms of Ahuviya.

Ahuviya From the Hebrew, meaning "beloved of God." HEBREW EQUIVALENT: Ahuviya.

Aida From the Latin and Old French, meaning "to help." HEBREW EQUIVALENT: Eliezra.

Aidel A variant spelling of Eidel.

Aileen From the Greek, meaning "light." HEBREW EQUIVALENT: Eliora.

Ailene A variant spelling of Aileen.

Aimee From the French and Latin, meaning "love, friendship." HEBREW EQUIVALENT: Ahava.

Alaina, Alaine Variant forms of the masculine Alan. HEBREW EQUIVALENT: Na'ama.

Alberta The feminine form of Albert.

Albertina, Albertine Pet forms of Alberta.

Alcina A pet form of Alice.

Alda From the Old German, meaning "old" or "rich."
HEBREW EQUIVALENT: Ashira.

Aldora From the Anglo-Saxon, meaning "noble gift."
HEBREW EQUIVALENT: Darona.

Aleeza From the Hebrew, meaning "joy, joyous one."
HEBREW EQUIVALENT: Aliza.

Alene A variant spelling of Allene.

Aletta From the Latin, meaning "the winged one." HEBREW
EQUIVALENT: Tzipora.

Alexa A variant form of Alexandra.

Alexandra A feminine form of the Greek name Alexander.
HEBREW EQUIVALENT: Aleksondra.

Alexandrina A pet form of Alexandra.

Alexia A variant form of Alexandra.

Alexis A variant form of Alexandra.

Alfreda The feminine form of Alfred, meaning "all peace"
or "wise counsellor." HEBREW EQUIVALENT: Bina.

Ali A pet form of Alice and Alison.

Alia A variant spelling of Aliya.

Alice From the Middle English and Old French, meaning
"of noble birth." HEBREW EQUIVALENT: Malka.

Alisa A variant form of Alice.

Alison A matronymic form, meaning "son of Alice."

Alissa A variant form of Alice.

Alita From the Hebrew, meaning "high, above" or
"excellent." HEBREW EQUIVALENT: Alita.

Alitza, Alitzah From the Hebrew, meaning "joy, happiness."
HEBREW EQUIVALENT: Alitza.

Aliya, Aliyah From the Hebrew, meaning "to ascend, to go
up." HEBREW EQUIVALENT: Aliya.

Alix A variant form of Alexandra.

Aliza, Alizah Variant spellings of Aleeza and Alitza.

Allegra From the Latin, meaning "cheerful." HEBREW
EQUIVALENT: Alisa.

Allene A feminine form of the masculine Allen. HEBREW
   EQUIVALENT: Shulamit.
Ally A variant spelling of Ali.
Allyn A feminine form of Alan. HEBREW EQUIVALENT:
   Na'ama.
Alma From the Hebrew, meaning "maiden." HEBREW
   EQUIVALENT: Alma.
Almana From the Hebrew, meaning "alone, lonely, widow."
   HEBREW EQUIVALENT: Almana.
Alona From the Hebrew, meaning "oak tree." HEBREW
   EQUIVALENT: Alona.
Althea From the Greek and Latin, meaning "to heal" or
   "healer." HEBREW EQUIVALENT: Rofi.
Alufa From the Hebrew, meaning "leader" or "princess."
   HEBREW EQUIVALENT: Alufa.
Aluma, Alumah From the Hebrew, meaning "girl, maiden"
   or "secret." HEBREW EQUIVALENT: Aluma.
Alumit A variant form of Aluma.
Alyce A variant spelling of Alice.
Alysa, Alyssa A variant spelling of Alisa and Alissa.
Alyson A variant spelling of Allison.
Amabel A compounded form of the Latin *amor*, meaning
   "love," and the French *belle*, meaning "beautiful." HEBREW
   EQUIVALENT: Ahuva.
Amal Popular as a masculine name. HEBREW EQUIVALENT:
   Amal.
Amalia A variant spelling of Amalya.
Amalie A German variant form of Amelia.
Amalya From the Hebrew, meaning "work of the Lord."
   HEBREW EQUIVALENT: Amalya.
Amana From the Hebrew, meaning "faithful." HEBREW
   EQUIVALENT: Amana.
Amanda From the Latin, meaning "love." HEBREW EQUIVA-
   LENT: Ahada.
Amandalina A pet form of Amanda.
Amber From the Old French and Arabic, meaning "amber"
   or "golden." HEBREW EQUIVALENT: Ofira.

Amela From the Hebrew, meaning "to work." HEBREW EQUIVALENT: Amela.

Amelia From the Latin, meaning "to work, to be industrious." HEBREW EQUIVALENT: Amalya.

Ami From the Hebrew, meaning "my nation, my people." HEBREW EQUIVALENT: Ami.

Amia A variant form of Amy.

Amie A variant spelling of Ami.

Amila A variant form of Amela. HEBREW EQUIVALENT: Amila.

Amina From the Hebrew and Arabic, meaning "trusted, faithful." HEBREW EQUIVALENT: Amina.

Amira From the Hebrew, meaning "speech, utterance." HEBREW EQUIVALENT: Amira.

Amit From the Hebrew, meaning "upright, honest." HEBREW EQUIVALENT: Amit.

Amita A variant form of Amit. HEBREW EQUIVALENT: Amita.

Amity From the Latin, meaning "love, friendship." HEBREW EQUIVALENT: Amita.

Amitza, Amitzah From the Hebrew, meaning "strong, powerful." HEBREW EQUIVALENT: Amitza.

Amiza, Amizza Variant spellings of Amitza.

Amtza, Amtzah From the Hebrew, meaning "strength." HEBREW EQUIVALENT: Amtza.

Amy A variant spelling of Aimee.

Ana A variant spelling of Anna.

Anat From the Hebrew, meaning "to sing." HEBREW EQUIVALENT: Anat.

Anava, Anavah From the Hebrew, meaning "grape." HEBREW EQUIVALENT: Anava.

Anchelle A feminine form of the masculine Anshel. HEBREW EQUIVALENT: Ashira.

Andra From the Old Norse, meaning "breath." HEBREW EQUIVALENT: Chava.

Andrea The feminine form of the Greek name Andrew, meaning "valiant, strong, courageous." HEBREW EQUIVALENT: Amtza.

Andye A feminine form of Andy, meaning "strong, courageous." HEBREW EQUIVALENT: Nili.

Anett A variant spelling of Annette.

Angela From the Latin, meaning "angel," or from the
Greek, meaning "messenger." HEBREW EQUIVALENT: Erela.

Angelica The Latin form of Angela.

Angelina A pet form of Angela.

Angeline A pet form of Angela.

Angelique A pet form of Angela.

Angelita A pet form of Angela.

Aniela, Aniella Pet forms of Ann and Annie.

Anina A pet form of Anna. Also, from the Aramaic, meaning "answer my prayer." HEBREW EQUIVALENT: Anina.

Anita A pet form of Anna.

Aniya From the Hebrew, meaning "boat, ship." HEBREW
EQUIVALENT: Oniya.

Ann A variant form of Anna.

Anna The Greek form of the Hebrew name Chana, meaning "gracious." HEBREW EQUIVALENT: Chana.

Annabel Either a hybrid of Anna and Bela, meaning "gracious, beautiful," or a variant form of the Latin name
Amabel, meaning "lovable." HEBREW EQUIVALENT: Chana.

Anabella, Annabelle Variant forms of Annabel.

Anne A French form of Hannah.

Annetta A pet form of Anna.

Annette A French form of Anna.

Annie A pet form of Anna.

Annick A pet form of Anna.

Annique A pet form of Anna.

Anthea A feminine form of Anthony, meaning "flourishing." HEBREW EQUIVALENT: Poriya.

Antoinette From the Greek and Latin, meaning "of high
esteem, revered." HEBREW EQUIVALENT: Adonit.

Antonella A pet form of the masculine Anton, meaning
"worthy of praise." HEBREW EQUIVALENT: Yehudit.

Antoina The Italian and Swedish form of Antoinette.

Anya A variant form of Anna.

April From the Latin, meaning "to open," symbolic of springtime. HEBREW EQUIVALENT: Aviva.

Arabel From the German *ara*, meaning "eagle," and the Latin *bella*, meaning "beautiful." HEBREW EQUIVALENT: Hadura.

Arabela, Arabella Variant forms of Arabel.

Arabelle A variant spelling of Arabel.

Ardra From the Celtic, meaning "high, high one." HEBREW EQUIVALENT: Aharona.

Arela, Arella From the Hebrew, meaning "angel, messenger." HEBREW EQUIVALENT: Arela.

Ari A pet form of Ariel.

Ariana, Arianna From the Latin, meaning "song." HEBREW EQUIVALENT: Rina.

Ariel From the Hebrew, meaning "lioness of God." HEBREW EQUIVALENT: Ariel.

Ariela, Ariella Variant forms of Ariel. HEBREW EQUIVALENT: Ariela.

Arielle A variant spelling of Ariel.

Ariza From the Hebrew, meaning "cedar panels." HEBREW EQUIVALENT: Ariza.

Arleen A variant spelling of Arlene.

Arlene A variant spelling of Arline.

Arlett A pet form of Arlene.

Arline From the German, meaning "girl," and from the Celtic, meaning "pledge, oath." HEBREW EQUIVALENT: Alma.

Armanda Feminine form of Armand, meaning "warrior." HEBREW EQUIVALENT: Gavrila.

Arlyne A variant spelling of Arline.

Armona From the Hebrew, meaning "castle" or "fortress." HEBREW EQUIVALENT: Armona.

Armonit A variant form of Armona. HEBREW EQUIVALENT: Armonit.

Arni A pet form of Aharona.

Arnina A pet form of Arni.

Arninit A variant form of Arni.

Arnit A variant form of Arni.

Arnolde A variant form of Arnoldine.

Arnoldine A French variant form of Arnold meaning "eagle's rule," signifying power. HEBREW EQUIVALENT: Abira.

Arnona From the Hebrew, meaning "roaring stream." HEBREW EQUIVALENT: Arnona.

Arnonit A pet form of Arnona.

Arona A variant form of Aharona. Also, from the Greek, meaning "a chamber." HEBREW EQUIVALENT: Arona.

Aryr A feminine form of Aaron, meaning "mountain." HEBREW EQUIVALENT: Aharona.

Arza From the Hebrew, meaning "cedar panels." HEBREW EQUIVALENT: Arza.

Arzit A variant form of Arza. HEBREW EQUIVALENT: Arzit.

Asaela From the Hebrew, meaning "God has created." HEBREW EQUIVALENT: Asa'ela.

Asenath Joseph's wife. From the Egyptian, meaning "she who belongs to [the goddess] Neith." HEBREW EQUIVALENT: Asnat.

Ashera From the Hebrew, meaning, "blessed, fortunate" or "idol." HEBREW EQUIVALENT: Ashera.

Ashira From the Hebrew, meaning "wealthy." HEBREW EQUIVALENT: Ashira.

Ashley From the Old English, meaning "grove of ash trees." HEBREW EQUIVALENT: Ilana.

Asisa From the Hebrew, meaning "juicy, ripe." HEBREW EQUIVALENT: Asisa.

Asisya From the Hebrew, meaning "juice [fruit] of the Lord." A variant form of Asisa. HEBREW EQUIVALENT: Asisya.

Asnat A variant spelling of Osnat.

Asta A variant form of Astera.

Astera, Asteria From the Persian and Greek, meaning "star." Akin to Esther.

Atalia, Ataliah Variant spellings of Atalya.

Atalya From the Assyrian, meaning "to grow, to be great." Also, from the Hebrew, meaning "God is exalted." HEBREW EQUIVALENT: Atalya.

Atara From the Hebrew, meaning "crown, wreath." HEBREW EQUIVALENT: Atara.

Ateret A variant form of Atara. HEBREW EQUIVALENT: Ateret.

Athalia, Athaliah Variant spellings of Atalya.

Atida, Atidah From the Hebrew, meaning "future." HEBREW EQUIVALENT: Atida.

Atira From the Hebrew, meaning "prayer." HEBREW EQUIVALENT: Atira.

Atlit A variant form of Atalya. HEBREW EQUIVALENT: Atlit.

Atura From the Hebrew, meaning "ornamented, adorned with a crown." HEBREW EQUIVALENT: Atura.

Atzila From the Hebrew, meaning "honorable, noble." HEBREW EQUIVALENT: Atzila.

Audrey From the Old English, meaning "noble strength." HEBREW EQUIVALENT: Abira.

Audrina A pet form of Audrey.

Audris From the old German, meaning "fortunate" or "wealthy." HEBREW EQUIVALENT: Asherit.

Augusta From the Latin, meaning "revered, sacred." HEBREW EQUIVALENT: Berucha.

Augustina A German form of Augusta.

Augustine A French form of Augusta.

Aura From the Greek, meaning "air, atmosphere." HEBREW EQUIVALENT: Avirit.

Aurea A variant form of Aurelia.

Aurelia A feminine form of the Latin name Aurelius, meaning "gold." HEBREW EQUIVALENT: Ofira.

Aurora From the Latin, meaning "dawn." HEBREW EQUIVALENT: Tzefira.

Aury A pet form of Aurelia.

Ava From the Latin, meaning "bird." HEBREW EQUIVALENT: Tzipora.

Aveline From the French, meaning "hazelnut." HEBREW EQUIVALENT: Egoza.

Avella A pet form of Aveline.

Avi From the Assyrian and Hebrew, meaning "father."
HEBREW EQUIVALENT: Avi.

Avia, Aviah Variant spellings of Aviya.

Aviela, Aviella From the Hebrew, meaning "God is my
father." HEBREW EQUIVALENT: Aviela.

Avigal From the Hebrew, meaning "father of joy." HEBREW
EQUIVALENT: Avigal.

Avigayil From the Hebrew, meaning "father's joy" or "my
father is joy." HEBREW EQUIVALENT: Aviga'yil.

Avigdora The feminine form of the masculine Avigdor.
HEBREW EQUIVALENT: Avigdora.

Avirama From the Hebrew, meaning "my father is exalted."
HEBREW EQUIVALENT: Avirama.

Avirit From the Hebrew, meaning "air, atmosphere, spirit."
HEBREW EQUIVALENT: Avirit.

Avis An Old German name, meaning "refugee, fortress."
Also, from the Latin, meaning "bird." HEBREW EQUIVALENT:
Armona.

Avital From the Hebrew, meaning "father of dew." HEBREW
EQUIVALENT: Avital.

Aviva, Avivah From the Hebrew, meaning "springtime,"
connoting youthfulness. HEBREW EQUIVALENT: Aviva.

Avivi From the Hebrew, meaning "springlike." HEBREW
EQUIVALENT: Avivi.

Avivia A variant spelling of Aviviya.

Avivit A variant form of Aviva. HEBREW EQUIVALENT: Avivit.

Aviviya A variant form of Aviya. HEBREW EQUIVALENT:
Aviviya.

Aviya From the Hebrew, meaning "God is my father."
HEBREW EQUIVALENT: Aviya.

Avna From the Hebrew, meaning "stone, rock." HEBREW
EQUIVALENT: Avna.

Avuka From the Hebrew, meaning "torch, flame." HEBREW
EQUIVALENT: Avuka.

Aya, Ayah From the Hebrew, meaning "to fly swiftly."
HEBREW EQUIVALENT: A'ya.

Ayala, Ayalah From the Hebrew, meaning "deer, gazelle." HEBREW EQUIVALENT: A'yala.

Ayelet From the Hebrew, meaning "deer, gazelle." HEBREW EQUIVALENT: A'yelet.

Ayla From the Hebrew, meaning "oak tree." HEBREW EQUIVALENT: Ayla.

Aza, Azah From the Hebrew, meaning "strong, powerful." HEBREW EQUIVALENT: Aza.

Aziza, Azizah From the Hebrew, meaning "strong." HEBREW EQUIVALENT: Aziza.

BEST BABY NAMES   BEST BABY NAMES

Bab A pet form of Barbara and Elizabeth.

Babette A pet form of Barbara.

Babs A variant form of Bab.

Baila, Baile Variant spellings of Bayla and Bayle.

Bambi A pet form of the Italian name Bambalina, meaning "little doll." HEBREW EQUIVALENT: Buba.

Bara From the Hebrew, meaning "to choose." HEBREW EQUIVALENT: Bara.

Barbara From the Greek, meaning "strange, stranger, foreign." HEBREW EQUIVALENT: Hagar.

Barbi A pet form of Barbara.

Bari, Barrie Feminine forms of Barry. HEBREW EQUIVALENT: Sara.

Basha A Yiddish form of Batya and Bat-Sheva.

Bashe A variant form of Basha.

Bas-Sheva The Ashkenazic pronunciation of Bat-Sheva.

Basya The Ashkenazic pronunciation of Batya.

Bathsheba The Anglicized form of Bat-Sheva.

Batli From the Hebrew, meaning "I have a daughter." HEBREW EQUIVALENT: Batli.

Bat-Sheva, Batsheva From the Hebrew, meaning "daughter of an oath." HEBREW EQUIVALENT: Bat-Sheva.

Bat-Shir From the Hebrew, meaning "songbird." HEBREW EQUIVALENT: Bat-Shir.

Bat-Shua, Batshua A biblical variant form of Bat-Sheva. HEBREW EQUIVALENT: Bat-Shua.

Bat-Tziyon From the Hebrew, meaning "daughter of Zion" or "daughter of excellence." HEBREW EQUIVALENT: Bat-Tziyon.

Batya From the Hebrew, meaning "daughter of God." HEBREW EQUIVALENT: Batya.

Bat-Yam From the Hebrew, meaning "daughter of the sea." HEBREW EQUIVALENT: Bat-Yam.

Bayla A Yiddish form of the Hebrew name Bilha. Also, a Yiddish form of Bela.

Bayle A variant form of Bayla.

Bea, Beah Pet forms of Beatrice.

Beata From the Latin, meaning "blessed." A variant form of Beatrice.

Beate A short form of Beatrice.

Beatrice From the Latin, meaning "one who brings happiness and blessing." HEBREW EQUIVALENT: Beracha.

Beatrix The original form of Beatrice.

Beccie A variant spelling of Beckie.

Beckie, Becky Pet forms of Rebecca.

Behira From the Hebrew, meaning "light, clear, brilliant." HEBREW EQUIVALENT: Behira.

Bela Either a form of Isabella, meaning "God's oath," or from the Hungarian, meaning "nobly bright." Also, from the Latin, meaning "beautiful one." HEBREW EQUIVALENT: Bat-Sheva.

Belinda An Old German name derived from the Latin, meaning "beautiful serpent." HEBREW EQUIVALENT: Yafa.

Belita A Spanish pet form of Belle.

Bella A short form of Isabella.

Belle A variant form of Bella.

Belva From the Latin, meaning "beautiful view." HEBREW EQUIVALENT: Adina.

Benedicta A feminine form of the Latin name Benedict, meaning "blessed." HEBREW EQUIVALENT: Berucha.

Benette A femine form of the masculine Ben and Benjamin. HEBREW EQUIVALENT: Batya.

Benjamina A feminine form of Benjamin. HEBREW EQUIVALENT: Binyamina.

Beracha A variant form of Bracha.

Berenice From the Greek, meaning "bringer of victory." HEBREW EQUIVALENT: Dafna.

Bernadette From the French and German, meaning "bold as a bear." HEBREW EQUIVALENT: Duba.

Bernadina A pet form of Bernadette.

Bernadine A pet form of Bernadette.

Bernette A variant form of Bernadette.

Bernice A variant form of Berenice.

Bernine A pet form of Bernice and Bernadette.

Bernita A pet form of Berenice.

Berta A variant spelling of Bertha.

Bertha From the Anglo-Saxon, meaning "bright, beautiful, famous." HEBREW EQUIVALENT: Behira.

Bertina A feminine form of the masculine Bert. HEBREW EQUIVALENT: Meira.

Berucha From the Hebrew, meaning "blessed." HEBREW EQUIVALENT: Berucha.

Beruchiya A variant form of Beruchya.

Beruchya From the Hebrew, meaning "blessed of the Lord." HEBREW EQUIVALENT: Beruchya.

Berura From the Hebrew, meaning "pure, clean." HEBREW EQUIVALENT: Berura.

Berurit A variant form of Berura.

Beruria, Beruriya A variant form of Berura. HEBREW EQUIVALENT: Beruriya.

Berurya A variant form of Berura. HEBREW EQUIVALENT: Berurya.

Beryl From the Greek and the Sanskrit, meaning "precious stone." Also, from the Persian and Arabic, meaning "crystal clear." HEBREW EQUIVALENT: Berura.

Bess A popular pet form of Elizabeth.

Bessie A pet form of Elizabeth.

Bet From the Hebrew, meaning "daughter." A variant form of Beth. HEBREW EQUIVALENT: Bat.

Beth A short form of Elizabeth.

Bethuel The Anglicized form of Betuel. HEBREW EQUIVALENT: Betuel.

Betsey, Betsy Pet forms of Elizabeth.

Bette A pet form of Elizabeth.

Bettina A pet form of Elizabeth.

Betty, Bettye Pet forms of Elizabeth.

Betuel From the Hebrew, meaning "daughter of God." HEBREW EQUIVALENT: Betuel.

Betula, Betulah From the Hebrew, meaning "maiden girl." HEBREW EQUIVALENT: Betula.

Beula, Beulah From the Hebrew, meaning "married" or "possessed." HEBREW EQUIVALENT: Be'ula.

Beverlee A variant spelling of Beverly.

Beverley, Beverly From the Old English, meaning "beaver's meadow." HEBREW EQUIVALENT: Nava.

Bilha, Bilhah From the Hebrew, meaning "old, weak, troubled." HEBREW EQUIVALENT: Bilha.

Billie A feminine form of William. Also, a pet form of Wilhelmina.

Bina From the Hebrew, meaning "understanding, intelligence, wisdom." HEBREW EQUIVALENT: Bina.

Binyamina A feminine form of Binyamin (Benjamin). HEBREW EQUIVALENT: Binyamina.

Bira From the Hebrew, meaning "fortified city" or "capital." HEBREW EQUIVALENT: Bira.

Biranit A variant Hebrew form of Bira. HEBREW EQUIVALENT: Biranit.

Bird, Birdie From the English, meaning "bird." HEBREW EQUIVALENT: Efrona.

Blair, Blaire From the Gaelic, meaning "field" or "battle." HEBREW EQUIVALENT: Nirit.

Blanca The Spanish form of the Old French *blanc*, meaning "white, fair," or from the Latin, meaning "pure." HEBREW EQUIVALENT: Levana.

Blanch, Blanche Variant forms of Blanca.

Blima A variant form of Bluma.

Blossom From the Old English, meaning "blooming flower." HEBREW EQUIVALENT: Shoshana.

Blu A pet form of Bluma.

Bluma From the German and Yiddish, meaning "flower." HEBREW EQUIVALENT: Shoshana.

Blume A variant form of Bluma.

Blythe From the Anglo-Saxon, meaning "happy." HEBREW EQUIVALENT: Gila.

Bobbe, Bobbie A pet form of Babette, Barbara, Roberta.

Bona From the Hebrew, meaning "builder." HEBREW EQUIVALENT: Bona.

Bonita A Spanish form of Bonnie.

Bonnie, Bonny From the Latin and the French, meaning "good" or "pretty." HEBREW EQUIVALENT: Na'ama.

Bracha From the Hebrew, meaning "blessing." HEBREW EQUIVALENT: Bracha.

Bree A pet form of Gabriela.

Breindel A pet form of the Yiddish name Bruna.

Brenda From the Celtic, meaning "dark-haired." HEBREW EQUIVALENT: Tzila.

Bridget From the Celtic, meaning "strong" or "lofty." HEBREW EQUIVALENT: Abira.

Bridgit, Bridgitte Variant forms of Bridget.

Brigit, Brigitte Variant spellings of Bridget.

Brina, Brine Variant forms of Bruna and Brune.

Brit, Brita Pet forms of Bridget.

Brook, Brooke From the Old English and Middle English, meaning "to break out," referring to a stream of water. HEBREW EQUIVALENT: Arnona.

Bruna, Brune Yiddish forms, from the German, meaning "brunette" or "brown." HEBREW EQUIVALENT: Chuma.

Bruria A variant spelling of Beruria.

Bryna A variant form of Bruna.

Buba From the Hebrew, meaning "doll." HEBREW EQUIVALENT: Buba.

Bubati From the Hebrew, meaning "my doll." HEBREW EQUIVALENT: Bubati.

Buna From the Hebrew, meaning "understanding, intelligence." HEBREW EQUIVALENT: Buna.

Buni, Bunie A variant form of Buna. HEBREW EQUIVALENT: Buni.

Bunny A nickname for Barbara and Roberta.

Byrd A variant spelling of Bird.

Byrdie A variant spelling of Birdie.

Caasi A pet form of Catherine.

Camilla, Camille From the Latin, meaning "servant, helper." HEBREW EQUIVALENT: Ezriela.

Candace From the Greek, meaning "fire-white, incandescent." Also, from the Latin, meaning "pure, unsullied." HEBREW EQUIVALENT: Avuka.

Candance A variant form of Candace.

Candi A pet form of Candance.

Candice A variant spelling of Candace.

Candida, Candide Variant forms of Candace.

Candy A pet form of Candace.

Candyce A variant spelling of Candace.

Cara A pet form of Caroline and Charlotte.

Caren A pet form of Catherine.

Caressa From the Latin, meaning "caring, loving." HEBREW EQUIVALENT: Chiba.

Carla, Carlana Feminine forms of Carl or Charles. Also, pet forms of Caroline.

Carlena A pet form of Caroline.

Carli, Carlie, Carley Pet forms of Caroline.

Carlina A pet form of Caroline.

Carlita An Italian pet form of Caroline.

Carly A variant spelling of Carley.

Carma A variant form of Carmel.

Carmela From the Hebrew, meaning "garden, orchard." HEBREW EQUIVALENT: Carmela.

Carmelit A variant form of Carmela. HEBREW EQUIVALENT: Carmelit.

Carmen The Spanish form of Carmel.

Cameron From the Greek, meaning "a vaulted chamber." HEBREW EQUIVALENT: Arona.

Carmia A variant spelling of Carmiya.

Carmiela A variant form of Carmiya. HEBREW EQUIVALENT: Carmiela.

Carmit A variant Hebrew form of Carmiya. HEBREW EQUIVALENT: Carmit.

Carmiya From the Hebrew, meaning "vineyard of the Lord." HEBREW EQUIVALENT: Carmiya.

Carna From the Aramaic, meaning "horn," symbolizing strength. HEBREW EQUIVALENT: Carna.

Carni A variant form of Carna. HEBREW EQUIVALENT: Carni.

Carnia A variant form of Carniya.

Carniela, Carniella Variant forms of Carniya. HEBREW EQUIVALENT: Carniela.

Carniya From the Hebrew, meaning "horn of God." A variant form of Carna. HEBREW EQUIVALENT: Carniya.

Carol From the Gaelic, meaning "melody, song." Also, a pet form of Caroline. HEBREW EQUIVALENT: Lirona.

Caroline From the French, meaning "strong, virile." HEBREW EQUIVALENT: Chasina.

Carolyn A variant spelling of Caroline.

Caron A variant spelling of Caren.

Carren A variant spelling of Caren.

Carrie A pet form of Caroline.

Carroll A variant spelling of Carol.

Carry, Cary Pet forms of Caroline.

Caryl A variant spelling of Carol.

Caryn A variant spelling of Caren.

Catherine From the Greek, meaning "pure, unsullied."
HEBREW EQUIVALENT: Beruriya.

Cathleen A variant form of Catherine.

Cathryn A variant spelling of Catherine.

Cathy A pet form of Catherine and Cathleen.

Cecelia From the Latin, meaning "blind" or "dim-sighted."
EUPHEMISTIC HEBREW EQUIVALENT: Me'ira.

Cecil A variant form of Cecelia.

Cecile, Cecille Variant spellings of Cecil.

Cecily A variant form of Cecilia.

Ceil A pet form of Cecelia.

Cela A variant form of Cecilia.

Cele A variant spelling of Ceil.

Celeste From the Latin, meaning "heavenly." HEBREW
EQUIVALENT: Ester.

Celia A variant form of Cecilia.

Cerena A variant spelling of Serena.

Cesca A pet form of Francesca.

Chagit From the Aramaic, meaning "fest, festival, festive
celebration." HEBREW EQUIVALENT: Chagit.

Chagiya From the Hebrew, meaning "God's festival."
HEBREW EQUIVALENT: Chagiya.

Chamuda From the Hebrew, meaning "desired one."
HEBREW EQUIVALENT: Chamuda.

Chamutal From the Hebrew, meaning "warm dew." HEBREW
EQUIVALENT: Chamutal.

Chana, Chanah From the Hebrew, meaning "gracious,
merciful." Hannah is the Anglicized form. HEBREW
EQUIVALENT: Chana.

Charity From the Latin, meaning "love, affection." HEBREW EQUIVALENT: Chaviva.

Charlayne A variant form of Charlene.

Charleen A variant spelling of Charlene.

Charlene A variant form of Caroline, meaning "strong, valiant." HEBREW EQUIVALENT: Aziza.

Charlet A variant form of Charlotte.

Charlot A variant spelling of Charlotte.

Charlotta The Italian form of Charlotte.

Charlotte The feminine form of Charles, meaning "strong." HEBREW EQUIVALENT: Chasina.

Charyl A variant form of Cheryl.

Chasida, Chasidah From the Hebrew, meaning "stork" or "righteous." HEBREW EQUIVALENT: Chasida.

Chasina From the Aramaic, meaning "strong, powerful." HEBREW EQUIVALENT: Chasina.

Chasna From the Aramaic, meaning "strong, powerful." HEBREW EQUIVALENT: Chasna.

Chasya From the Hebrew, meaning "protected by God." HEBREW EQUIVALENT: Chasya.

Chava From the Hebrew, meaning "life." HEBREW EQUIVALENT: Chava.

Chaviva From the Hebrew, meaning "beloved." HEBREW EQUIVALENT: Chaviva.

Chaya From the Hebrew, meaning "alive, living." HEBREW EQUIVALENT: Cha'ya.

Chayele A pet form of Chaya.

Cheftzi-Ba From the Hebrew, meaning "she is my desire." HEBREW EQUIVALENT: Cheftzi-Ba.

Chemda From the Hebrew, meaning "desirable, charming." HEBREW EQUIVALENT: Chemda.

Cher, Chere Pet forms of Cheryl.

Cheri, Cherie French pet forms of Cheryl.

Cherlene A variant form of Charlene.

Cherri, Cherrie Pet forms of Cheryl.

Cheryl, Cheryle From the French, meaning "dear, beloved." HEBREW EQUIVALENT: Chaviva.

Chesna From the Slavic, meaning "peaceful." HEBREW
EQUIVALENT: Shulamit.

Chita From the Aramaic and Hebrew, meaning "grain,
wheat." HEBREW EQUIVALENT: Chita.

Chloe From the Greek, meaning "blooming, verdant."
HEBREW EQUIVALENT: Poriya.

Chloris A variant form of Chloe. *See* Chloe.

Choma From the Hebrew, meaning "wall." HEBREW EQUIVA-
LENT: Choma.

Chrystal Variant spellings of Crystal.

Cicely A variant form of Cecilia.

Cicily A variant form of Cecilia.

Cindy A pet form of Cynthia.

Cipora A variant spelling of Tzipora.

Ciporit A variant spelling of Tziporit.

Cis, Ciss, Cissy Pet forms of Cecilia.

Civia A variant spelling of Tzivya.

Claire A French form of Clara.

Clara From the Latin, meaning "clear, bright." HEBREW
EQUIVALENT: Me'ira.

Clarabella, Clarabelle Names compounded of the Latin,
meaning "bright" and "beautiful." HEBREW EQUIVALENT:
Behira.

Clare A variant spelling of Claire.

Clarette A variant form of Clara.

Clarissa, Clarisse Italian forms of Clara.

Claudette A French pet form of Claudia.

Claudia From the Latin, meaning "lame." EUPHEMISTIC
HEBREW EQUIVALENT: A'yelet.

Claudine A French pet form of Claudia.

Clementine A French form of the Latin, meaning "merciful." HEBREW EQUIVALENT: Chana.

Clio From the Greek, meaning "to celebrate, glorify."
HEBREW EQUIVALENT: Chagiga.

Cloe A variant spelling of Chloe.

Colette From the Latin, meaning "victorious." HEBREW
EQUIVALENT: Gibora.

Colleen From the Irish, meaning "girl." HEBREW EQUIVALENT: Alma.

Collette A variant spelling of Colette.

Connie A pet form of Constance.

Constance From the Latin, meaning "constant, firm, faithful." HEBREW EQUIVALENT: Tikva.

Cora From the Greek, meaning "maiden." HEBREW EQUIVALENT: Alma.

Coral From the Hebrew and Greek, meaning "small stone, pebble." HEBREW EQUIVALENT: Gorala.

Coralee A variant form of Coral.

Coralie A variant form of Coral.

Coreen A pet form of Cora.

Coretta A pet form of Cora.

Corette A variant form of Coretta.

Corey From the Gaelic, meaning "ravine, enclosed place." HEBREW EQUIVALENT: Afeka.

Cori, Corie Variant spellings of Corey.

Corinna, Corinne From the Greek, meaning "hummingbird." Also, French forms of Cora.

Corita A pet form of Cora.

Corna A pet form of Cornelia.

Cornelia From the Greek, meaning "cornell tree," or from the Latin, meaning "horn of the sun," symbol of royalty. HEBREW EQUIVALENT: Malka.

Correy A variant spelling of Corey.

Corri, Corrie Variant spellings of Corey.

Cory, Corry Variant spellings of Corey.

Courteny, Courtney Variant forms of Corey.

Crystal From the Greek, meaning "clear glass." HEBREW EQUIVALENT: Zaka.

Cybil, Cybill From the Latin, meaning "soothsayer." HEBREW EQUIVALENT: Amira.

Cyma From the Greek and Latin, meaning to sprout, grow, flourish." HEBREW EQUIVALENT: Carmel.

Cyndi A pet form of Cynthia.

Cynthia From the Greek, meaning "the moon personified." HEBREW EQUIVALENT: Levana.

Dafna A variant spelling of Daphna.

Dafne A variant spelling of Daphne.

Dafnit The Hebrew form of the Greek Daphne. HEBREW EQUIVALENT: Dafnit.

Deganya A variant spelling of Deganya.

Dahlia A variant spelling of Dalya.

Daisy Usually taken as a nickname for Margaret.

Dalia A variant spelling of Daliya and Dalya.

Dalgia A variant spelling of Dalgiya.

Dalgiya From the Hebrew, meaning "rope." HEBREW EQUIVALENT: Dalgiya.

Dalika A pet form of Dalia.

Dalit From the Hebrew, meaning "to draw water" or "bough, branch." HEBREW EQUIVALENT: Dalit.

Daliya A variant form of Dalya. HEBREW EQUIVALENT: Daliya.

Dalya From the Hebrew, meaning "branch, bough" or "to draw water." HEBREW EQUIVALENT: Dalya.

Dama From the Latin, meaning "lady." HEBREW EQUIVALENT: Adiva.

Dame A variant form of Dama.

Damita A Spanish form of Dama.

Dana From the Latin, meaning "bright, pure as day." Also, from the Hebrew, meaning "to judge." HEBREW EQUIVALENT: Dana.

Danette A pet form of Dana.

Dania, Daniah Variant spellings of Danya.

Daniela, Daniella Feminine forms of Daniel, meaning "God is my judge." HEBREW EQUIVALENT: Daniela.

Daniele, Danielle Variant spellings of Daniela.

Danit A variant form of Daniela. HEBREW EQUIVALENT: Danit.

Danita A variant form of Daniela. HEBREW EQUIVALENT: Danita.

Danna A variant spelling of Dana.

Danya A feminine form of Dan, meaning "judgment of the Lord." HEBREW EQUIVALENT: Danya.

Daphna, Daphne From the Greek, meaning "laurel" or "baytree," symbols of victory. HEBREW EQUIVALENT: Dafna.

Daphnit A variant spelling of Dafnit.

Dapna A variant form of Daphne.

Darcie From the Celtic, meaning "dark." HEBREW EQUIVALENT: Chachila.

Daria The feminine form of the Persian Darius, meaning "wealth." HHEBREW EQUIVALENT: Ashira.

Darla From the Middle English, meaning "dear, loved one." HEBREW EQUIVALENT: Ahuva.

Daroma From the Hebrew, meaning "south, southward." HEBREW EQUIVALENT: Daroma.

Darona A Hebrew form of the Greek, meaning "gift." HEBREW EQUIVALENT: Darona.

Daryl From the Old English, meaning "dear, beloved." HEBREW EQUIVALENT: Davida.

Dasi, Dassi Pet forms of Hadassah. HEBREW EQUIVALENT: Dasi.

Dati From the Hebrew, meaning "religious, observant." HEBREW EQUIVALENT: Dati.

Datit A variant form of Dati. HEBREW EQUIVALENT: Datit.

Datya From the Hebrew, meaning "faith in God" or "law of the Lord." HEBREW EQUIVALENT: Datya.

Davene A feminine form of David, meaning "beloved, friend." HEBREW EQUIVALENT: Davida.

Davida, Davide Feminine forms of David. HEBREW EQUIVALENT: Davida.

Davina A Scottish form of David used in the seventeenth century. HEBREW EQUIVALENT: Davida.

Davita A Spanish form of David. HEBREW EQUIVALENT: David.

Dayana From the Hebrew, meaning "judge." HEBREW EQUIVALENT: Da'yana.

Dawn, Dawne From the Old Norse and Old English, meaning "dawn." HEBREW EQUIVALENT: Bat-Shachar.

Daya The Hebrew name of a bird of prey. HEBREW EQUIVALENT: Da'ya.

Dean, Deane Feminine forms of Dean. HEBREW EQUIVALENT: Rosh.

Deanna, Deanne Variant forms of Diana or Dinah.

Debbe, Debbi, Debby Pet forms of Deborah.

Debi A pet form of Deborah.

Debora A variant spelling of Deborah.

Deborah The Anglicized form of Devora.

Debra A variant form of Deborah.

Deena From the Anglo-Saxon, meaning "from the valley." Also a variant spelling of Dinah.

Deenie A pet form of Dinah.

Degania, Deganiah Variant spellings of Deganya.

Deganit A variant form of Deganya. HEBREW EQUIVALENT: Deganit.

Deganya From the Hebrew, meaning "grain." HEBREW EQUIVALENT: Deganya.

Degula From the Hebrew, meaning "honored, famous." HEBREW EQUIVALENT: Degula.

Deidra A variant spelling of Deidre.

Deidre From the Middle Irish, meaning "young girl." HEBREW EQUIVALENT: Tze'ira.

Deirdre A variant form of Deidre.

Delila, Delilah From the Hebrew, meaning "hair" or "poor." HEBREW EQUIVALENT: Delila.

Dell, Della, Delle Variant pet forms of Adela and Adeline.

Dena A variant spelling of Dinah.

Delta A Greek and Latin form of the Hebrew *dalet*, meaning "door." HEBREW EQUIVALENT: Dalet.

Denice, Deniece, Deniese Variant spellings of Denise.

Denise A feminine form of Denis. HEBREW EQUIVALENT: Anava.

Denna From the Anglo-Saxon, meaning "valley." HEBREW EQUIVALENT: Ga'ya.

Denyse A variant spelling of Denise.

Derora, Derorah From the Hebrew, meaning "freedom, liberty." HEBREW EQUIVALENT: Derora.

Derorina A pet form of Derora.

Deuela, Deuella From the Hebrew, meaning "knowledge of the Lord." HEBREW EQUIVALENT: De'uela.

Devir From the Hebrew, meaning sanctuary. HEBREW EQUIVALENT: Devir.

Devira A variant form of Devir. HEBREW EQUIVALENT: Devira.

Devora, Devorah From the Hebrew, meaning "swarm of bees" HEBREW EQUIVALENT: Devora.

Devorit A variant form of Devora. HEBREW EQUIVALENT: Devorit.

Devra A variant form of Devora.

Di A pet form of Diana.

Diana, Diane, Dianne From the Latin, meaning "bright as a day." HEBREW EQUIVALENT: Behira.

Diedre A variant spelling of Deidre.

Digla From the Hebrew, meaning "flag." HEBREW EQUIVALENT: Digla.

Diglat A variant form of Digla. HEBREW EQUIVALENT: Diglat.

Dikla, Diklah The Aramaic form of the Hebrew, meaning "palm [date] tree." HEBREW EQUIVALENT: Dikla.

Diklit A variant form of Dikla. HEBREW EQUIVALENT: Diklit.

Dina, Dinah From the Hebrew, meaning "judgment." HEBREW EQUIVALENT: Deena.

Disa, Dissa Pet Yiddish forms of Yehudit (Judith).

Ditza, Ditzah From the Hebrew, meaning "joy." HEBREW EQUIVALENT: Ditza.

Diza, Dizah Variant spellings of Ditza.

Dobe A pet form of Devora.

Dobra, Dobrah Variant Yiddish forms of Deborah. Also from the Slavic, meaning "good." HEBREW EQUIVALENT: Tova.

Doda, Dodah From the Hebrew, meaning "beloved" or "aunt." HEBREW EQUIVALENT: Doda.

Dodi, Dodie From the Hebrew, meaning "my friend, my beloved." HEBREW EQUIVALENT: Dodi.

Dodo A pet form of Dorothy. Also, a variant form of Doda.

Dody A variant spelling of Dodi.

Dodye A pet form of Dodi.

Doe From the Old English, meaning "female deer." HEBREW EQUIVALENT: Tzivya.

Dolley A variant spelling of Dolly.

Dollie A variant spelling of Dolly.

Dolly A variant form of Dorothy.

Dona A variant spelling of Donna.

Donna From the Latin and Italian, meaning "lady of nobility." HEBREW EQUIVALENT: Adina.

Dora A diminutive form of Dorothy.

Doraleen, Doralene Pet forms of Dora.

Dore A German form of Dorothea.

Dorea A variant form of Doris.

Doreen A pet form of Dorothy.

Doreet A variant spelling of Dorit.

Dorene A variant spelling of Doreen.

Doretha A variant form of Dorothy.

Doretta, Dorette A French form of Dorothy.

Dorina A pet form of Dora.

Doris From the Greek, meaning "sacrificial knife." In Greek mythology, the mother of sea gods. HEBREW EQUIVALENT: Bat-Yam.

Dorisa A variant form of Doris.

Dorit From the Greek, meaning "to heap, to pile" or "dwelling place." Also, from the Hebrew, meaning "generation." HEBREW EQUIVALENT: Dorit.

Dorona From the Greek, meaning "gift." HEBREW EQUIVALENT: Dorona.

Doronit A variant form of Dorona. HEBREW EQUIVALENT: Doronit.

Dorothea A variant form of Dorothy.

Dorothy From the Greek, meaning "gift of God." HEBREW EQUIVALENT: Netanya.

Dorri, Dorrie Pet forms of Dorothy.

Dorris A variant spelling of Doris.

Dorrit A variant spelling of Dorit.

Dot, Dottie, Dotty Pet forms of Dorothy.

Dovie A pet form of Devora.

Dovrat A variant form of Devora. HEBREW EQUIVALENT: Dovrat.

Duba From the Hebrew, meaning "bear." HEBREW EQUIVALENT: Duba.

Dulcie From the Latin, meaning "charming, sweet." HEBREW EQUIVALENT: Metuka.

Durene From the Latin, meaning "enduring, lasting." HEBREW EQUIVALENT: Nitzcha.

Dvora, Dvorah A variant spelling of Devora.

Dvorit A variant spelling of Devorit.

Dyana A variant spelling of Diana.

BEST BABY NAMES   BEST BABY NAMES

Earla A feminine form of the masculine Earl, meaning "nobility." HEBREW EQUIVALENT: Milka.

Earlene A pet form of Earla.

Eda, Edda From the Icelandic, meaning "poet" or "songwriter." HEBREW EQUIVALENT: Lirit.

Ede A pet form of Edith.

Edel A variant spelling of Eidel.

Edia, Ediah Variant spellings of Edya.

Edie A popular Scottish pet form of Edith.

Edina From the Anglo-Saxon, meaning "rich friend." HEBREW EQUIVALENT: Chaviva.

Edith From the Anglo-Saxon, meaning "rich, prosperous, happy warrior." HEBREW EQUIVALENT: Ashira.

Edna, Ednah From the Hebrew, meaning "desired, adorned, voluptuous." Also, a contracted form of the Anglo-Saxon name Edwina, meaning "rich friend." HEBREW EQUIVALENT: Ashira.

Edya, Edyah From the Hebrew, meaning "adornment of the Lord." HEBREW EQUIVALENT: Edya.

Edyth, Edythe Variant spellings of Edith.

Efrat From the Hebrew, meaning "honored, distinguished" or "fruitful." Also, from the Aramaic, meaning "mantle, turban." HEBREW EQUIVALENT: Efrat.

Efrata A variant form of Efrat. HEBREW EQUIVALENT: Efrata.

Efrona From the Hebrew, meaning "bird." HEBREW EQUIVALENT: Efrona.

Eidel From the Yiddish, meaning "delicate, gentle." HEBREW EQUIVALENT: Adina.

Eila, Eilah From the Hebrew, meaning "oak tree, terebinth tree." HEBREW EQUIVALENT: Eila (Ayla).

Eilat From the Hebrew, meaning "gazelle" or "tree." HEBREW EQUIVALENT: Aylat.

Eileen A popular Irish form of Helen.

Elain, Elaine French forms of Helen, meaning "light."

Elana A variant spelling of Ilana, meaning "tree."

Elayne A variant spelling of Elaine.

Elberta The feminine form of Albert.

Eldora From the Spanish, meaning "gilded." HEBREW EQUIVALENT: Ofira.

Ele A pet form of Eleanor.

Eleanor A German form of Helen, from the Greek, meaning "light." HEBREW EQUIVALENT: Me'ira.

Eleanora A variant form of Eleanor.

Eleanore A variant spelling of Eleanor.

Elen A variant spelling of Ellen.

Elena From the Greek, meaning "light." HEBREW EQUIVA-
LENT: Meira.

Elenor A variant spelling of Eleanor.

Eleora A variant spelling of Eliora.

Elfrieda A variant spelling of Alfreda.

Eliana, Eliane, Elianna From the Hebrew, meaning "My
God has answered." HEBREW EQUIVALENT: Eliana.

Eliava, Eliavah From the Hebrew, meaning "My God is
willing." HEBREW EQUIVALENT: Eliava.

Elie A pet form of Eleanor.

Eliezra From the Hebrew, meaning "My God is salvation."
HEBREW EQUIVALENT: Eliezra.

Elinoar From the Hebrew, meaning "God is my youth."
HEBREW EQUIVALENT: Elino'ar.

Elin A variant spelling of Ellen.

Elinor A variant spelling of Eleanor.

Elinora A variant spelling of Eleanora.

Elinore A variant spelling of Eleanor.

Eliora From the Hebrew, meaning "My God is light."
HEBREW EQUIVALENT: Eliora.

Eliraz From the Hebrew, meaning "My God is my secret."
HEBREW EQUIVALENT: Eliraz.

Elisa A short form of Elisabeth.

Elisabeta The Hawaiian form of Elisabeth.

Elisabeth A variant spelling of Elizabeth.

Elise A pet form of Elisabeth.

Elisheva From the Hebrew, meaning "God is my oath."
HEBREW EQUIVALENT: Elisheva.

Elissa A pet form of Elisabeth.

Eliza A short form of Elizabeth.

Elizabeth From the Hebrew, meaning "God's oath." HEBREW
EQUIVALENT: Elisheva.

Elize A short form of Elizabeth.

Elka, Elke A pet form of Alice and Alexandra.

Elki, Elkie Variant forms of Elka.

Ella A short form of Eleanor.

Ellen A short form of Eleanor.

Ellette A pet form of Ella.

Ellie A pet form of Eleanor.

Ellin A variant spelling of Ellen.

Ellyn, Ellynne Variant spellings of Ellen.

Elma From the Greek and Latin, meaning "pleasant, fair, kind." HEBREW EQUIVALENT: Na'ama.

Elona From the Hebrew, meaning "oak tree." HEBREW EQUIVALENT: Elona (Aylona).

Elsa, Else German pet forms of Elizabeth.

Elsie A variant form of Elisabeth.

Elvera, Elvira From the Latin, meaning "noble truth." HEBREW EQUIVALENT: Amita.

Elvita From the Latin, meaning "noble life." HEBREW EQUIVALENT: Chava.

Elyn, Elynn Variant spellings of Ellen.

Elysa, Elyse Variant spelling of Elisabeth.

Elyssa, Elysse Variant forms of Elisabeth.

Elza A pet form of Elizabeth. Also, from the Hebrew, meaning "joy." HEBREW EQUIVALENT: Elza.

Em A pet form of Emma.

Emanuela, Emanuella Feminine forms of Emanuel, meaning "God is with us." HEBREW EQUIVALENT: Imanuela.

Emila An Italian form of Emilie.

Emilie From the Anglo-Saxon, meaning "flatterer." Also, a variant spelling of Emily.

Emily From the Latin, meaning "industrious, ambitious." HEBREW EQUIVALENT: Mehira.

Emma From the Anglo-Saxon, meaning "big one" or "grandmother." HEBREW EQUIVALENT: Ima.

Emmie A pet form of Emma.

Emuna, Emunah From the Hebrew, meaning "faith, faithful." HEBREW EQUIVALENT: Emuna.

Ena A variant spelling of Ina. Also, a pet form of Eugenia.

Enid From the Anglo-Saxon, meaning "fair," or from the Celtic, meaning "soul, life." HEBREW EQUIVALENT: Chava.

Erela From the Hebrew, meaning "angel, messenger." HEBREW EQUIVALENT: Erela.

Eretz From the Hebrew, meaning "land, earth." HEBREW EQUIVALENT: Eretz.

Erez A variant spelling of Eretz. Also from the Hebrew, meaning "cedar." HEBREW EQUIVALENT: Erez.

Erga From the Hebrew, meaning "yearning, hope, longing." HEBREW EQUIVALENT: Erga.

Erica The feminine form of Eric, meaning "ever-kingly, brave, powerful." HEBREW EQUIVALENT: Malka.

Erika A variant spelling of Erica.

Erin From the Irish, meaning "peace." HEBREW EQUIVALENT: Shlomit.

Erma A variant spelling of Irma.

Erna From the Anglo-Saxon, meaning "retiring, peaceful." HEBREW EQUIVALENT: Menucha.

Ernesta, Ernestine Feminine forms of Ernest. HEBREW EQUIVALENT: Amana.

Essie A pet form of Esther.

Esta, Estee Variant forms of Esther.

Estella A Spanish form of Esther.

Estelle A variant form of Esther.

Ester, Esther From the Persian, meaning "star." HEBREW EQUIVALENT: Ester.

Esti A pet form of Esther.

Etana From the Hebrew, meaning "strong." HEBREW EQUIVALENT: Etana.

Ethel From the Anglo-Saxon, meaning "noble." HEBREW EQUIVALENT: Atzila.

Eti A pet form of Esther.

Etka The Yiddish pet form of Ita and Yetta.

Etta A pet form of Harriet and Henrietta.

Etta-Jo A combination of Etta and Josephine.

Etti, Etty Pet forms of Esther.

Eudice A variant spelling of Eudit.

Eudit A variant form of Yehudit (Judith).

Eudora From the Greek, meaning "good gift." HEBREW EQUIVALENT: Dorona.

Eugenia From the Greek, meaning "well-born." HEBREW EQUIVALENT: Adina.

Eugenie The French form of Eugenia.

Eunice From the Greek, meaning "happy victory." HEBREW EQUIVALENT: Dafna.

Eva A variant form of Eve.

Evangeline From the Greek, meaning "bearer of glad tidings, messenger." HEBREW EQUIVALENT: Gila.

Eve A Latin and German form, from the Hebrew, meaning "life." HEBREW EQUIVALENT: Chava.

Evelyn A pet form of Eve. Also, from the Celtic, meaning "pleasant, good." HEBREW EQUIVALENT: Tova.

Evelyne A variant spelling of Evelyn.

Evita A Spanish pet form of Eve.

Evonne A pet form of Eva, Evelyn or Yvonne.

Evrona From the Hebrew, meaning "overflowing anger, fury." HEBREW EQUIVALENT: Evrona.

Evy A variant spelling of Evie.

Ezraela, Ezraella From the Hebrew, meaning "God is my help." HEBREW EQUIVALENT: Ezra'ela.

Ezriela, Ezriella From the Hebrew, meaning "God is my help." HEBREW EQUIVALENT: Ezriela.

BEST BABY NAMES BEST BABY NAMES

Fabia From the Greek, meaning "bean farmer." HEBREW EQUIVALENT: Adama.

Fabiana A variant form of Fabia.

Faga A variant spelling of Feiga.

Faiga A Yiddish form of the German *Vogel*, meaning "bird." HEBREW EQUIVALENT: Efrona.

Faige A variant spelling of Faiga.

Faigel A Yiddish pet form of Faiga.

Faith   From the Anglo-Saxon, meaning "unswerving trust, hope." HEBREW EQUIVALENT: Emuna.

Falice, Falicia   Variant spellings of Felice and Felicia.

Fani   A variant spelling of Fannie.

Fania   A pet form of Frances.

Fannie, Fanny, Fannye   Pet forms of Frances.

Fanya   A variant spelling of Fania.

Fawn   From the Latin, meaning "young deer," or from the Middle English, meaning "friendly." HEBREW EQUIVALENT: Tzivya.

Fawna   A variant form of Fawn.

Fawne   A variant spelling of Fawn.

Fawnia   A variant form of Fawn.

Fay, Faye   From the Old French, meaning "fidelity." HEBREW EQUIVALENT: Ne'emana.

Fayette   A pet form of Fay.

Feiga   A variant form of Feige.

Feige   From the Yiddish *feig*, meaning "fig." Also, a variant form of Feigel and Faiga.

Feigel   A variant spelling of Faigel.

Felecia   A variant spelling of Felicia.

Felice, Felicia   From the Latin, meaning "happy, fortunate." HEBREW EQUIVALENT: Ashera.

Feliciana   A Spanish form of Felice.

Felicite, Felicity   French and Spanish forms of Felice.

Felisa, Felise, Felisse   Variant spellings of Felice.

Fern, Ferne   From the Anglo-Saxon, meaning "strong, brave." Also, a plant name. HEBREW EQUIVALENT: Gavriela.

Fidelia   From the Latin, meaning "faithful." HEBREW EQUIVALENT: Emuna.

Fidella   A variant form of Fidelia.

Fiona   From the Celtic, meaning "white." HEBREW EQUIVALENT: Livna.

Flavia   From the Latin, meaning "yellow-haired, blond." HEBREW EQUIVALENT: Paziya.

Fleur   A French form of the Latin, meaning "flower." HEBREW EQUIVALENT: Pericha.

Fleurette A pet form of Fleur.

Flora From the Latin, meaning "flower." HEBREW EQUIVA-
LENT: Shoshana.

Floreen A variant form of Florence.

Florella A pet form of Florence.

Floren A short form of Florence.

Florence From the Latin, meaning "blooming, flowery,
flourishing." HEBREW EQUIVALENT: Irit.

Florentina A pet form of Florence.

Floria A variant form of Flora.

Florrie A pet form of Flora and Florence.

Floryn A pet form of Flora and Florence.

Flossie A pet form of Flora and Florence.

Fortuna A popular Ladino name, meaning "fortunate."
HEBREW EQUIVALENT: Mazala.

Fradel A pet form of Frayda.

Fran A pet form of Frances.

Francene A pet form of Frances.

Frances From the Anglo-Saxon, meaning "free, liberal."
HEBREW EQUIVALENT: Derorit.

Francesca An Italian form of Frances.

Francie A pet form of Frances.

Francine A pet form of Frances.

Frani A pet form of Frances.

Frankie A pet form of Frances.

Frayda, Frayde From the Yiddish, meaning "joy." HEBREW
EQUIVALENT: Aliza.

Freda A variant form of Frieda.

Fredda A pet form of Frederica and Frieda.

Frederica The feminine form of Frederick, meaning "peaceful ruler." HEBREW EQUIVALENT: Malka.

Freida, Freide Variant forms of Frieda. Also, variant spellings of Frayda.

Frieda From the Old High German, meaning "peace."
HEBREW EQUIVALENT: Sha'anana.

Friedel A pet form of Frieda.

Fritzi A pet form of Frederica and Frieda.

Fruma From the Yiddish, meaning "pious one." HEBREW
EQUIVALENT: Chasida.

Frume A variant form of Fruma.

Frumet, Frumeth Variant forms of Frume.

Gabi A pet form of Gabriella. HEBREW EQUIVALENT: Gabi.

Gabriela, Gabriella Anglicized forms of Gavriela.

Gabriele, Gabrielle Variant French forms of Gabriela and
Gabriella.

Gada The feminine form of Gad. HEBREW EQUIVALENT:
Gada.

Gadiela, Gadiella Variant forms of Gadiel.

Gadit A variant form of Gada. HEBREW EQUIVALENT: Gadit.

Gafna The Aramaic form of Gefen. HEBREW EQUIVALENT:
Gafna.

Gafnit A variant form of Gafna. HEBREW EQUIVALENT:
Gafnit.

Gail A short form of Abigail.

Gal From the Hebrew, meaning "mound, hill" or "wave."
HEBREW EQUIVALENT: Gal.

Gala A variant form of Gal.

Gale A variant form of Gail.

Gali A variant form of Gal. HEBREW EQUIVALENT: Gali.

Galia A variant spelling of Galiya.

Galila From the Hebrew, meaning "roll up, roll away."
HEBREW EQUIVALENT: Galila.

Galina The Russian form of Helen.

Galit A variant form of Gal. HEBREW EQUIVALENT: Galit.

Galiya A variant form of Galya. HEBREW EQUIVALENT: Galiya.

Galya From the Hebrew, meaning "hill of God." HEBREW
EQUIVALENT: Galya.

Gamliela A feminine form of Gamliel. HEBREW EQUIVALENT: Gamliela.

Gana From the Hebrew, meaning "garden." HEBREW EQUIVALENT: Gana.

Gania A variant spelling of Ganya.

Ganit A variant form of Gana. HEBREW EQUIVALENT: Ganit.

Ganya From the Hebrew, meaning "garden of the Lord." HEBREW EQUIVALENT: Ganya.

Garnit From the Hebrew, meaning "granary." HEBREW EQUIVALENT: Garnit.

Gavi A pet form of Gavriela.

Gavriela, Gavriella From the Hebrew, meaning "heroine." HEBREW EQUIVALENT: Gavriela.

Gavrila Variant forms of Gavriela. HEBREW EQUIVALENT: Gavrila.

Gay From the Anglo-Saxon, meaning "gay, merry." HEBREW EQUIVALENT: Gila.

Gayle A variant spelling of Gail.

Gayora From the Hebrew, meaning "valley of light." HEBREW EQUIVALENT: Gayora.

Gazella From the Latin, meaning "gazelle, deer." HEBREW EQUIVALENT: A'yala.

Gazit From the Hebrew, meaning "hewn stone." HEBREW EQUIVALENT: Gazit.

Geela, Geelah Variant spellings of Gila.

Gefen, Geffen From the Hebrew, meaning "vine." HEBREW EQUIVALENT: Gefen.

Gemma From the Latin, meaning "swelling bud" or "precious stone." HEBREW EQUIVALENT: Yahaloma.

Gena, Gene Variant spellings of Gina.

Genevieve From the Celtic, meaning "white wave." HEBREW EQUIVALENT: Bat-Galim.

Georgeanne A hybrid form of the masculine George and Anne. HEBREW EQUIVALENT: Gana.

Georgette A pet form of Georgia.

Georgia From the Greek, meaning "husbandman, farmer." HEBREW EQUIVALENT: Gana.

Georgiana A variant form of Georgeanne.

Georgina, Georgine Pet forms of Georgia.

Geraldene, Geraldine From the Old High German, meaning "spearwielder, warrior." HEBREW EQUIVALENT: Chanit.

Geralyn A hybrid of Geraldine and Lynn.

Gerda From the Old High German, meaning "protected one." HEBREW EQUIVALENT: Shimrit.

Gerrie, Gerry Pet forms of Geraldine and Gerardine.

Gershona The feminine form of Gershon. HEBREW EQUIVALENT: Gershona.

Gertrude From the Old High German, meaning "battlemaid" or "adored warrior." HEBREW EQUIVALENT: Gibora.

Geula, Geulah From the Hebrew, meaning "redemption." HEBREW EQUIVALENT: Ge'ula.

Gevira, Gevirah From the Hebrew, meaning "lady" or "queen." HEBREW EQUIVALENT: Gevira.

Gevura, Gevurah From the Hebrew, meaning "strength." HEBREW EQUIVALENT: Gevura.

Ghila A variant spelling of Gila.

Ghity, Ghitty Pet forms of Gitel.

Gibora, Giborah From the Hebrew, meaning "strong, heroine." HEBREW EQUIVALENT: Gibora.

Gidona The feminine form of Gidon. HEBREW EQUIVALENT: Gidona.

Gila, Gilah From the Hebrew, meaning "joy." HEBREW EQUIVALENT: Gila.

Gilada, Giladah From the Hebrew, meaning "[the] hill is [my] witness" or "joy is forever." HEBREW EQUIVALENT: Gilada.

Gilana, Gilanah From the Hebrew, meaning "joy." HEBREW EQUIVALENT: Gilana.

Gilat A variant form of Gilana. HEBREW EQUIVALENT: Gilat.

Gilberta The feminine form of Gilbert. HEBREW EQUIVALENT: Behira.

Gilda From the Celtic, meaning "servant of God," or from the Old English, meaning "coated with gold." HEBREW EQUIVALENT: Zehava.

Gili From the Hebrew, meaning "my joy." HEBREW EQUIVA-
LENT: Gili.

Gilit A variant form of Gilana. HEBREW EQUIVALENT: Gilit.

Gill From the Old English, meaning "girl." HEBREW
EQUIVALENT: Alma.

Gilla A variant spelling of Gill.

Gillian A variant form of the Latin name Juliana.

Gina From the Hebrew, meaning "garden." HEBREW
EQUIVALENT: Gina.

Ginat A variant form of Gina. HEBREW EQUIVALENT: Ginat.

Ginger A pet form of Virginia.

Gisa From the Anglo-Saxon, meaning "gift." HEBREW
EQUIVALENT: Migdana.

Gisela, Gisella From the Anglo-Saxon, meaning "the bright
hope of the people" or "sword." HEBREW EQUIVALENT:
Zahara.

Giselle A variant form of Gisela.

Gita A variant form of Gitit. HEBREW EQUIVALENT: Gita.

Gitel, Gitele, Gittel From the Yiddish, meaning "good."
HEBREW EQUIVALENT: Tova.

Gitit From the Hebrew, meaning "wine press." HEBREW
EQUIVALENT: Gitit.

Gittie, Gitty Pet forms of Gitel.

Giva, Givah From the Hebrew, meaning "hill, high place."
HEBREW EQUIVALENT: Giva.

Givona A variant form of Giva. HEBREW EQUIVALENT:
Givona.

Giza From the Hebrew, meaning "cut stone." HEBREW
EQUIVALENT: Giza.

Gizela A variant spelling of Gisela.

Gladys A Welsh form of the Latin name Claudia, meaning
"lame." Also, from the Celtic, meaning "brilliant,
splendid." HEBREW EQUIVALENT: Behira.

Gladyce A variant spelling of Gladys.

Glenda A variant form of Glendora or Glenna.

Glendora A hybrid of Glenna and Dora.

Glenna The feminine form of Glenn. HEBREW EQUIVALENT: Ganit.

Glikel A pet form of Glukel.

Glora A variant form of Gloria.

Gloria From the Latin, meaning "glory, glorious." HEBREW EQUIVALENT: Hillela.

Gloriana A variant form of Gloria.

Glory A variant form of Gloria.

Gloryette A pet form of Glory.

Glukel From the German and Yiddish, meaning "luck, good fortune." HEBREW EQUIVALENT: Mazal.

Glynda A variant form of Glenda.

Glynis, Glynnis From the Brittish, meaning "glen, narrow valley." HEBREW EQUIVALENT: Ga'ya.

Golda A popular Yiddish name, from the Old English and German, meaning "gold, golden." HEBREW EQUIVALENT: Zehava.

Goldie, Goldy Pet forms of Golda.

Gomer From the Hebrew, meaning "to finish, complete." HEBREW EQUIVALENT: Gomer.

Gorala From the Hebrew, meaning "lot, lottery." HEBREW EQUIVALENT: Gorala.

Gozala From the Hebrew, meaning "young bird." HEBREW EQUIVALENT: Gozala.

Grace From the Latin, meaning "grace." HEBREW EQUIVALENT: Chana.

Graciela A variant form of Grace.

Greer From the Greek and Latin, meaning "guard, guardian." HEBREW EQUIVALENT: Mishmeret.

Greta A Swedish pet form of Margaret.

Gretchen A German pet form of Margaret.

Gretel A variant form of Gretchen.

Gurit From the Hebrew, meaning "young lion." HEBREW EQUIVALENT: Gurit.

Gussie, Gussy Popular pet forms of Augusta.

Gustine A variant form of Augusta.

Guta, Gute From the Yiddish, meaning "good." HEBREW
EQUIVALENT: Tova.

Gwen From the Welsh, meaning "white, fair" or "beautiful."
HEBREW EQUIVALENT: Berucha.

Gwenn, Gwenne Variant spellings of Gwen.

Gwyn, Gwynn, Gwynne Variant forms of Gwen.

BEST BABY NAMES   BEST BABY NAMES

Hada A pet form of Hadasa.

Hadar From the Hebrew, meaning "ornamented, beautiful,
honored." HEBREW EQUIVALENT: Hadar.

Hadara A variant form of Hadar. HEBREW EQUIVALENT:
Hadara.

Hadarit A variant form of Hadar. HEBREW EQUIVALENT:
Hadarit.

Hadas A short form of Hadasa. HEBREW EQUIVALENT: Hadas.

Hadasa, Hadassa, Hadassah From the Hebrew, meaning
"myrtle tree." HEBREW EQUIVALENT: Hadasa.

Hadura From the Hebrew, meaning "ornamented, beautiful." HEBREW EQUIVALENT: Hadura.

Hagar From the Hebrew, meaning "stranger." HEBREW
EQUIVALENT: Hagar.

Hagia, Haggiah Variant spellings of Chagiya.

Hagit A variant spelling of Chagit.

Hallela From the Hebrew, meaning "praise." HEBREW
EQUIVALENT: Hallela.

Haley From the Norse, meaning "hero." HEBREW EQUIVA-
LENT: Gavriela.

Halie A variant spelling of Haley.

Halina A Polish form of Helen.

Hallie, Hally Variant spellings of Haley.

Hana A variant spelling of Chana.

Hania A variant spelling of Chaniya.

Hanina A variant spelling of Chanina.

Hanit A variant spelling of Chanit.

Hanita A variant spelling of Chanita.

Haniya A variant spelling of Chaniya.

Hanna, Hannah Variant spellings of Chana.

Hanni A pet form of Chana.

Hanny A pet form of Chana.

Happy A modern English name, meaning "joyful." HEBREW EQUIVALENT: Aliza.

Happi A variant spelling of Happy.

Harela The feminine form of Harel, meaning "mountain of God." HEBREW EQUIVALENT: Harela.

Harmony From the Greek, meaning "unity, peace." HEBREW EQUIVALENT: Shlomit.

Harriet, Harriette From the Old English, meaning "mistress of the house, ruler, lord." HEBREW EQUIVALENT: Sara.

Hasida A variant spelling of Chasida.

Hasina A variant spelling of Chasina.

Hasna A variant spelling of Chasna.

Hasya A variant spelling of Chasya.

Hava A variant spelling of Chava.

Haviva A variant spelling of Chaviva.

Haya A variant spelling of Chaya.

Hazel From the Old English, meaning "hazel tree." HEBREW EQUIVALENT: Alona.

Hazelbelle A hybrid of Hazel and Belle.

Heather From the Anglo-Saxon, meaning "heath, plant, shrub." HEBREW EQUIVALENT: Ketzia.

Hedda From the German, meaning "strife, warfare." HEBREW EQUIVALENT: Amtza.

Hedva, Hedvah Variant spellings of Chedva.

Hedy, Heddy Pet forms of Hedda, Hester, and Esther.

Hedya From the Hebrew, meaning "echo [voice] of the Lord." HEBREW EQUIVALENT: Hedya.

Hefziba, Hefzibah Anglicized forms of Chefzi-Ba.

Heidi Probably a variant form of Hester and Esther.

Helaine A variant form of Helen.

Helen From the Greek, meaning "light." HEBREW EQUIVA-
LENT: Nahara.

Helena A variant form of Helen.

Helene The French form of Helen.

Heleni A variant form of Helene.

Helenmae A combination of Helen and Mae.

Heline The Hawaiian form of Helen.

Hella A variant form of Helen.

Hemda A variant spelling of Chemda.

Hen A variant spelling of Chein.

Henda, Hende Variant Yiddish forms of Hene.

Hendel A Yiddish pet form of Chana.

Hene, Heneh Yiddish pet forms of Chana.

Henia A Yiddish pet form of Henrietta.

Henna A Yiddish form of Hannah.

Henrietta, Henriette Variant forms of Harriet.

Henya A Yiddish pet form of Henrietta.

Hephziba, Hephzibah Variant spellings of Cheftzi-Ba.

Hepzi, Hepzia Pet forms of Hephziba.

Hepziba, Hepzibah Variant forms of Hefziba.

Herma From the Latin, meaning "stone pillar, signpost."
HEBREW EQUIVALENT: Giva.

Hermine A variant form of Hermione.

Hermione In Greek mythology, the messenger and servant
of gods. HEBREW EQUIVALENT: Shimshona.

Hermona A feminine form of Hermon. HEBREW EQUIVALENT:
Chermona.

Hertzela The feminine form of Herzl. HEBREW EQUIVALENT:
Hertzela.

Hertzliya A variant form of Hertzela. HEBREW EQUIVALENT:
Hertzliya.

Herzlia, Herzliah Variant spellings of Hertzliya.

Hester The Latin form of Esther.

Hesther A variant form of Hester.

Hetta A pet form of Harriet.

Hetty A pet form of Harriet.

Hila, Hilah From the Hebrew, meaning "praise." HEBREW EQUIVALENT: Hila.

Hilaire The French form of Hilary.

Hilana A variant form of Hila. HEBREW EQUIVALENT: Hilana.

Hilary, Hillary From the Greek and the Latin, meaning "cheerful." HEBREW EQUIVALENT: Gilana.

Hilda, Hilde Short forms of Hildegard.

Hildegard, Hildegarde, Hildergarde From the German, meaning "warrior, battlemaid." HEBREW EQUIVALENT: Gavriela.

Hildi, Hildy Pet forms of Hildegard.

Hili A pet form of Hilda and Hillela.

Hilla, Hillah Variant spellings of Hila.

Hillary A variant spelling of Hilary.

Hillela The feminine form of Hillel, meaning "praise." HEBREW EQUIVALENT: Hillela.

Hilma Probably a variant form of Wilhelmina.

Hinda From the German and Yiddish, meaning "hind, deer." HEBREW EQUIVALENT: A'yala.

Hindee A pet form of Hinda.

Hindel, Hindelle Yiddish pet forms of Hinda.

Hindi, Hindie Pet forms of Hinda.

Hode, Hodeh Yiddish forms of Hadasah.

Hodel A Yiddish pet form of Hadasah.

Hodi A Yiddish form of Hadasah.

Hodia, Hodiah Variant spellings of Hodiya.

Hodiya From the Hebrew, meaning "praise the Lord." HEBREW EQUIVALENT: Hodiya.

Holiday From the Anglo-Saxon, meaning "festive day, holiday." HEBREW EQUIVALENT: Chagit.

Holis A variant spelling of Hollace.

Hollace A variant form of Haley.

Holli A variant form of Holly.

Hollis A variant spelling of Hollace.

Holly, Hollye From the Anglo-Saxon, meaning "holy." HEBREW EQUIVALENT: Chagiya.

Honey From the Anglo-Saxon, meaning "honey." HEBREW EQUIVALENT: Devash.

Honor From the Latin, meaning "glory" or "respect." HEBREW EQUIVALENT: Adra.

Honora A variant form of Honor.

Honorine A pet form of Honor.

Hope From the Anglo-Saxon, meaning "trust, faith." HEBREW EQUIVALENT: Emuna.

Horia, Horiah Variant spellings of Horiya.

Horiya, Horiyah From the Hebrew, meaning "teaching of the Lord." HEBREW EQUIVALENT: Horiya.

Hortense From the Latin, meaning "gardener." HEBREW EQUIVALENT: Gana.

Hude, Hudes Yiddish forms of Hadasah. Also, nicknames for Yehudit.

Hudel A pet form of Hude.

Hulda, Huldah Variant spellings of Chulda.

Ida From the Old Norse, meaning "industrious." Also, from the Greek, meaning "happy." HEBREW EQUIVALENT: Ditza.

Idalee A combination of Ida and Lee.

Idel, Idelle Pet forms of Ida.

Idena A hybrid name of Ida and Dena.

Idette A pet form of Ida.

Idit A Yiddish form of the Hebrew name Yehudit.

Idra From the Aramaic, meaning "bone of a fish" or "fig tree." HEBREW EQUIVALENT: Idra.

Idria A variant spelling of Idriya.

Idrit A variant form of Idriya. HEBREW EQUIVALENT: Idrit.

Idriya From the Hebrew, meaning "duck." HEBREW EQUIVALENT: Idriya.

Ila A variant form of Ilit.

Ilana From the Hebrew, meaning "tree." HEBREW EQUIVA-
LENT: Ilana.

Ilanit A variant form of Ilana. HEBREW EQUIVALENT: Ilanit.

Ilene A variant spelling of Eileen.

Ilisa, Ilise Variant forms of Elisabeth.

Ilit From the Aramaic, meaning "uppermost, superlative."
HEBREW EQUIVALENT: Ilit.

Ilita A variant form of Ilit. HEBREW EQUIVALENT: Ilita.

Ilsa, Ilse Variant forms of Elisabeth.

Ilyse A variant form of Elisabeth.

Ima A variant spelling of Imma.

Imma From the Hebrew, meaning "mother." HEBREW
EQUIVALENT: Imma.

Imogen, Imogene From the Latin, meaning "image, likeness." HEBREW EQUIVALENT: Michal.

Ina From the Latin, meaning "mother." HEBREW EQUIVALENT:
Imma.

Inez From the Greek and Portuguese, meaning "pure."
HEBREW EQUIVALENT: Penuya.

Inga, Inge From the Old English, meaning "meadow."
HEBREW EQUIVALENT: Ganit.

Inger A variant form of Inga.

Ingrid In Norse mythology, Ing is the god of fertility and
peace. HEBREW EQUIVALENT: Pora.

Irena A Polish form of Irene.

Irene From the Greek, meaning "peace." HEBREW EQUIVA-
LENT: Margaya.

Irenee A variant form of Irene.

Irina A variant form of Irena.

Iris In Greek mythology, the goddess of the rainbow. From
the Latin, meaning "faith, hope." HEBREW EQUIVALENT:
Amana.

Irit The name of a flower from the lily family. HEBREW
EQUIVALENT: Irit.

Irma From the Anglo-Saxon, meaning "noble maid."
HEBREW EQUIVALENT: Alma.

Isa A pet form of Isabel, used chiefly in Scotland.

Isaaca The feminine form of Isaac, meaning "laughter." HEBREW EQUIVALENT: Yitzchaka.

Isabel, Isabele, Isabella, Isabelle Variant forms of Elisabeth.

Isadora, Isidora Feminine forms of the masculine Isadore. HEBREW EQUIVALENT: Matana.

Isobel A variant Scottish spelling of Isabel.

Israela A variant spelling of Yisraela.

Israelit A variant spelling of Yisraela.

Ita From the Celtic, meaning "thirsty." Also, a corrupt Yiddish form of Yehudit (Judith).

Iti From the Hebrew, meaning "with me." HEBREW EQUIVALENT: Iti.

Itia A variant spelling of Itiya.

Itiya From the Hebrew, meaning "God is with me." HEBREW EQUIVALENT: Itiya.

Itta A variant spelling of Ita.

Itti A variant spelling of Itti.

Ivana, Ivanna Feminine forms of Ivan, the Russian form of John. HEBREW EQUIVALENT: Yochana.

Ivette A variant spelling of Yvette.

Ivria, Ivriah Variant spellings of Ivriya.

Ivrit From the Hebrew, meaning "Hebrew [language]." HEBREW EQUIVALENT: Ivrit.

Ivrita A variant form of Ivrit.

Ivriya The feminine form of Ivri, meaning "Hebrew." HEBREW EQUIVALENT: Ivriya.

Ivy From the Middle English, meaning "vine." HEBREW EQUIVALENT: Karmela.

Jacalyn A variant spelling of Jacqueline.

Jackee A pet form of Jacoba and Jacqueline.

Jacklyn, Jaclyn, Jaclynn Variant forms of Jacqueline.

Jacoba The feminine form of Jacob, meaning "supplant" or "protect." HEBREW EQUIVALENT: Ya'akova.

Jacqueline A French form of Jacoba.

Jacquelyn, Jacquelynne Variant spellings of Jacqueline.

Jael From the Hebrew, meaning "mountain goat." HEBREW EQUIVALENT: Ya'el.

Jaen A variant spelling of Ya'en.

Jaffa A variant spelling of Yafa.

Jafit A variant spelling of Yafit.

Jaime, Jaimee, Jaimie Feminine forms of James, derived from Jacob, meaning "to supplant" or "to protect." HEBREW EQUIVALENT: Ya'akova.

Jamie A variant spelling of Jaime.

Jan A pet form of Janice or Jeanette.

Jane A variant English form of Johanna.

Janet An English and Scottish form of Johanna.

Janetta An English form of Johanna.

Janette A variant spelling of Janet.

Jani A pet form of Jane.

Janice A variant form of Jane.

Janie A pet form of Jane.

Janiece A variant spelling of Janice.

Janina, Janine Pet forms of Jane.

Janis A variant spelling of Janice.

Janita A Spanish pet form of Jane.

Janna A pet form of Johanna.

Jannette A variant spelling of Janet.

Jannie A pet form of Janet.

Jardena A variant spelling of Yardena.

Jardenia A variant spelling of Yardeniya.

Jasmina A variant form of Jasmine. HEBREW EQUIVALENT: Yasmina.

Jasmine A Persian flower-name, usually referring to a flower in the olive family. HEBREW EQUIVALENT: Yasmin.

Jean, Jeane Scottish forms of Johanna.

Jeanetta A variant form of Jeanette.

Jeanette A French form of Johanna.

Jeanice A variant form of Jean.

Jeanie A pet form of Jean.

Jeanine A pet form of Jean.

Jeanne A French form of Johanna.

Jeannette A variant spelling of Jeanette.

Jeannine A variant spelling of Jeanine.

Jeannye A variant spelling of Jennie.

Jedida, Jedidah French forms of Yedida.

Jehane, Jehanne French forms of Johanna.

Jemima A variant spelling of Yemima.

Jemina A variant spelling of Yemina.

Jen A short form of Jeanette. Also, a pet form of Jennifer.

Jenat A variant form of Jeanette.

Jene A variant spelling of Jean.

Jenerette A pet form of Jane.

Jenine A pet form of Jane.

Jenna A variant form of Jeanette.

Jennie A pet form of Jean, Jeanette, and Jennifer.

Jennifer From the Welsh, meaning "friend of peace." HEBREW EQUIVALENT: Menucha.

Jennilee A name created by combining Jennifer and Lee.

Jenny An English and Scottish pet form of Johanna.

Jeralyn A variant spelling of Geralyn.

Jeri, Jerri Pet forms of Geraldene.

Jerriann A name created by combining Jerri and Ann.

Jerrilyn A name created by combining Jerri and Lyn.

Jessica A variant form of Jessie.

Jessie A Scottish form of Johanna. Also, a feminine form of Jesse.

Jethra A feminine form of Jethro, meaning "abundance, riches." HEBREW EQUIVALENT: Yitra.

Jewel, Jewell From the Old French, meaning "joy." HEBREW EQUIVALENT: Aliza.

Jill A variant spelling of Gill.

Joan A variant form of Johanna.

Joana, Jo Ann Short forms of Joanna.

Joanna A short form of Johanna.

Joanne A variant spelling of Joann.

Jo-Anne A hybrid name compounded of Jo (Josephine) and Ann(e).

Jocelin, Joceline German forms of the Hebrew Jacoba, the feminine form of Jacob, meaning "supplant" or "protect." HEBREW EQUIVALENT: Ya'akova.

Jocelyn, Jocelyne Variant spellings of Jocelin.

Jodette A French form of Jodi or Jocelin.

Jodi, Jodie, Jody Pet forms of Judith and Josephine.

Joela, Joella Feminine forms of Joel, meaning "God is willing." HEBREW EQUIVALENT: Yo'ela.

Joelle A variant form of Joela.

Joellen A variant form of Joelynn.

Joely A pet form of Joela.

Joelynn A hybrid form of Joela and Lynn.

Joette A pet form from the masculine Joseph. HEBREW EQUIVALENT: Yosifa.

Johan, Johanna, Johanne German and English forms of the masculine Yochanan, meaning "God is gracious." HEBREW EQUIVALENT: Yochanana.

Johanne A variant form of Johanna.

Johnetta A pet form of Johanna.

Johnine A pet form of Johana.

Johnna A variant form of Johanna.

Joice A variant spelling of Joyce.

Jolanda A variant spelling of Yolande.

Jolene A pet form of Jolie.

Joletta A pet form of Jolie.

Jolie From the French, meaning "high spirits, good humor, pleasant." HEBREW EQUIVALENT: Na'ama.

Joliet A variant form of Jolie or Juliet.

Jonea A variant form of Johan.

Jonelle A feminine form of Jonah. HEBREW EQUIVALENT: Yonina.

Jonina A variant spelling of Yonina.

Jonit, Jonita Variant spellings of Yonit and Yonita.

Jordana, Jordena Feminine forms of Jordan. HEBREW EQUIVA-LENT: Yardena.

Jordi, Jordie Pet forms of Jordana.

Joscelin An Old French form of Jocelin.

Joscelind A variant form of Jocelin.

Josefa, Josepha Variant spellings of Yosifa.

Josephine A feminine French form of Joseph. HEBREW EQUIVALENT: Yosifa.

Josetta, Josette Pet forms of Jocelyn and Josephine.

Joslyn A variant spelling of Jocelyn.

Jovita A Spanish pet form of Joy.

Joy A short form of Joyce.

Joya A variant form of Joy.

Joyce From the Latin, meaning "jovial, merry." HEBREW EQUIVALENT: Gila.

Judi, Judie Pet forms of Judith.

Judith An Anglicized form of Yehudit.

Judy A pet form of Judith.

Jule A variant form of Julia.

Julee A variant spelling of Julie.

Juleen A variant form of Julia.

Jules A variant form of Julia.

Julia From the Greek, meaning "soft-haired," symbolizing youth. HEBREW EQUIVALENT: Alma.

Julian, Juliana Variant forms of Julia.

Julie A pet form of Julia.

Julienne The French form of Julia.

Juliet A French pet form of Julia.

Julieta A variant form of Julia.

Juliette A French pet form of Julia.

June From the Latin, meaning "ever youthful." HEBREW EQUIVALENT: Aviva.

Justina, Justine Feminine forms of Justin. HEBREW EQUIVALENT: Danya.

Justyna A variant spelling of Justina.

Jyll A variant spelling of Jill.

BEST BABY NAMES   BEST BABY NAMES

Kadia A variant spelling of Kadiya.

Kadisha From the Hebrew, meaning "holy." HEBREW EQUIVALENT: Kadisha.

Kadiya From the Hebrew, meaning "pitcher." HEBREW EQUIVALENT: Kadiya.

Kadya A variant form of Kadiya.

Kaethe A variant form of Kathy.

Kaile, Kaille Variant forms of Kelila.

Kalanit From the Hebrew, meaning "an anemon," a flower in the buttercup family. HEBREW EQUIVALENT: Kalanit.

Kaley A variant form of Kelly.

Kalia A variant form of Kelila.

Kara A pet form of Katherine.

Karen A Danish form of Katherine.

Kari A variant spelling of Carrie.

Karin A variant spelling of Karen.

Karla A feminine form of Karl. HEBREW EQUIVALENT: Ariela.

Karleen A pet form of Karla.

Karlene A pet form of Karla.

Karma A variant spelling of Carma.

Karmel A variant spelling of Carmel.

Karmela A variant spelling of Carmela.

Karmeli A variant spelling of Carmeli.

Karmelit A variant spelling of Carmelit.

Karmit A variant spelling of Carmit.

Karmiya A variant spelling of Carmia.

Karna A variant spelling of Carna.

Karni A variant spelling of Carni.

Karnia A variant spelling of Carnia.

Karniela, Karniella Variant spellings of Carniela.

Kanit A variant spelling of Carnit.

Karol, Karole Variant spellings of Carol.

Karolina The Polish form of Karolyn.

Karolyn A variant spelling of Carolyn and Caroline.

Karon A variant spelling of Karen.

Karyl A variant spelling of Carol.

Karyn A variant spelling of Karen.

Kaspit From the Hebrew, meaning "silver." HEBREW
    EQUIVALENT: Kaspit.

Katania, Kataniya From the Hebrew, meaning "small."
    HEBREW EQUIVALENT: Kataniya.

Kate A pet form of Katherine.

Katharine A variant spelling of Katherine.

Kathe A pet form of Katherine.

Katherine From the Greek, meaning "pure, unsullied."
    HEBREW EQUIVALENT: Berura.

Kathie A pet form of Katherine.

Kathleen A variant spelling of Cathleen.

Kathryn A variant spelling of Katherine.

Kathy A pet form of Katherine.

Kati, Katie Pet forms of Katherine.

Katrin, Katrina, Katrine, Katryn Variant forms of
    Katherine.

Katy A pet form of Katherine.

Kay From the Greek, meaning "rejoice." HEBREW EQUIVA-
    LENT: Rina.

Kayla, Kayle Variant forms of Kelila. Or, a Yiddish form of
    Celia.

Kedma From the Hebrew, meaning "east, eastward." HEBREW EQUIVALENT: Kedma.

Kefira From the Hebrew, meaning "young lioness." HEBREW EQUIVALENT: Kefira.

Kelila From the Hebrew, meaning "crown" or "laurels." HEBREW EQUIVALENT: Kelila.

Kelula A variant form of Kelila. HEBREW EQUIVALENT: Kelula.

Kenna From the Old Norse, meaning "to have knowledge." HEBREW EQUIVALENT: Buna.

Kerem From the Hebrew, meaning "vineyard." HEBREW EQUIVALENT: Kerem.

Keren, Keryn From the Hebrew, meaning "horn." HEBREW EQUIVALENT: Keren.

Keret From the Hebrew, meaning "city, settlement." HEBREW EQUIVALENT: Keret.

Kerry A variant form of Katherine or Carrie.

Keshet From the Hebrew, meaning "bow, rainbow." HEBREW EQUIVALENT: Keshet.

Keshisha From the Hebrew, meaning "old, elder." HEBREW EQUIVALENT: Keshisha.

Ketaniya A variant form of Kataniya. HEBREW EQUIVALENT: Ketaniya.

Ketifa From the Hebrew and Arabic, meaning "to pluck [fruit]." HEBREW EQUIVALENT: Ketifa.

Ketana From the Hebrew, meaning "small." HEBREW EQUIVALENT: Ketana.

Ketina From the Aramaic, meaning "minor" or "small child." HEBREW EQUIVALENT: Ketina.

Ketzia, Ketziah From the Hebrew, meaning "a powdered, fragrant, cinnamon-like bark." HEBREW EQUIVALENT: Ketzia.

Kevuda From the Hebrew, meaning "precious" or "respected." HEBREW EQUIVALENT: Kevuda.

Kezi A pet form of Ketzia.

Kezia, Keziah Variant spellings of Ketzia.

Kezzi, Kezzie, Kezzy Pet forms of Ketzia.

Kim A pet form of Kimberly.

Kimberley, Kimberly From "kimberlite," a type of rock formation containing diamonds. HEBREW EQUIVALENT: Yahalomit.

Kinneret Probably from the Hebrew, meaning "harp." HEBREW EQUIVALENT: Kinneret.

Kirsten From the Old English, meaning "stone, church." HEBREW EQUIVALENT: Devira.

Kit A pet form of Katherine.

Kitra From the Aramaic, meaning "crown." HEBREW EQUIVALENT: Kitra.

Kitrit A variant form of Kitra. HEBREW EQUIVALENT: Kitrit.

Kitron From the Hebrew, meaning "crown." HEBREW EQUIVALENT: Kitron.

Kitty A pet form of Katherine.

Klara A variant spelling of Clara.

Kosbi A variant spelling of Kozvi.

Kozvi From the Hebrew, meaning "lie, falsehood." HEBREW EQUIVALENT: Kosvi.

Kochava From the Hebrew, meaning "star." HEBREW EQUIVALENT: Kochava.

Kochavit A variant form of Kochava.

Koranit From the Hebrew, meaning "thyme" or "thistle." HEBREW EQUIVALENT: Koranit.

Korenet From the Hebrew, meaning "to shine, emit rays." HEBREW EQUIVALENT: Korenet.

Kori A variant spelling of Corey.

Krayna, Krayne Variant forms of Kreine.

Kreindel A pet form of Kreine.

Kreine A Yiddish form of the German *Krone*, meaning "crown." HEBREW EQUIVALENT: Atara.

Kryna A variant spelling of Kreine.

Kyla, Kyle Variant forms of Kelila.

Laeh A variant spelling of Leah.

Laila A variant spelling of Leila.

Laili, Lailie Variant spellings of Leili and Leilie.

Lala A variant form of Leila.

Lana From the Latin, meaning "woolly." HEBREW EQUIVA-
LENT: Tzameret.

Lani From the Hawaiian, meaning "sky, heaven." HEBREW
EQUIVALENT: Ramit.

Lara A variant spelling of Laura.

Laraine, Larainne From the Latin, meaning "sea bird."
HEBREW EQUIVALENT: Tzipora.

Laris, Larisa, Larissa From the Latin, meaning "cheerful."
HEBREW EQUIVALENT: Aviga'yil.

Lark From the Old English, meaning "old" or "large." Also,
a name applied to a large family of songbirds. HEBREW
EQUIVALENT: Tzipora.

Laura A variant form of the masculine Laurel, meaning
"laurel," a symbol of victory. HEBREW EQUIVALENT: Dafna.

Lauraine A variant form of Laura.

Laure A variant form of Laura.

Laurel A variant form of Laura.

Lauren A variant form of Laura.

Lauretta, Laurette Pet forms of Laura.

Lauri, Laurie Pet forms of Laura.

Laurice A variant form of Laurel.

Laverne From the Latin and French, meaning "springlike"
or "verdant." HEBREW EQUIVALENT: Aviva.

Lavina A variant form of Lavinia.

Lavinia From the Latin, meaning "woman of Rome,"
symbolizing sophistication. HEBREW EQUIVALENT: Nediva.

Laya The Hebrew form of Leah.

Laylie A variant spelling of Leili.

Lea A French form of Leah.

Leah From the Hebrew, meaning "to be weary." HEBREW EQUIVALENT: Laya.

Leana A variant spelling of Liana.

Leanne A name created by combining Leah and Anne.

Leanor, Leanore Variant forms of Eleanor.

Leatrice A name created by combining Leah and Beatrice.

Lee From the Anglo-Saxon, meaning "field, meadow." HEBREW EQUIVALENT: Nirit.

Leeba A variant spelling of Liba.

Leesa, Leeza Variant spellings of Lisa.

Leila, Leilah From the Arabic and Hebrew, meaning "night" or "dark, oriental beauty." HEBREW EQUIVALENT: Laila.

Leilani From the Hawaiian, meaning "heavenly flower." HEBREW EQUIVALENT: Chelmit.

Leili, Leilie A variant form of Leila.

Lela From the Anglo-Saxon, meaning "loyal, faithful." HEBREW EQUIVALENT: Emuna.

Leland From the Old English, meaning "meadowland." HEBREW EQUIVALENT: Gana.

Lelani A variant spelling of Leilani.

Lelia A variant form of Lela.

Lena A pet form of Eleanor, Helen, and Magdalene. Also, from the Hebrew, meaning "lodging." HEBREW EQUIVALENT: Lina.

Lennie A pet form of Eleanor.

Lenora, Lenore Pet forms of Eleanor.

Leola From the Anglo-Saxon, meaning "deer." HEBREW EQUIVALENT: A'yelet.

Leona From the Greek, meaning "lion-like." HEBREW EQUIVALENT: Ariela.

Leonia A variant seplling of Leona.

Leonie A pet form of Leona.

Leonora, Leonore Variant forms of Eleanor.

Leontine, Leontyne From the Latin, meaning "lion-like." HEBREW EQUIVALENT: Ariela.

Leora A variant spelling of Liora.

Leorit A variant spelling of Liorit.

Leron, Lerone Variant spellings of Liron.

Lesley, Leslie From the Anglo-Saxon, meaning "meadow-land." HEBREW EQUIVALENT: Karmela.

Leta Probably a form of Elizabeth.

Letifa, Letipha From the Hebrew, meaning "caress." HEBREW EQUIVALENT: Letifa.

Letitia From the Latin, meaning "joy." HEBREW EQUIVALENT: Aliza.

Lettie, Letty Pet forms of Elizabeth.

Leuma From the Hebrew, meaning "nation." HEBREW EQUIVALENT: Le'uma.

Leumi From the Hebrew, meaning "national." HEBREW EQUIVALENT: Le'umi.

Levana From the Hebrew, meaning "white" or "moon." HEBREW EQUIVALENT: Levana.

Levani From the Fijian, meaning "anointed with oil." Also, a variant form of Levana. HEBREW EQUIVALENT: Levani.

Levia, Leviah From the Hebrew, meaning "lioness of the Lord." HEBREW EQUIVALENT: Levia.

Levina From the Middle English, meaning "to shine." HEBREW EQUIVALENT: Meira.

Leviva From the Hebrew, meaning "pancake." HEBREW EQUIVALENT: Leviva.

Levona From the Hebrew, meaning "frankincense," so called because of its white color. HEBREW EQUIVALENT: Levona.

Leya A variant spelling of Leah.

Leyla A variant spelling of Leila.

Li From the Hebrew, meaning "to me." HEBREW EQUIVALENT: Li (Lee).

Lia, Liah Variant spellings of Leah.

Liba A variant Yiddish form of Libe.

Libbie, Libby Diminutive forms of Elizabeth.

Libe A Yiddish form of the German *liebe*, meaning "loved one, dear one." HEBREW EQUIVALENT: Ahava.

Liberty From the Latin, meaning "freedom." HEBREW
EQUIVALENT: Li-Dror.

Libi A variant form of Liba.

Libke, Libkeh Yiddish pet forms of Libe.

Lieba A variant Yiddish form of Libe.

Liebe A variant spelling of Libe.

Lila, Lilac, Lilah Flower names of Persian origin. HEBREW
EQUIVALENT: Lilach.

Lilach From the Hebrew, meaning "a plant from the olive
family." HEBREW EQUIVALENT: Lilach.

Lili, Lilia Variant forms of Lilian.

Lilian From the Greek and Latin, meaning "lily." HEBREW
EQUIVALENT: Chavatzelet.

Lilibet A pet form of Elizabeth.

Lilita A pet form of Lilian.

Lilli A pet form of Lillian.

Lillian A variant spelling of Lilian.

Lilo From the Hebrew, meaning "to be generous." HEBREW
EQUIVALENT: Nediva.

Lilly A pet form of Lillian.

Lily A pet form of Lilian.

Lilya A variant form of Lilian.

Lilyan A variant spelling of Lilian.

Lilybeth A hybrid name of Lily (Lilian) and Beth (Elizabeth).

Limor From the Hebrew and Arabic, meaning "myrhh,
bitter," a Middle Eastern plant. HEBREW EQUIVALENT:
Limor.

Lina A pet form of Caroline and Adelina. Also, a variant
spelling of Lena.

Linda From the Latin and Spanish, meaning "handsome,
pretty," or from the Anglo-Saxon, meaning "gentle maid."
HEBREW EQUIVALENT: Na'omi.

Linn, Linne From the Welsh, meaning "waterfall, lake."
HEBREW EQUIVALENT: Silona.

Linnet From the Latin, meaning "flaxen or golden-haired."
HEBREW EQUIVALENT: Zehuva.

Lior From the Hebrew, meaning "I have light." HEBREW EQUIVALENT: Lior.

Liora From the Hebrew, meaning "Light is mine." HEBREW EQUIVALENT: Liora.

Liorit A variant form of Liora. HEBREW EQUIVALENT: Liorit.

Lipke, Lipkeh Variant forms of the Yiddish Libke.

Lirit A Hebrew form of the Greek, meaning "lyrical, musical, poetic." HEBREW EQUIVALENT: Lirit.

Liron From the Hebrew, meaning "song is mine." HEBREW EQUIVALENT: Liron.

Lirona A variant form of Liron.

Lirone A variant spelling of Liron.

Lisa A pet form of Elizabeth.

Lital From the Hebrew, meaning "dew [rain] is mine." HEBREW EQUIVALENT: Lital.

Livana A variant spelling of Levana.

Livia A short form of Olivia.

Liviya A variant form of Levia.

Livna From the Hebrew, meaning "white." HEBREW EQUIVALENT: Livna.

Livnat A variant form of Livna. HEBREW EQUIVALENT: Livnat.

Livya From the Hebrew, meaning "crown." HEBREW EQUIVALENT: Livya.

Liza A pet form of Elizabeth.

Lizbeth A pet form of Elizabeth.

Lize A variant spelling of Liza.

Lizette A pet form of Elizabeth.

Lizzie, Lizzy Pet forms of Elizabeth.

Lois From the Greek, meaning "good, desirable." HEBREW EQUIVALENT: Bat-Tziyon.

Lola A pet form of the Italian Carlotta.

Lora From the Latin, meaning "she who weeps, sorrowful," or from the Old High German, meaning "famous warrior." HEBREW EQUIVALENT: Mara.

Loraine A variant form of Lora.

Loran, Lorann Hybrid forms of Laura and Ann.

Loree A variant spelling of Laurie.

Lorelei From the German, meaning "melody, song." HEBREW EQUIVALENT: Lirit.

Loren From the Latin, meaning "crowned with laurel." HEBREW EQUIVALENT: Kelila.

Loretta, Lorette From the Anglo-Saxon, meaning "ignorant." HEBREW EQUIVALENT: Datiela.

Lori A pet form of Lora.

Lorna From the Anglo-Saxon, meaning "lost, forlorn, forsaken." HEBREW EQUIVALENT: Azuva.

Lorraine A variant spelling of Loraine.

Lorri A pet form of Laura.

Lorrin A variant form of Lora.

Loryn A variant form of Lora.

Lota, Lotta, Lotte Pet forms of Charlotte.

Lottie A pet form of Charlotte.

Louisa From the Anglo-Saxon, meaning "refuge of the people, warrior-prince." HEBREW EQUIVALENT: Gavriela.

Lotus A plant in the water lily family. HEBREW EQUIVALENT: Shoshana.

Louise A French form of Louisa.

Loura A variant spelling of Laura.

Luan, Luann, Luanne Hybrid forms of Laura and Ann.

Luba A variant Yiddish form of Liba.

Lucette A pet form of Lucille.

Luci A pet form of Lucile.

Lucia A diminutive form of Lucile.

Lucie A pet form of Lucile.

Lucile, Lucille From the Latin, meaning "light" or "daybreak." HEBREW EQUIVALENT: Liora.

Lucinda An English form of Lucia.

Lucy An English form of Lucia.

Luella A hybrid of Louise and Ella.

Luisa An italian and Spanish form of Louise.

Luise A variant French form of Louise.

Lula A pet form of Louise.

Lulu A pet form of Louise.

Luna From the Latin, meaning "moon" or "singing one." HEBREW EQUIVALENT: Levana.

Lunetta, Lunette Pet forms of Luna.

Lupita From the Latin, meaning "wolf." HEBREW EQUIVALENT: Alma.

Lyadia A variant form of Lyda.

Lyala A variant spelling of Lila.

Lyda A Greek place-name, meaning "maiden from Lydia." HEBREW EQUIVALENT: Alma.

Lydia A variant form of Lyda.

Lyn A variant spelling of Linn.

Lynette A pet form of Lyn.

Lynn, Lynne Variant spellings of Linn.

Lys A pet form of Elisabeth.

BEST BABY NAMES   BEST BABY NAMES

Mabel From the Latin, meaning "my beautifyl one," or from the Old Irish, meaning "merry." HEBREW EQUIVALENT: Na'omi.

Mabella, Mabelle Variant forms of Mabel.

Mable A variant spelling of Mabel.

Madelaine A variant form of Magdalene.

Madeleine, Madeline French forms of Magdalene.

Madelon A variant form of Magdalene.

Madelyn A variant form of Magdalene.

Madge A pet form of Margaret.

Mady A pet form of Madge or Magdalene.

Mae A variant form of Mary and a variant spelling of May.

Mag A pet form of Margaret or Magdalene.

Magda A pet form of Magdalene.

Migdala From the Hebrew, meaning "tower." HEBREW EQUIVALENT: Migdala.

Magdalen A variant spelling of Magdalene.

Magdalene A Greek form of the Hebrew *migdal*, meaning "high tower." HEBREW EQUIVALENT: Migdala.

Magdaline A variant spelling of Magdalene.

Magena From the Hebrew, meaning "covering" or "protector." HEBREW EQUIVALENT: Magena.

Maggie A pet form of Margaret.

Magina A variant form of Magena. HEBREW EQUIVALENT: Magina.

Magna From the Latin, meaning "great." HEBREW EQUIVALENT: Gedola.

Magnolia From Modern Latin, meaning "the big laurel tree." HEBREW EQUIVALENT: Dafna.

Mahira A variant spelling of Mehira.

Maia In Roman mythology, goddess of the earth and growth. HEBREW EQUIVALENT: Adama.

Maida, Maide From the Anglo-Saxon, meaning "maiden." HEBREW EQUIVALENT: Alma.

Maire An Irish form of Mary. HEBREW EQUIVALENT: Adama.

Maisie From the British, meaning "field." HEBREW EQUIVALENT: Adama. Also, a Scottish pet form of Margaret.

Maital A variant spelling of Meital.

Maksima From the Hebrew, meaning "diviner, performer of miracles." HEBREW EQUIVALENT: Maksima.

Malbina From the Hebrew, meaning "to whiten" or "embarass." HEBREW EQUIVALENT: Malbina.

Malia The Hawaiian form of Mary.

Malinda A variant spelling of Melinda.

Malka, Malkah From the Hebrew, meaning "queen." HEBREW EQUIVALENT: Malka.

Malkia, Malkiah Variant spellings of Malkiya.

Malkie A pet form of Malka.

Malkit From the Hebrew, meaning "queen, queenly." HEBREW EQUIVALENT: Malkit.

Malkiya From the Hebrew, meaning "God is my king." HEBREW EQUIVALENT: Malkiya.

Malvina A variant spelling of Melvina.

Mamie A pet form of Mary.

Mana From the Hebrew, meaning "share, portion, gift."
HEBREW EQUIVALENT: Mana.

Manda A pet form of Amanda.

Mandy A pet form of Amanda.

Manette A pet form of Marion.

Mangena A variant spelling of Mangina.

Mangina From the Hebrew, meaning "song, melody."
HEBREW EQUIVALENT: Mangina.

Manuela A Spanish feminine form of Manuel. HEBREW
EQUIVALENT: Imanuela.

Mara, Marah From the Hebrew, meaning "bitter, bitterness."
HEBREW EQUIVALENT: Mara.

Maralee A hybrid form of Mara and Lee.

Maralyn A variant spelling of Marilyn.

Marata The Aramaic form of Mara. HEBREW EQUIVALENT:
Marata.

Marcella From the Latin, meaning "brave, martial" or
"hammer." HEBREW EQUIVALENT: Amtza.

Marcelyn A variant form of Marcella.

Marcia A variant form of Marcella.

Marcie A variant form of Marcia.

Marcilen A variant form of Marcella.

Marcy A variant form of Marcia.

Mardi A pet form of Martha.

Maree A variant spelling of Marie.

Mareea A variant spelling of Maria.

Maren, Marena From the Latin, meaning "sea." HEBREW
EQUIVALENT: Bat-Yam.

Marenda A variant form of Miranda.

Margalit A Hebrew form of the Greek *margarit*, meaning
"pearl." HEBREW EQUIVALENT: Margalit.

Margalita A variant form of Margalit. HEBREW EQUIVALENT:
Margalita.

Marganit A blue, gold, and red flower in the daisy family.
HEBREW EQUIVALENT: Marganit.

Margaret From the Greek, meaning "pearl" or "child of light." HEBREW EQUIVALENT: Margalit.

Margarete A German form of Margaret.

Margaretta A Spanish pet form of Margaret.

Margarita A Spanish form of Margaret.

Marge A pet form of Margaret.

Margene A variant form of Margaret.

Margerie A variant spelling of Margery.

Margery A variant form of Margaret.

Marget A pet form of Margaret.

Margie A pet form of Margaret.

Margo A variant form of Margaret.

Margy A pet form of Margaret.

Mari A variant spelling of Mary.

Maria A variant spelling of Mary.

Mariah A variant spelling of Maria.

Mariamne An early form of Mary.

Marian, Mariane, Marianne Variant hybrid forms of Mary and Ann.

Maribel A variant form of Mary, meaning "beautiful Mary."

Marie The French and Old German form of Mary.

Mariel A Dutch form of Mary.

Mariele A variant form of Mary.

Marien, Marienne Variant forms of Marion.

Marietta An Italian pet form of Mary.

Mariette A French pet form of Mary.

Marilyn, Marilynn Variant forms of Mary, meaning "Mary's line, descendants of Mary."

Marina, Marinna From the Latin, meaning "sea." HEBREW EQUIVALENT: Miryam.

Marion A pet form of the French name Marie. Also, a variant form of Mary.

Maris, Marisa, Marise From the Latin, meaning "sea." HEBREW EQUIVALENT: Miryam.

Marissa A variant spelling of Marisa.

Marita A pet form of Martha.

Marjorie, Marjory Variant spellings of Margery, popular in Scotland.

Malca A variant spelling of Malka.

Marlee A pet form of Marleen.

Marleen A Slavic form of Magdalene.

Marlena A variant form of Marleen.

Marlene A variant form of Marleen.

Marli, Marlie A pet form of Marleen.

Marlo A variant form of Marleen.

Marlyn, Marlynn Contracted forms of Marilyn.

Marna, Marne A variant form of Marina.

Marni A pet form of Marina.

Marnina From the Hebrew, meaning "rejoice." HEBREW EQUIVALENT: Marnina.

Marona From the Hebrew, meaning "flock of sheep." HEBREW EQUIVALENT: Marona.

Marra A variant spelling of Mara.

Marsha, Marshe Variant spellings of Marcia.

Marta A variant form of Martha.

Martelle A French feminine form of Martin. HEBREW EQUIVALENT: Amtza.

Martha From the Aramaic, meaning "sorrowful" or "mistress." HEBREW EQUIVALENT: Marata.

Marthe A French form of Martha.

Marti A pet form of Martina.

Martina, Martine Feminine forms of Martin. HEBREW EQUIVALENT: Amtza.

Marva From the Hebrew, referring to the sage plant of the mint family. HEBREW EQUIVALENT: Marva.

Marvel, Marvella From the Middle English and the Latin, meaning "to wonder, admire." HEBREW EQUIVALENT: Maksima.

Mary The Greek form of Miriam, from the Hebrew, meaning "sea of bitterness." HEBREW EQUIVALENT: Miryam.

Marya A Russian and Polish form of Mary.

Maryanne A hybrid of Mary and Anne.

Maryashe A Yiddish form of Miriam.

Marylin, Maryline Variant spellings of Marilyn.

Masada, Massada From the Hebrew, meaning "foundation, support." HEBREW EQUIVALENT: Masada.

Matana From the Hebrew, meaning "gift." HEBREW EQUIVALENT: Matana.

Matat From the Hebrew, meaning "gift." HEBREW EQUIVALENT: Matat. Also, a short form of Matityahu.

Mathilda, Mathilde From the Old High German and Anglo-Saxon, meaning "powerful in battle" or "battlemaid." HEBREW EQUIVALENT: Alma.

Matilda A variant spelling of Mathilda.

Matti, Mattie Pet forms of Mathilda.

Matty, Mattye Pet forms of Mathilda.

Matya A Yiddish pet form of Mathilda.

Maud, Maude French pet forms of Mathilda.

Maura A form of Mary commonly used in Ireland. Also, from the Celtic, meaning "dark." HEBREW EQUIVALENT: Tzila.

Maureen, Maurine Variant forms of Maura.

Mavis A bird-name that evolved in France from an Old English word meaning "song thrush." HEBREW EQUIVALENT: Efrona.

Maxa A feminine form of Max.

Maxene A variant spelling of Maxine.

Maxima A variant spelling of Maksima.

Maxime A feminine form of Maximilian. HEBREW EQUIVALENT: Migdala.

Maxine A variant form of Maxine.

May A pet form of Mary and Margaret. Also, a month of the year connoting spring, youth, growth. HEBREW EQUIVALENT: Aviva.

Maya A variant spelling of Maia.

Mazal From the Hebrew, meaning "star." HEBREW EQUIVALENT: Mazal.

Mazala A variant form of Mazal. HEBREW EQUIVALENT: Mazala.

Mazalit A variant form of Mazal. HEBREW EQUIVALENT: Mazalit.

Mazhira From the Hebrew, meaning "shining." HEBREW EQUIVALENT: Mazhira.

Meg A pet form of Margaret.

Megan A Welsh form of Margaret.

Mehira From the Hebrew, meaning "swift, energetic." HEBREW EQUIVALENT: Mehira.

Meira From the Hebrew, meaning "light." HEBREW EQUIVALENT: Me'ira.

Meirav From the Hebrew, meaning "the best" or "maximum." HEBREW EQUIVALENT: Meirav.

Meirit A variant form of Meiri. HEBREW EQUIVALENT: Me'irit.

Meirona From the Aramaic, meaning "sheep," or from the Hebrew, meaning "troops, soldiers." HEBREW EQUIVALENT: Meirona (Mayrona).

Meital From the Hebrew, meaning "dew drops." HEBREW EQUIVALENT: Meital (Maytal.)

Melanie From the Greek, meaning "black, dark." HEBREW EQUIVALENT: Adara.

Melba A variant feminine form of Melvin. HEBREW EQUIVALENT: Amalya.

Melina From the Greek, meaning "song." HEBREW EQUIVALENT: Mangina.

Melinda From the Greek and Old English, meaning "gentle." HEBREW EQUIVALENT: Na'ama.

Melissa, Melisse From the Greek, meaning "bee, honey." HEBREW EQUIVALENT: Metuka.

Melody From the Greek, meaning "melody, song." HEBREW EQUIVALENT: Mangena.

Melva A feminine form of Melvin. HEBREW EQUIVALENT: Amalya.

Melveen, Melvene Variant forms of Melva.

Melvina A variant form of Melva.

Menora, Menorah From the Hebrew, meaning "candelabrum." HEBREW EQUIVALENT: Menora.

Mercedes From the Latin, meaning "mercy, pity." HEBREW EQUIVALENT: Nechama.

Meredith From the Old Celtic, meaning "protector of the sea." HEBREW EQUIVALENT: Migdala.

Meri From the Hebrew, meaning "rebelliousness, bitterness." HEBREW EQUIVALENT: Meri.

Merideth A variant spelling of Meredith.

Merie A variant spelling of Meri.

Merla A variant form of Merle.

Merle From the Latin and the French, meaning "bird," specifically a blackbird. HEBREW EQUIVALENT: Gozala.

Merlin From the Old High German, meaning "falcon." HEBREW EQUIVALENT: Gozala.

Meroma From the Hebrew, meaning "elevated, high, noble." HEBREW EQUIVALENT: Meroma.

Merona A variant spelling of Meirona.

Merrie From the Anglo-Saxon, meaning "joyous, pleasant." HEBREW EQUIVALENT: Marnina.

Merrielle A pet form of Merrie.

Merril, Merrill Variant forms of Merle and Muriel.

Merry A variant spelling of Merrie.

Merryl A variant spelling of Meryl.

Merta A variant form of Marta (Martha).

Meryl, Meryle Variant spellings of Merril.

Metuka From the Hebrew, meaning "sweet." HEBREW EQUIVALENT: Metuka.

Mia A short form of Michaela. HEBREW EQUIVALENT: Miya.

Mica A short form of Michal.

Micha A short form of Michal.

Michaela The feminine form of Michael. HEBREW EQUIVALENT: Michaela.

Michaelita A diminutive feminine form of Michaela.

Michaelann A hybrid of Michaela and Ann.

Michaele A variant form of Michaela.

Michal A contracted form of Michael, meaning "Who is like God?" HEBREW EQUIVALENT: Michal.

Michalina A pet form of Michal.

Michel, Michele, Michelle Variant French forms of Michal.

Micke, Mickey, Micki Pet forms of Michal.

Midge A variant form of Madge.

Migda From the Hebrew, meaning "choice thing, gift" or "excellent." HEBREW EQUIVALENT: Migda.

Migdala From the Hebrew, meaning "fortress, tower." HEBREW EQUIVALENT: Migdala.

Migdana From the Hebrew, meaning "gift." HEBREW EQUIVALENT: Migdana.

Mignon From the French, meaning "delicate, graceful, petite." HEBREW EQUIVALENT: Adina.

Mikaela A variant spelling of Michaela.

Mildred From the Anglo-Saxon, meaning "gentle of speech" or "gentle counselor." HEBREW EQUIVALENT: Milka.

Mili From the Hebrew, meaning "Who is for me?" or an Hebraized form of Millie. HEBREW EQUIVALENT: Mili.

Milka From the Hebrew, meaning "divine" or "queen." Akin to Malka. HEBREW EQUIVALENT: Milka.

Millicent From the Latin, meaning "sweet singer," or from the Old French and Old High German, meaning "work" or "strength." HEBREW EQUIVALENT: Amalya.

Millie, Milly Pet forms of Mildred and Millicent.

Mim A pet form of Miryam.

Mimi A pet form of Miryam.

Mina A variant spelling of Minna.

Minda A Yiddish form of Minna.

Mindel A Yiddish pet form of Minda.

Mindi A variant spelling of Mindy.

Mindy A pet form of Melinda and Mildred.

Minerva The Roman goddess of wisdom. HEBREW EQUIVALENT: Milka.

Minette A French pet form of Mary.

Minna A pet form of Wilhelmina.

Minnie, Minny Pet forms of Minna, Miriam, and Wilhelmina.

Minta From the Greek, meaning "mint," an aromatic leaf. HEBREW EQUIVALENT: Ketzia.

Mira A pet form of Miryam.

Miranda From the Latin, meaning "wonderful" or "adored one." HEBREW EQUIVALENT: Mechubada.

Mirel, Mirele Yiddish pet forms of Miryam.

Miri A short form of Mirit and Miryam.

Miriam The Anglicized spelling of Miryam.

Miril A Yiddish pet form of Miryam.

Mirit From the Hebrew, meaning "sweet wine." HEBREW EQUIVALENT: Mirit.

Mirra A variant spelling of Mira.

Miryam From the Hebrew, meaning "sea of bitterness, sorrow," or from the Chaldaic, meaning "mistress of the sea." HEBREW EQUIVALENT: Miryam.

Miryom A variant spelling of Miryam.

Missie, Missy A modern American name, meaning "young girl." HEBREW EQUIVALENT: Batya.

Mitzi A pet form of Mary.

Mitzpa, Mitzpah From the Hebrew, meaning "tower." HEBREW EQUIVALENT: Mitzpa.

Mizpa, Mizpah Variant spellings of Mitzpa.

Mollie, Molly, Mollye Pet forms of Mary, Millicent, and Miriam.

Mona From the Irish, meaning "noble, pure." HEBREW EQUIVALENT: Malka.

Monica A variant form of Mona.

Monique A French form of Mona.

Mor From the Hebrew, referring to a plant used in making perfumes and medicines.

Moraga The feminine form of Moreg. HEBREW EQUIVALENT: Moraga.

Moran From the Hebrew, meaning "teacher." Also, a shrub or tree in the honeysuckle family. HEBREW EQUIVALENT: Moran.

Morasha From the Hebrew, meaning "legacy." HEBREW EQUIVALENT: Morasha.

Morena A variant form of Maura.

Morgan From the Welsh, meaning "sea dweller." HEBREW EQUIVALENT: Miryam.

Moria, Moriah Variant spellings of Moriya.

Moriel From the Hebrew, meaning "God is my teacher." HEBREW EQUIVALENT: Moriel.

Morine A variant form of Maureen.

Morit From the Hebrew, meaning "teacher." HEBREW EQUIVALENT: Morit.

Moriya From the Hebrew, meaning "teacher," also the "sage" plant known as salvia. HEBREW EQUIVALENT: Moriya.

Morna From the Middle English and German, meaning "morning," or from the Celtic, meaning "gentle, beloved." HEBREW EQUIVALENT: Bat-Shachar.

Morrisa, Morrissa The feminine form of Morris, meaning "moorish, dark-skinned." HEBREW EQUIVALENT: Tzila.

Muriel From the Irish, meaning "bright sea," or from the Middle English, meaning "merry." HEBREW EQUIVALENT: Marnina.

Myra From the Greek and Arabic, meaning "myrrh," connoting bitterness. Also, from the Celtic, meaning "gentle, beloved." HEBREW EQUIVALENT: Talmor.

Myrel A variant spelling of Mirel.

Myriam A variant spelling of Miryam.

Myrna A variant form of Myra.

Myrtle From the Persian, meaning "myrtle tree," a symbol of victory. HEBREW EQUIVALENT: Hadas.

Naama, Naamah From the Hebrew, meaning "pleasant, beautiful." HEBREW EQUIVALENT: Na'ama.

Naamana From the Hebrew, meaning "pleasant." HEBREW EQUIVALENT: Na'amana.

Naami A variant form of Naomi. HEBREW EQUIVALENT: Na'ami.

Naamia, Naamiah Variant spellings of Naamiya.

Naamit From the Hebrew, meaning "an ostrich-like bird." HEBREW EQUIVALENT: Na'amit.

Naamiya From the Hebrew, meaning "pleasant, sweet." HEBREW EQUIVALENT: Na'amiya.

Nada From the Slavic, meaning "hope." HEBREW EQUIVALENT: Emuna.

Nadia A variant form of Nada.

Nadine A French form of Nada.

Nadya A Hebrew form of Nada. HEBREW EQUIVALENT: Nadya.

Nafshiya From the Hebrew, meaning "soul" or "friendship." HEBREW EQUIVALENT: Nafshiya.

Naftala From the Hebrew, meaning "to wrestle." HEBREW EQUIVALENT: Naftala.

Nagida From the Hebrew, meaning "noble, prosperous person." HEBREW EQUIVALENT: Nagida.

Nahara From the Hebrew and Aramaic, meaning "light." HEBREW EQUIVALENT: Nahara.

Nan, Nana Pet forms of Nancy.

Nanci A variant spelling of Nancy.

Nancy A pet form of Hannah.

Nanette A pet form of Anna and Hannah.

Nanine A variant pet form of Nanette.

Nanna A pet form of Hannah.

Naoma A variant form of Naomi.

Naomi From the Hebrew, meaning "beautiful, pleasant, delightful." HEBREW EQUIVALENT: Na'omi.

Natalie A Christian name referring to the birth of Jesus.

Natania, Nataniah Variant spellings of Natanya.

Nataniela, Nataniella, Natanielle From the Hebrew, meaning "gift of God." HEBREW EQUIVALENT: Nataniela.

Netanya The feminine form of Natan (Nathan). HEBREW EQUIVALENT: Natanya.

Nava, Navah From the Hebrew, meaning "beautiful, pleasant." HEBREW EQUIVALENT: Nava.

Navit A variant form of Nava. HEBREW EQUIVALENT: Navit.

Neala A feminine form of Neal. HEBREW EQUIVALENT: No'aza.

Nechama From the Hebrew, meaning "comfort." HEBREW EQUIVALENT: Nechama.

Nedara From the Hebrew, meaning "oath, promise." HEBREW EQUIVALENT: Nedara.

Nedavia, Nedaviah Variant spellings of Nedavya.

Nedavya From the Hebrew, meaning "generosity of the Lord." HEBREW EQUIVALENT: Nedavya.

Nediva From the Hebrew, meaning "noble, generous." HEBREW EQUIVALENT: Nadiv.

Ne'ema From the Hebrew, meaning "faithful." HEBREW EQUIVALENT: Ne'ema.

Neena A variant spelling of Nina.

Negida A variant form of Nagida. HEBREW EQUIVALENT: Negida.

Negina From the Hebrew, meaning "song, melody." HEBREW EQUIVALENT: Negina.

Nehama A variant spelling of Nechama.

Nehara A variant form of Nahara. HEBREW EQUIVALENT: Nehara.

Nehira A variant form of Nehora. HEBREW EQUIVALENT: Nehira.

Nehora From the Aramaic, meaning "light." HEBREW EQUIVALENT: Nehora.

Nehura A variant form of Nehora. HEBREW EQUIVALENT: Nehura.

Ne'ila From the Hebrew, meaning "closing [of the gates on Yom Kippur]." HEBREW EQUIVALENT: Ne'ila.

Ne'ima From the Hebrew, meaning "pleasant one." HEBREW EQUIVALENT: Ne'ima.

Nell, Nella Pet forms of Eleanor and Helen.

Nellie A pet form of Eleanor.

Nelly A pet form of Eleanor.

Nema A variant spelling of Nima.

Neora From the Aramaic and Hebrew, meaning "light" or "shine." HEBREW EQUIVALENT: Ne'ora.

Neria From the Hebrew, meaning "light of God." HEBREW EQUIVALENT: Neria.

Nerya From the Hebrew, meaning "light of the Lord." HEBREW EQUIVALENT: Nerya.

Neshama From the Hebrew, meaning "soul." HEBREW EQUIVALENT: Neshama.

Nessa From the Old Norse, meaning "promontory, headland." Also, a short form of Vanessa. HEBREW EQUIVALENT: Artzit.

Nessia A variant spelling of Nesya.

Nessie A Welsh pet form of Agnes.

Nesya From the Hebrew, meaning "miracle of God." HEBREW EQUIVALENT: Nesya.

Neta From the Hebrew, meaning "a bud, plant, or shrub." HEBREW EQUIVALENT: Neta.

Netana From the Hebrew, meaning "gift." HEBREW EQUIVALENT: Netana.

Netania, Netaniah Variant spellings of Netanya.

Netaniela, Netaniella From the Hebrew, meaning "the gift of God." Variant forms of Netanya. HEBREW EQUIVALENT: Netaniela.

Netanya From the Hebrew, meaning "gift of God." HEBREW EQUIVALENT: Netanya.

Netiva From the Hebrew, meaning "path." HEBREW EQUIVALENT: Netiva.

Netta A variant spelling of Neta.

Netti A variant spelling of Neti.

Nettie, Netty Pet forms of Antoinette and Annette.

Neva From the Spanish, meaning "snow," or from the Old English, meaning "new." HEBREW EQUIVALENT: Chadasha.

Nicci An Italian form of the Latin, meaning "victory." HEBREW EQUIVALENT: Nitzcha.

Nichelle A variant form of Nicci.

Nicola, Nicole Italian and French feminine forms of Nicholas. HEBREW EQUIVALENT: Dafna.

Nicolette A pet form of Nicola.

Nicolle A variant spelling of Nicole.

Nili Used most commonly as a masculine name. HEBREW EQUIVALENT: Nili.

Nilit A variant form of Nili. HEBREW EQUIVALENT: Nilit.

Nima From the Hebrew, meaning "picture, portrait, appearance." HEBREW EQUIVALENT: Nima.

Nina A French and Russian pet form of Nanine, which is a form of Anne.

Ninette A variant form of Nanette.

Nirel From the Hebrew, meaning "uncultivated field" or "light of God." HEBREW EQUIVALENT: Nirel.

Nirit An annual plant with yellow flowers, found in Israel. HEBREW EQUIVALENT: Nirit.

Nirtza From the Hebrew, meaning "desirable." HEBREW EQUIVALENT: Nirtza.

Nisa, Nissa From the Hebrew, meaning "to test." HEBREW EQUIVALENT: Nisa.

Nita From the Hebrew, meaning "to plant." HEBREW EQUIVALENT: Nit'a.

Nitza, Nitzah From the Hebrew, meaning "bud of a flower." HEBREW EQUIVALENT: Nitza.

Nitzana A variant form of Nitza. HEBREW EQUIVALENT: Nitzana.

Nitzanit A variant form of Nitza. *See* Nitza. HEBREW EQUIVALENT: Nitzanit.

Nitzra From the Hebrew, meaning "guard." HEBREW EQUIVALENT: Nitzra.

Niva From the Hebrew, meaning "speech." HEBREW EQUIVALENT: Niva.

Noa From the Hebrew meaning "peace," or "rest." HEBREW EQUIVALENT: No'a.

Noemi A variant form of Naomi.

Nofiya From the Hebrew, meaning "beautiful landscape." HEBREW EQUIVALENT: Nofiya.

Noga From the Hebrew, meaning "morning light, brightness." HEBREW EQUIVALENT: Noga.

Nola From the Celtic, meaning "famous." HEBREW EQUIVALENT: Hillela.

Nomi A variant spelling of Naomi.

Nophia A variant spelling of Nofia.

Nora, Norah From the Latin, meaning "honor, respect." HEBREW EQUIVALENT: Nediva.

Noreen A variant Irish form of Nora.

Norene A variant spelling of Noreen.

Nori A pet form of Noreen.

Norma From the Latin, meaning "exact to the pattern, normal, peaceful." HEBREW EQUIVALENT: Menucha.

Norrie A pet form of Nora.

Novela, Novella From the Latin, meaning "new, unusual." HEBREW EQUIVALENT: Rishona.

Noya From the Hebrew, meaning "beautiful, ornamented." HEBREW EQUIVALENT: No'ya.

Nufar, Nuphar From the Hebrew, meaning "a yellow water lily." HEBREW EQUIVALENT: Nufar.

Nura From the Aramaic, meaning "light, bright." HEBREW EQUIVALENT: Nura.

Nuriah A variant spelling of Nuriya.

Nurit From the Hebrew, meaning "a buttercup [plant]." HEBREW EQUIVALENT: Nurit.

Nurita A variant form of Nurit. HEBREW EQUIVALENT: Nurita.

Nuriya From the Hebrew, meaning "light of the Lord." HEBREW EQUIVALENT: Nuriya.

BEST BABY NAMES   **O**   BEST BABY NAMES

Oda, Odah From the Greek, meaning "song, ode." HEBREW EQUIVALENT: Zimra.

Odeda From the Hebrew, meaning "strong, courageous." HEBREW EQUIVALENT: Odeda.

Odedia A variant form of Odela.

Odeh From the Hebrew, meaning "I will praise." HEBREW
EQUIVALENT: Odeh.

Odele From the Greek, meaning "ode, melody." HEBREW
EQUIVALENT: Negina.

Odeleya From the Hebrew, meaning "I will praise God."
HEBREW EQUIVALENT: Odeh'le'ya.

Odelia A variant spelling of Odeleya.

Odell A variant spelling of Odele.

Odera From the Hebrew, meaning "plough." HEBREW
EQUIVALENT: Odera.

Odetta A pet form of Odele.

Odette A variant form of Odetta.

Odiya From the Hebrew, meaning "song of praise to God."
HEBREW EQUIVALENT: Odiya.

Ofira From the Hebrew, meaning "gold." HEBREW EQUIVA-
LENT: Ofira.

Ofna From the Aramaic, meaning "appearance." HEBREW
EQUIVALENT: Ofna.

Ofnat From the Hebrew, meaning "wheel." HEBREW EQUIVA-
LENT: Ofnat.

Ofniya A variant form of Ofna. HEBREW EQUIVALENT: Ofniya.

Ofra From the Hebrew, meaning "young mountain goat" or
"young deer." HEBREW EQUIVALENT: Ofra.

Ofrat A variant form of Ofra. HEBREW EQUIVALENT: Ofrat.

Ofrit A variant form of Ofra. HEBREW EQUIVALENT: Ofrit.

Ola, Olah From the Hebrew, meaning "immigrant." Also,
from the Old Norse, meaning "ancestor." HEBREW EQUIVA-
LENT: Ola.

Olga From the Russian and Old Norse, meaning "holy" or
"peace." HEBREW EQUIVALENT: Chagit.

Olive From the Latin, meaning "olive," symbol of peace.
HEBREW EQUIVALENT: Za'yit.

Oliva A variant form of Olive.

Olympia From the Greek Olympus, the mountain on which
the gods resided. HEBREW EQUIVALENT: Bat-El.

Oona A variant form of the Latin name Una, meaning "the
one." HEBREW EQUIVALENT: Rishona.

Ophelia From the Greek, meaning "serpent" or "to help."
HEBREW EQUIVALENT: Eli'ezra.

Ophira A variant spelling of Ofira.

Ophnat A variant spelling of Ofnat.

Ophra A variant spelling of Ofra.

Ophrat A variant spelling of Ofrat.

Opra, Oprah Variant forms of Ofra.

Ora, Orah From the Hebrew, meaning "light." Also, from
the Latin, meaning "gold." HEBREW EQUIVALENT: Ora.

Oralee, Orali From the Hebrew, meaning "my light."
HEBREW EQUIVALENT: Orali.

Oriel From the Old French and the Latin, meaning "gold."
HEBREW EQUIVALENT: Ofira.

Orit A variant form of Ora. HEBREW EQUIVALENT: Orit.

Orlanda A variant form of the masculine Orlando. HEBREW
EQUIVALENT: Yehudit.

Or-Li, Orli From the Hebrew, meaning "light is mine."
HEBREW EQUIVALENT: Orli.

Orlit A variant form of Or-Li. HEBREW EQUIVALENT: Orlit.

Orly A variant spelling of Orli.

Orna From the Hebrew, meaning "Let there be light" or
"pine tree." HEBREW EQUIVALENT: Orna.

Orni From the Hebrew, meaning "pine tree." HEBREW
EQUIVALENT: Orni.

Ornina A variant form of Orni. HEBREW EQUIVALENT: Ornina.

Ornit A variant form of Orni. HEBREW EQUIVALENT: Ornit.

Osnat A variant spelling of Asenath.

BEST BABY NAMES   BEST BABY NAMES

Paloma A Spanish name from the Latin, meaning "dove."
HEBREW EQUIVALENT: Yona.

Pam A diminutive form of Pamela.

Pamela From the Greek and the Anglo-Saxon, meaning "loved one, sweet one." HEBREW EQUIVALENT: Mirit.

Pansy An English flower-name. Also, from the French, meaning "to think." HEBREW EQUIVALENT: Pericha.

Pat A pet form of Patricia.

Patience From the Latin, meaning "to suffer, endure." HEBREW EQUIVALENT: Nitzcha.

Patrice A variant form of Patricia.

Patricia The feminine form of Patrick. HEBREW EQUIVALENT: Yisr'ela.

Patsy A pet form of Patricia.

Patti, Pattie, Patty Pet forms of Patricia.

Paula From the Greek, meaning "small." HEBREW EQUIVALENT: Ketana.

Prudence From the Latin, meaning "prudent, wise." HEBREW EQUIVALENT: Buna.

Paulette A French pet form of Paula.

Paulina The Spanish form of Pauline. HEBREW EQUIVALENT: Ketana.

Pauline The French form of Paula.

Paz From the Hebrew, meaning "gold." HEBREW EQUIVALENT: Paz.

Paza A variant form of Paz. HEBREW EQUIVALENT: Paza.

Pazit A variant form of Paz. HEBREW EQUIVALENT: Pazit.

Paziya A variant form of Pazya. HEBREW EQUIVALENT: Paziya.

Pazya From the Hebrew, meaning "God's gold." HEBREW EQUIVALENT: Pazya.

Pearl From the Latin and Middle English, meaning "pearl." HEBREW EQUIVALENT: Penina.

Peg, Peggie, Peggy Pet forms of Margaret and Pearl.

Peggity A variant form of Peggy.

Pelia, Peliah From the Hebrew, meaning "wonder, miracle." HEBREW EQUIVALENT: Pelia.

Penelope From the Greek, meaning "worker in cloth" or "silent worker." HEBREW EQUIVALENT: Amalya.

Penina From the Hebrew, meaning "coral" or "pearl." HEBREW EQUIVALENT: Penina.

Penini A variant form of Penina. HEBREW EQUIVALENT: Penini.

Peninia A variant spelling of Peniniya.

Peninit From the Hebrew, meaning "pearly." HEBREW EQUIVALENT: Peninit.

Peniniya From the Hebrew, meaning "hen, fowl." HEBREW EQUIVALENT: Peniniya.

Penney, Pennie, Penny Pet forms of Penelope.

Peninah A variant spelling of Penina.

Pepita A Spanish pet form of Josephine.

Peri From the Hebrew, meaning "fruit." HEBREW EQUIVALENT: Peri (P'ri).

Perl A Yiddish form of Pearl.

Peshe, Peshy A Yiddish form of Bashe.

Pessel A Yiddish form of Bashe.

Petra A feminine form of Peter, from the Greek, meaning "rock." HEBREW EQUIVALENT: Ritzpa.

Phebe A variant spelling of Pheobe.

Philippa From the Greek, meaning "lover of horses." The feminine form of Philip. HEBREW EQUIVALENT: Ahuva.

Phoebe From the Greek, meaning "bright, shining one." HEBREW EQUIVALENT: Behira.

Phylicia A variant spelling of Felicia.

Phylis, Phyllis From the Greek, meaning "little leaf, green bough." HEBREW EQUIVALENT: Nitza.

Pia From the Latin, meaning "pious." HEBREW EQUIVALENT: Chasida.

Pier A feminine form of Pierre, the French form of Peter. HEBREW EQUIVALENT: Tzuriya.

Pita From the Hebrew, meaning "bread." HEBREW EQUIVALENT: Pita.

Piuta A variant form of Piyuta.

Piyuta A Hebrew form of the Greek, meaning "poet, poetry." HEBREW EQUIVALENT: Piyuta.

Poda From the Hebrew, meaning "redeemed." HEBREW EQUIVALENT: Poda.

Pola The Italian form of Pula (a seaport in Yugoslavia), meaning "rain." HEBREW EQUIVALENT: Malkosha.

Polly A variant form of Molly.

Pora From the Hebrew, meaning "fruitful." HEBREW EQUIVALENT: Pora.

Porat A variant form of Pora. HEBREW EQUIVALENT: Porat.

Poria, Poriah Variant spellings of Poriya.

Poriya A variant form of Pora. HEBREW EQUIVALENT: Poriya.

Portia From the Latin, meaning "hog." There are no Hebrew equivalents.

Priscilla From the Latin, meaning "ancient, old." HEBREW EQUIVALENT: Keshisha.

Prudence From the Latin, meaning "prudent, wise." HEBREW EQUIVALENT: Tushiya.

Prue A pet form of Prudence.

Pua, Puah From the Hebrew, meaning "to groan, cry out." HEBREW EQUIVALENT: Pua.

BEST BABY NAMES **Q–R** BEST BABY NAMES

Queena, Queene Variant forms of Queenie.

Queenie A nickname for Regina, from the Latin, meaning "queen." HEBREW EQUIVALENT: Malka.

Raanana From the Hebrew, meaning "fresh, luscious, beautiful." HEBREW EQUIVALENT: Ra'anana.

Rachel, Rachaele Variant spellings of Rachel.

Rachel From the Hebrew, meaning "ewe," a symbol of purity and gentility. HEBREW EQUIVALENT: Rachel.

Rachela A variant form of Rachel. HEBREW EQUIVALENT: Rachel.

Rachelle A variant spelling of Rachel.

Rae A pet form of Rachel.

Rafaela, Rafaele Varaint spellings of Refaela.

Rafia A variant spelling of Rafya.

Rafya From the Hebrew, meaning "the healing of the Lord."
HEBREW EQUIVALENT: Rafya.

Rahel A variant spelling of Rachel.

Raina, Raine From the Latin, meaning "to rule." Akin to
Regina. Also, from the Yiddish, meaning "clean, pure."
HEBREW EQUIVALENT: Beruriya.

Raisa From the Yiddish, meaning "rose." HEBREW EQUIVA-
LENT: Shoshana.

Raise A variant form of Rasia.

Raisel A pet form of Raise.

Raissa, Raisse Variant spellings of Raisa.

Raize A variant form of Raise.

Raizel A pet form of Raize.

Raizi A pet form of Raizel.

Rakefet The name of a plant in the primrose family. HEBREW
EQUIVALENT: Rakefet.

Rama From the Hebrew, meaning "lofty, exalted." HEBREW
EQUIVALENT: Rama.

Rami A variant form of Rama. HEBREW EQUIVALENT: Rami.

Ramit A variant form of Rama. HEBREW EQUIVALENT: Ramit.

Ramona A short form of Raymonda, meaning "peace" or
"protection." HEBREW EQUIVALENT: Efrat.

Ramot A variant form of Rama. HEBREW EQUIVALENT:
Ramot.

Rana A variant spelling of Raina.

Ranana A variant spelling of Raanana.

Randi, Randy Feminine pet forms of Randolph. HEBREW
EQUIVALENT: Nevona.

Rani From the Hebrew, meaning "my song." HEBREW
EQUIVALENT: Rani.

Ranit From the Hebrew, meaning "joy" or "song." HEBREW
EQUIVALENT: Ranit.

Ranita A variant form of Ranit. HEBREW EQUIVALENT: Ranita.

Ranny A pet form of Frances.

Ranya From the Hebrew, meaning "song of the Lord." HEBREW EQUIVALENT: Ranya.

Raoul A variant form of Randolph and Jack. HEBREW EQUIVALENT: Buna.

Raphaela A variant spelling of Refaela.

Raquel A variant Spanish form of Rachel.

Raviva A variant form of Reviva. HEBREW EQUIVALENT: Raviva.

Ravital From the Hebrew, meaning "abundance of dew." HEBREW EQUIVALENT: Ravital.

Ray, Raye Pet forms of Rachel. Also, from the Celtic, meaning "grace, gracious." HEBREW EQUIVALENT: Chana.

Raya From the Hebrew, meaning "my friend." HEBREW EQUIVALENT: Raya.

Rayna A Yiddish form of Catherine meaning "pure, clean." HEBREW EQUIVALENT: Berura.

Rayne A variant form of Rayna.

Rayzel A pet form of Raize.

Raz From the Aramaic, meaning "secret." HEBREW EQUIVALENT: Raz.

Razi From the Hebrew, meaning "my secret." HEBREW EQUIVALENT: Razi.

Razia, Raziah Variant spellings of Raziya.

Raziela, Raziella From the Hebrew, meaning "God is my secret." HEBREW EQUIVALENT: Razi'ela.

Razil A variant spelling of Raisel.

Razilee A variant spelling of Razili.

Razili From the Aramaic and Hebrew, meaning "my secret." HEBREW EQUIVALENT: Razili.

Razina An Hebraized form of Rosina. HEBREW EQUIVALENT: Razina.

Raziya From the Hebrew, meaning "secret of the Lord." HEBREW EQUIVALENT: Raziya.

Reba A pet form of Rebecca. HEBREW EQUIVALENT: Riba.

Rebecca From the Hebrew, meaning "to tie, bind." HEBREW EQUIVALENT: Rivka.

Reda A variant form of Rita.

Reena A variant spelling of Rina.

Reesa A pet form of Theresa.

Reeta A variant spelling of Rita.

Refaela From the Hebrew, meaning "God has healed."
HEBREW EQUIVALENT: Refa'ela.

Regan A variant form of Regina.

Regina From the Latin, meaning "to rule," or from the
Anglo-Saxon, meaning "pure." HEBREW EQUIVALENT:
Berura.

Reina, Reine Variant spellings of Rayna.

Reita A variant spelling of Rita.

Reitha A variant spelling of Reatha.

Reizel A variant spelling of Raisel.

Reizl A variant spelling of Raisel.

Remiza Fom the Hebrew, meaning "sign, hint." HEBREW
EQUIVALENT: Remiza.

Rena, Renah Short forms of Regina or Serena. Also, variant
spellings of Rina.

Renana From the Hebrew, meaning "joy" or "song," HEBREW
EQUIVALENT: Renana.

Renanit A variant form of Renana. *See* Renana. The exact
Hebrew equivalent is Renanit.

Renat, Renata From the Latin, meaning "to be born again."
HEBREW EQUIVALENT: Cha'ya.

Rene, Renee French forms of Renata.

Renette A French pet form of Rene.

Renina A variant form of Renana. HEBREW EQUIVALENT:
Renina.

Renita A Spanish pet form of Rene.

Rephaela A variant spelling of Refaela.

Resa A pet form of Theresa.

Reubena A variant spelling of Reuvena.

Reuvat A feminine form of Reuven, meaning "Behold, a
son!" HEBREW EQUIVALENT: Re'uvat.

Reuvena A feminine form of Reuven (Reuben), meaning

"Behold, a son!" HEBREW EQUIVALENT: Re'uvena.

Reva A pet form of Rebecca. HEBREW EQUIVALENT: Riva.

Reviva From the Hebrew, meaning "dew" or "rain." HEBREW EQUIVALENT: Reviva.

Rexana The feminine form of Rex, meaning "king." HEBREW EQUIVALENT: Atara.

Reyna A variant spelling of Rayna.

Rhea From the Greek, meaning "protector of cities." HEBREW EQUIVALENT: Shimrit.

Rheta A variant spelling of Rita. Also, from the Greek, meaning "one who speaks well." HEBREW EQUIVALENT: Amira.

Rhoda From the Greek, meaning "rose." HEBREW EQUIVALENT: Vered.

Rhode A variant form of Rhoda.

Rhona A hybrid of Rose and Anna.

Rhonda From the Celtic, meaning "powerful river." HEBREW EQUIVALENT: Arnona.

Rica A pet form of Ricarda.

Ricarda A feminine Italian form of Ricardo (Richard). HEBREW EQUIVALENT: Ashira.

Richarda A variant form of Ricarda.

Ricka, Ricki Pet forms of Patricia, Rebecca, Ricarda, and Roberta.

Rickma From the Hebrew, meaning "woven product." HEBREW EQUIVALENT: Rikma.

Ricky A variant spelling of Ricki.

Rifka A Yiddish form of Rivka.

Rifke A Yiddish form of Rivka.

Riki, Rikki Pet forms of Erica.

Rikma A variant spelling of Rickma.

Rimon From the Hebrew, meaning "pomegranate." HEBREW EQUIVALENT: Rimon.

Rimona The feminine form of Rimon. HEBREW EQUIVALENT: Rimona.

Rina From the Hebrew, meaning "joy." HEBREW EQUIVALENT: Rina.

Risa A pet form of Theresa.

Rishona From the Hebrew, meaning "first." HEBREW EQUIVA-
LENT: Rishona.

Rita From the Sanskrit, meaning "brave" or "honest."
HEBREW EQUIVALENT: Abira.

Riva From the Old French, meaning "coastline, shore."
Also, a pet form of Rivka.

Rivi A pet form of Rivka. HEBREW EQUIVALENT: Rivi.

Rivka, Rivkah From the Hebrew, meaning "to bind."
Rebecca is the Anglicized form. HEBREW EQUIVALENT:
Rivka.

Rivke, Rivkie A Yiddish form of Rivka.

Roanna, Roanna A hybrid of Rose and Ann.

Robbi, Robbie Pet forms of Roberta.

Roberta The feminine form of Robert, meaning "bright,
wise counsel." HEBREW EQUIVALENT: Meira.

Robertina A pet form of Roberta.

Robin, Robyn Pet forms of Roberta. *See* Roberta.

Rochel A Yiddish form of Rachel.

Rochelle From the Old French, meaning "small rock."
HEBREW EQUIVALENT: Ritzpa.

Rofi From the Hebrew, meaning "healing, healer." HEBREW
EQUIVALENT: Rofi.

Rolanda A feminine form of Roland. HEBREW EQUIVALENT:
Yehudit.

Roma From the Hebrew, meaning "heights, lofty, exalted."
HEBREW EQUIVALENT: Roma.

Romema From the Hebrew, meaning "heights, lofty, exalted." HEBREW EQUIVALENT: Romeima.

Romia A variant spelling of Romiya.

Romit A variant form of Roma. HEBREW EQUIVALENT: Romit.

Romiya A variant spelling of Romema. HEBREW EQUIVALENT:
Romiya.

Ron From the Hebrew, meaning "song" or "joy." HEBREW
EQUIVALENT: Ron.

Rona From the Gaelic, meaning "seal," or from the Hebrew,
meanig "joy." HEBREW EQUIVALENT: Rona.

Ronalda A feminine form of Ronald. HEBREW EQUIVALENT: Atara.

Ronela, Ronella Variant forms of Ron. HEBREW EQUIVALENT: Ronela.

Roni A variant form of Ron. HEBREW EQUIVALENT: Roni.

Ronia A variant spelling of Roniya.

Ronili From the Hebrew, meaning "Joy is mine." HEBREW EQUIVALENT: Ronili.

Roniya A variant form of Ron, meaning "joy of the Lord." HEBREW EQUIVALENT: Roniya.

Ronli A variant form of Ron, meaning "Joy is mine." HEBREW EQUIVALENT: Ronli.

Ronne, Ronni, Ronnie Feminine pet forms of Ronald, meaning "wise, powerful ruler." HEBREW EQUIVALENT: Gevira.

Ronnit A variant spelling of Ronit.

Ronny A variant spelling of Ronnie.

Ronya From the Hebrew, meaning "song of God." HEBREW EQUIVALENT: Ronya.

Rori, Rory Irish feminine forms of Roderick and Robert, meaning "bright, wise counsel." HEBREW EQUIVALENT: Bina.

Rosabel From the Latin and French, meaning "beautiful rose." HEBREW EQUIVALENT: Vered.

Rosalie A variant French pet form of Rose.

Rosalind A pet form of Rose.

Rosalinda A Spanish form of Rosalind.

Rosaline A variant form of Rosalind.

Rosalyn A variant form of Rosalind.

Rosanne A hybrid form of Rose and Anne.

Rose The English form of the Latin Rosa, meaning "rose." HEBREW EQUIVALENT: Vered.

Roselotte A combination of Rose and Lotte.

Roselyn A variant form of Rosalind.

Rosemary A hybrid form of Rose and Mary.

Rosetta An Italian pet form of Rose.

Rosette A French pet form of Rose.

Rosi, Rosie Pet forms of Rose.

Rosina, Rosine Pet forms of Rose.

Rosita A pet form of Rose.

Roslyn A variant spelling of Rosalyn.

Rotem From the Hebrew, meaning "to bind." Also, from the Aramaic meaning "a plant in the pea family." HEBREW EQUIVALENT: Rotem.

Rowena From the Old English, meaning "rugged land," and from the Celtic, meaning "flowery white hair." HEBREW EQUIVALENT: Artzit.

Roxane, Roxanna, Roxanne From the Persian, meaning "dawn, brilliant light." HEBREW EQUIVALENT: Tzafra.

Roxie A variant spelling of Roxy.

Roxine A variant form of Roxanne.

Roxy A pet form of Roxanne.

Roz A pet form of Rosalyn.

Rozelin A variant spelling of Rosaline.

Rozella A hybrid form of Rose and Ella.

Rozina A variant spelling of Rosina.

Ruby From the Latin and French, meaning "a precious reddish stone." HEBREW EQUIVALENT: Bareket.

Ruchama, Ruhama From the Hebrew, meaning "compassionate." HEBREW EQUIVALENT: Ruchama.

Rudelle From the Old High German, meaning "famous one." HEBREW EQUIVALENT: Yehudit.

Rue From the Old High German, meaning "fame." A variant form of Rudelle.

Rula From the Middle English and the Latin, meaning "ruler." HEBREW EQUIVALENT: Sara.

Rut The Hebraized form of Ruth.

Ruth From the Syriac and Hebrew, meaning "friendship." HEBREW EQUIVALENT: Rut.

Ruthanna A hybrid of Ruth and Anna.

Ruti A pet form of Rut. HEBREW EQUIVALENT: Ruti.

Saada From the Hebrew, meaning "support, help." HEBREW EQUIVALENT: Sa'ada.

Sabaria A variant spelling of Tzabaria.

Saba From the Hebrew and Aramaic, meaning "old, aged." HEBREW EQUIVALENT: Saba.

Sabra From the Hebrew, meaning "thorny cactus." HEBREW EQUIVALENT: Tzabara.

Sabrina A pet form of Sabra.

Sacha A pet form of Alexandra, popular in Russia.

Sadi A modern spelling of Sadie.

Sadie A pet form of Sarah.

Sadira From the Arabic and Hebrew, meaning "organized, regulated." HEBREW EQUIVALENT: Sadira.

Sady, Sadye Variant spellings of Sadie.

Sahara From the Hebrew, meaning "moon." HEBREW EQUIVALENT: Sahara.

Salida From the Old German, meaning "happiness, joy." HEBREW EQUIVALENT: Sasona.

Salit From the Hebrew, meaning "rock, rocky." HEBREW EQUIVALENT: Salit.

Sallie, Sally Variant forms of Sarah.

Salome From the Hebrew, meaning "peaceful." HEBREW EQUIVALENT: Shelomit (Shlomit).

Samantha From the Aramaic, meaning "listener." Akin to Samuela.

Samara From the Latin, meaning "seed of the elm," and from the Hebrew, meaning "guardian." HEBREW EQUIVALENT: Shomrona.

Sammy, Sammye A pet form of Samuela and Samantha.

Samuela The feminine form of Samuel. HEBREW EQUIVALENT: Shemuela.

Sandee, Sandi, Sandie Pet forms of Sandra.

Sandra A pet form of Alexandra.

Sandy A pet form of Sandra.

Sapir From the Hebrew, meaning "sapphire." HEBREW
EQUIVALENT: Sapir.

Sapira A variant form of Sapir. HEBREW EQUIVALENT: Sapira.

Sapirit A variant form of Sapir. HEBREW EQUIVALENT: Sapira.

Sara, Sarah From the Hebrew, meaning "noble" or "princess." HEBREW EQUIVALENT: Sara.

Sarai The original biblical form of Sara.

Sarali A pet form of Sara. HEBREW EQUIVALENT: Sarali.

Saran, Sarann, Saranne Hybrid forms of Sarah and Ann.

Sareli A variant spelling of Sarali.

Sarene A variant form of Sara.

Sarida From the Hebrew, meaning "refugee, leftover."
HEBREW EQUIVALENT: Sarida.

Saretta, Sarette Pet forms of Sara.

Sari A variant spelling of Sarai.

Sarina, Sarine Variant forms of Sara.

Sarit A variant form of Sara. HEBREW EQUIVALENT: Sarit.

Sarita A variant form of Sara. HEBREW EQUIVALENT: Sarita.

Saryl A variant Yiddish form of Sara.

Saundra A variant spelling of Sandra.

Savrina A variant form of Sabra. HEBREW EQUIVALENT: Savrina.

Savta From the Aramaic, meaning "grandmother." HEBREW
EQUIVALENT: Savta.

Scarlet, Scarlett From the Middle English, meaning "red,
ruby-colored." HEBREW EQUIVALENT: Almoga.

Schifra A variant spelling of Shifra.

Seema From the Greek, meaning "sprout." HEBREW EQUIVA-
LENT: Nitza.

Segula From the Hebrew, meaning "treasure" or "precious."
HEBREW EQUIVALENT: Segula.

Sela From the Greek and Hebrew, meaning "rock." HEBREW
EQUIVALENT: Sela.

Selda, Selde From the Anglo-Saxon, meaning "precious,
rare." HEBREW EQUIVALENT: Segula.

Selena, Selene From the Greek, meaning "moon." HEBREW EQUIVALENT: Sahara.

Selila From the Hebrew, meaning "path." HEBREW EQUIVALENT: Selila.

Selima, Selimah Arabic feminine forms of Solomon, meaning "peace." HEBREW EQUIVALENT: Shlomit.

Selina A variant spelling of Selena.

Selma From the Celtic, meaning "fair." HEBREW EQUIVALENT: Na'ama.

Sema A variant spelling of Seema.

Serena From the Latin, meaning "peaceful" or "cheerful." HEBREW EQUIVALENT: Shalviya.

Serita A variant spelling of Sarita.

Severina From the Latin, meaning "friendly, friendship." HEBREW EQUIVALENT: Yedida.

Shafrira From the Hebrew, meaning a "protective canopy." HEBREW EQUIVALENT: Shafrira.

Shaindi A variant form of Shaina.

Shalhevet From the Hebrew, meaning "fiery flame." HEBREW EQUIVALENT: Shalhevet.

Shaina From the Yiddish, meaning "beautiful." HEBREW EQUIVALENT: Yaffa.

Shaindel A pet form of Shaina.

Shalva, Shalvah From the Hebrew, meaning "peace, tranquility." HEBREW EQUIVALENT: Shalva.

Shamira From the Hebrew, meaning "guard, protector." HEBREW EQUIVALENT: Shamira.

Shana A variant spelling of Shaina.

Shane A variant spelling of Shaine.

Shani, Shanie Pet forms of Shaine.

Shanit From the Hebrew, the name of a plant that grows in the wild in damp areas. HEBREW EQUIVALENT: Shanit.

Shannen A variant spelling of Shannon.

Shannon A feminine form of Sean, a variant form of John. HEBREW EQUIVALENT: Yochana.

Shareen A variant form of Sharon.

Sharelle A variant form of Sharon.

Shari A pet form of Sharon.

Sharin A variant spelling of Sharon.

Sharleen A variant spelling of Charlene.

Sharlene A variant spelling of Charlene.

Sharon From the Hebrew, referring to Palestine in Israel, extending from Mount Carmel southward to where roses grew in abundance. HEBREW EQUIVALENT: Sharon.

Sharona A variant form of Sharon. HEBREW EQUIVALENT: Sharona.

Sharoni A variant form of Sharon. HEBREW EQUIVALENT: Sharoni.

Sharonit A variant form of Sharon. HEBREW EQUIVALENT: Sharonit.

Sharyl A variant form of Cheryl.

Sharyn A variant spelling of Sharon.

Shaula A feminine form of Shaul (Saul). HEBREW EQUIVALENT: Sha'ula.

Shaulit A variant form of Shaula.

Shayna A variant spelling of Sheina.

Shayndel A variant spelling of Shaindel.

Shayne A variant spelling of Shaine.

Sheba The Anglicized form of Sheva.

Sheena A Gaelic form of Jane.

Sheila, Sheilah Variant forms of Cecelia and Celia.

Sheina A variant form of Shaina.

Sheindel A pet form of Sheina.

Shelby From the Anglo-Saxon, meaning "sheltered town." HEBREW EQUIVALENT: Shamira.

Sheli A variant form of Shelley. Also from the Hebrew, meaning "mine." HEBREW EQUIVALENT: Sheli.

Shelia A variant spelling of Sheliya.

Sheliya, Sheli-Ya From the Hebrew, meaning "Mine is God's." HEBREW EQUIVALENT: Sheliya.

Shelley, Shelly Irish pet forms of Cecelia.

Shelomit A variant spelling of Shlomit.

Shemuela A variant spelling of Shmuela.

Sheree A variant form of Cheryl.

Sherelle, Sherrelle A variant spelling of Cheryl.

Sherelyn A pet form of Sherry.

Sheri A variant spelling of Cheri.

Sherry A variant form of Caesarina, the feminine form of the Latin Caesar, meaning "king." HEBREW EQUIVALENT: Malka.

Sheryl A variant form of Sherry.

Sheva From the Hebrew, meaning "oath." HEBREW EQUIVALENT: Sheva.

Shifra, Shifrah From the Hebrew, meaning "good, handsome, beautiful" or from the Aramaic, meaning "trumpet." HEBREW EQUIVALENT: Shifra.

Shimra From the Hebrew, meaning "guarded, protected." HEBREW EQUIVALENT: Shimra.

Shimrat From the Aramaic, meaning "protected, guarded." HEBREW EQUIVALENT: Shimrat.

Shimrit From the Hebrew, meaning "guarded, protected." HEBREW EQUIVALENT: Shimrit.

Shimriya From the Hebrew, meaning "God is my protector." HEBREW EQUIVALENT: Shimriya.

Shimshona The feminine form of Shimshon (Samson), meaning "sun." HEBREW EQUIVALENT: Shimshona.

Shiphra A variant spelling of Shifra.

Shira, Shirah From the Hebrew, meaning "song." HEBREW EQUIVALENT: Shira.

Shiraz From the Hebrew, meaning "mighty song." HEBREW EQUIVALENT: Shiraz.

Shirel From the Hebrew, meaning "God's song." HEBREW EQUIVALENT: Shirel.

Shirl A pet form of Shirley.

Shirlee, Shir-Lee Variant spellings of Shirli.

Shirley From the Old English, meaning "from the white meadow." HEBREW EQUIVALENT: Sharona.

Shirli, Shir-Li From the Hebrew, meaning "Song is mine." HEBREW EQUIVALENT: Shirli.

Shirra A variant spelling of Shira.

Shiva From the Hebrew, meaning "seven." HEBREW EQUIVALENT: Shiva.

Shlomit From the Hebrew, meaning "peaceful." HEBREW EQUIVALENT: Shlomit (Shelomit).

Shmuela The feminine form of Shmuel (Samuel). HEBREW EQUIVALENT: Shmu'ela.

Shona A variant form of Sheina.

Shoni, Shonie Variant forms of Sheina.

Shosh A pet form of Shoshana.

Shoshan From the Hebrew, meaning "lily," or from the Egyptian and Coptic, meaning "lotus." HEBREW EQUIVALENT: Shoshan.

Shoshana, Shoshanah Variant forms of Shoshan. HEBREW EQUIVALENT: Shoshana.

Shprintza, Shprintze Yiddish forms from the Esperanto, meaning "hope." HEBREW EQUIVALENT: Tikva.

Shuala From the Hebrew, meaning "fox." HEBREW EQUIVALENT: Shu'ala.

Shula A pet form of Shulamit. HEBREW EQUIVALENT: Shula.

Shulamit From the Hebrew, meaning "peace, peaceful." HEBREW EQUIVALENT: Shulamit.

Shuli, Shuly Pet forms of Shulamit. HEBREW EQUIVALENT: Shuli.

Sibyl From the Greek, meaning "counsel of God." Also, from the Old Italian, meaning "wise old woman." HEBREW EQUIVALENT: Bina.

Sidra From the Latin, meaning "starlike." Also, from the Hebrew, meaning "order, sequence." HEBREW EQUIVALENT: Sidra.

Sigal From the Hebrew, meaning "treasure." HEBREW EQUIVALENT: Sigal.

Sigalia A variant spelling of Sigaliya.

Sigalit From the Hebrew, meaning "a violet." HEBREW EQUIVALENT: Sigalit.

Sigaliya A variant form of Sigal. HEBREW EQUIVALENT: Sigaliya.

Siglia A variant spelling of Sigaliya.

Siglit A variant form of Sigal. HEBREW EQUIVALENT: Siglit.

Signora From the Latin, meaning "Woman, lady." HEBREW EQUIVALENT: Gevira.

Silona From the Greek and Hebrew, meaning "water conduit, stream." HEBREW EQUIVALENT: Silona.

Silonit A variant form of Silona. HEBREW EQUIVALENT: Silonit.

Silva A variant form of Sylvia.

Silvia A variant spelling of Sylvia.

Sima From the Aramaic, meaning "treasure." HEBREW EQUIVALENT: Sima.

Simajean A hybrid of Sima and Jean.

Simcha From the Hebrew, meaning "joy." HEBREW EQUIVALENT: Simcha.

Simchit A variant form of Simcha. HEBREW EQUIVALENT: Simchit.

Simchona A variant form of Simcha.

Simeona A variant spelling of Simona.

Simona, Simone Feminine forms of Simon, meaning "to hear." HEBREW EQUIVALENT: Shimona.

Sindy A fanciful spelling of Cindy.

Siona A variant spelling of Tziyona.

Sirel A Yiddish form of Sara.

Sirena A variant spelling of Serena.

Sirke A Yiddish pet form of Sara.

Sisel From the Yiddish, meaning "sweet." HEBREW EQUIVALENT: Metuka.

Sisi A pet form of Cecilia.

Sisley A variant spelling of Cicely.

Sissie, Sissy Variant spellings of Sisi.

Sitvanit From the Hebrew, meaning "an autumn crocus." HEBREW EQUIVALENT: Sitvanit.

Sivana A variant form of the masculine Sivan. HEBREW EQUIVALENT: Sivana.

Sivia, Sivya Variant forms of Tzivya.

Sloan A unisex name, meaning "warrior." HEBREW EQUIVALENT: Gavrilla.

Soferet From the Hebrew, meaning "scribe." HEBREW EQUIVALENT: Soferet.

Sondra A variant spelling of Sandra.

Sonia A variant form of Sophia.

Sonja, Sonya Slavic forms of Sonia.

Sophia From the Greek, meaning "wisdom, wise one."
HEBREW EQUIVALENT: Tushiya.

Sophie A French form of Sophia.

Sorale A Yiddish pet form of Sarah.

Sorali, Soralie Yiddish pet forms of Sarah.

Soreka From the Hebrew, meaning "vine." HEBREW EQUIVA-
LENT: Sorcka.

Sorka, Sorke A Yiddish pet form of Sara.

Soroli A variant spelling of Sorali.

Stacey, Stacy Irish forms of the Greek name Anastasia,
mean-ing "resurrection, revival." HEBREW EQUIVALENT:
Cha'ya.

Staci, Stacia, Stacie Variant spellings of Stacey.

Star From the Old English, meaning "star." HEBREW EQUIVA-
LENT: Ester.

Staria A variant form of Star.

Starletta A pet form of Star.

Starr A variant spelling of Star.

Stefana, Stefania Feminine forms of Stephen, meaning
"crown." HEBREW EQUIVALENT: Malka.

Stefanie, Stefenie Variant forms of Stephana.

Steffi A pet form of Stefanie.

Stella From the Latin, meaning "star." HEBREW EQUIVALENT:
Ester.

Stephane A variant spelling of Stephanie.

Stephania, Stephanie, Stephenie Variant forms of Stefana.

Stevana, Stevena Variant forms of Stefana.

Su, Sue Pet forms of Susan.

Suellen A hybrid of Sue (Susan) and Ellen.

Sultana From the Arabic, meaning "ruler" or "victorious."
HEBREW EQUIVALENT: Nitzchiya.

Sunni, Sunny From Old English, meaning "shining, bright."
HEBREW EQUIVALENT: Me'ira.

Suri A variant form of Sara.

Surilee A hybrid form of Suri and Lee.

Susan From the Hebrew, meaning "lily." HEBREW EQUIVA-
LENT: Shoshan.

Susanna, Susannah Variant forms of Susan.

Susanne A variant form of Susan.

Susette A pet form of Susan.

Susi, Susie, Susy Pet forms of Susan.

Suzanne A variant form of Susan.

Suzette A French form of Susan.

Suzy A pet form of Susan.

Sybil, Sybille Variant spellings of Sibyl.

Sybyl, Sybyle Variant spellings of Sibyl.

Syd, Sydel, Sydelle Variant pet forms of Sydney.

Sydney A feminine form of the masculine Sidney. HEBREW
EQUIVALENT: Gitit.

Sylvia From the Latin, meaning "forest" or "one who dwells
in the woods." HEBREW EQUIVALENT: Ya'arit.

Sylvie A Norweigian form of Sylvia.

Syma A variant spelling of Cyma, Seema, and Sima.

BEST BABY NAMES   BEST BABY NAMES

Tabita, Tabitha From the Akkadian, meaning "goat."
HEBREW EQUIVALENT: Gadya.

Taffy The Welsh form of Vida, a variant form of David.
HEBREW EQUIVALENT: Davida.

Taga From the Aramaic and Arabic, meaning "crown."
HEBREW EQUIVALENT: Taga.

Tahl A variant spelling of Tal.

Tal From the Hebrew, meaning "dew." HEBREW EQUIVALENT:
Tal.

Tali From the Hebrew, meaning "my dew." HEBREW EQUIVA-
LENT: Tali.

Talia A variant spelling of Talya.

Talie A variant spelling of Tali.

Talma From the Hebrew, meaning "mound, hill." HEBREW EQUIVALENT: Talma.

Talmit A variant form of Talma. HEBREW EQUIVALENT: Talmit.

Talmor From the Hebrew, meaning "heaped" or "sprinkled with myrrh, perfumed." HEBREW EQUIVALENT: Talmor.

Talor, Tal-Or From the Hebrew, meaning "morning dew." HEBREW EQUIVALENT: Tal-Or.

Talora, Tal-Ora A variant form of Tal-Or. HEBREW EQUIVALENT: Tal-Ora.

Talya From the Hebrew, meaning "dew." HEBREW EQUIVALENT: Talya.

Tama, Tamah From the Hebrew, meaning "wonder, surprise" or "whole, complete." HEBREW EQUIVALENT: Tama.

Tamar From the Hebrew, meaning "palm tree" or "upright, righteous, graceful." HEBREW EQUIVALENT: Tamar.

Tamara, Tamarah From the East Indian, meaning "spice." HEBREW EQUIVALENT: Tamara.

Tami, Tammy Feminine forms of Thomas, meaning "twin" or "sun god." HEBREW EQUIVALENT: Orit.

Tania A variant spelling of Tanya.

Tanya From the Russian, meaning "fairy queen." HEBREW EQUIVALENT: Malkit.

Tara From the French and Aramaic, referring to a unit of measurement. Also, from the Aramaic, meaning "throw" or "carry." HEBREW EQUIVALENT: Tara.

Tari From the Hebrew, meaning "fresh, ripe, new." HEBREW EQUIVALENT: Tari.

Taryn A variant form of Tara.

Tate From the Anglo-Saxon, meaning "to be cheerful." HEBREW EQUIVALENT: Ditza.

Tauba, Taube Yiddish forms of the German, meaning "dove." HEBREW EQUIVALENT: Yonita.

Tavi A variant form of the masculine David. HEBREW EQUIVALENT: Davida.

Tavita A pet form of Tavi.

Taylor From the Late Latin, meaning "to cut." HEBREW EQUIVALENT: Gitit.

Techiya From the Hebrew, meaning "life, revival." HEBREW EQUIVALENT: Techiya.

Tehila, Tehilla From the Hebrew, meaning "praise, song of praise." HEBREW EQUIVALENT: Tehila (T'hila).

Tehiya A variant spelling of Techiya.

Tehora From the Hebrew, meaning "pure, clean." HEBREW EQUIVALENT: Tehora.

Telalit From the Hebrew, meaning "sundew." HEBREW EQUIVALENT: Telalit.

Teli From the Aramaic and Hebrew, meaning "lamb." HEBREW EQUIVALENT: Teli (T'li).

Tema A Yiddish form of Tamar.

Temara A variant form of Tamar. HEBREW EQUIVALENT: Temara.

Temima From the Hebrew, meaning "whole, honest." HEBREW EQUIVALENT: Temima.

Temira From the Hebrew, meaning "tall, stately." HEBREW EQUIVALENT: Temira.

Temma A variant spelling of Tema.

Teresa The Spanish and Italian form of Theresa.

Teri a pet form of Theresa.

Teriya A variant form of Tari. HEBREW EQUIVALENT: Teriya.

Terry A pet form of Theresa.

Teruma, Terumah From the Hebrew, meaning "offering, gift." HEBREW EQUIVALENT: Teruma.

Teshura, Teshurah From the Hebrew, meaning "gift." HEBREW EQUIVALENT: Teshura.

Tetty A pet form of Elizabeth.

Tevita A Fijian form of Davida.

Thalia From the Greek, meaning "luxurious, flourishing." HEBREW EQUIVALENT: Pircha.

Thea A short form of Althea.

Thelma From the Greek, meaning "nursing, infant."
HEBREW EQUIVALENT: Alma.

Theodora The feminine form of Theodore. HEBREW EQUIVA-
LENT: Matana.

Theora A short form of Theodora.

Theresa, Therese From the Greek, meaning "harvester,
farmer." HEBREW EQUIVALENT: Gana.

Tifara From the Hebrew, meaning "beauty" or "glory."
HEBREW EQUIVALENT: Tifara.

Tiferet A variant form of Tifara. HEBREW EQUIVALENT:
Tiferet.

Tiffany From the Latin, meaning "three, the trinity."
HEBREW EQUIVALENT: Shelosha.

Tikva From the Hebrew, meaning "hope." HEBREW EQUIVA-
LENT: Tikva.

Tilda A pet form of Mathilda.

Tilla A variant form of Tillie.

Tillamae A hybrid of Tilla and Mae.

Tillie, Tilly Pet forms of Mathilda. Also, from the Latin,
meaning "graceful linden tree." HEBREW EQUIVALENT:
Tirza.

Timi A pet form of Timora.

Timora From the Hebrew, meaning "tall," like the palm
tree. HEBREW EQUIVALENT: Timora.

Timura A variant form of Timora. HEBREW EQUIVALENT:
Timura.

Tina A pet form of names such as Christina and Bettina.

Tira From the Syriac, meaning "sheepfold," or from the
Hebrew, meaning "enclosure, encampment." HEBREW
EQUIVALENT: Tira.

Tiri A variant form of Tira. HEBREW EQUIVALENT: Tiri.

Tirtza, Tirtzah From the Hebrew, meaning "agreeable,
willing." HEBREW EQUIVALENT: Tirtza.

Tirza, Tirzah From the Hebrew, meaning "linden" or
"cypress tree." HEBREW EQUIVALENT: Tirza.

Tisha A pet form of Patricia.

Tita A variant form of Titania.

Titania From the Greek, meaning "great one." HEBREW EQUIVALENT: Atalya.

Tiva From the Hebrew, meaning "good." HEBREW EQUIVALENT: Tiva.

Tivona From the Hebrew, meaning "lover of nature." HEBREW EQUIVALENT: Tivona.

Tivoni A variant form of Tivona. HEBREW EQUIVALENT: Tivoni.

Toba A variant spelling of Tova.

Tobelle A pet form of Toba.

Tobey A variant form of Toba.

Tobi A variant spelling of Toby.

Tobit A variant spelling of Tovit.

Toby A pet form of Toba.

Toda, Todah From the Hebrew, meaning "thanks, thank you." HEBREW EQUIVALENT: Toda.

Toiba, Toibe From the Yiddish, meaning "dove." HEBREW EQUIVALENT: Yona.

Toni A pet form of Antoinette.

Tonia A variant form of Toni.

Tonise A variant form of Toni.

Tony A variant spelling of Toni.

Topaza From the Greek, referring to a yellow variety of sapphire. HEBREW EQUIVALENT: Sapira.

Tora, Torah From the Hebrew, meaning "teaching" or "law." HEBREW EQUIVALENT: Tora.

Tori From the Hebrew, meaning "my turtledove." HEBREW EQUIVALENT: Tori.

Tory A pet form of Victoria.

Totie A variant form of Dottie, a pet form of Dorothy.

Tova, Tovah From the Hebrew, meaning "good." HEBREW EQUIVALENT: Tova.

Tovat A variant form of Tova. HEBREW EQUIVALENT: Tovat.

Tovit From the Hebrew, meaning "good." HEBREW EQUIVALENT: Tovit.

Tracey, Traci Variant spellings of Tracy.

Tracy From the Anglo-Saxon, meaning "brave." Also, a pet form of Theresa. HEBREW EQUIVALENT: Abiri.

Trella A short form of Estella, the Spanish form of Esther.

Tricia A pet form of Patricia.

Trina A short form of Katrina.

Trish, Trisha Pet forms of Patricia.

Trix, Trixie, Trixy Pet forms of Beatrice and Beatrix.

Truda, Trude Pet forms of Gertrude.

Tumi From the Hebrew, meaning "whole, complete." HEBREW EQUIVALENT: Tumi.

Tuvit A variant form of Tova. HEBREW EQUIVALENT: Tuvit.

Tyna, Tyne From the British, meaning "river." HEBREW EQUIVALENT: Bat-Yam.

Tzabara From the Arabic, meaning "cactus." HEBREW EQUIVALENT: Tzabar.

Tzabaria A variant spelling of Tzabariya.

Tzabariya A variant form of Tzabara. HEBREW EQUIVALENT: Tzabariya.

Tzahal From the Hebrew, meaning "joy." HEBREW EQUIVALENT: Tzahal.

Tze'ela From the Hebrew, meaning "a poinciana," a shrub of the legume family. HEBREW EQUIVALENT: Tze'ela.

Tzeviya A variant form of Tzivya. HEBREW EQUIVALENT: Tzeviya.

Tziona A variant spelling of Tziyona.

Tzipi A pet form of Tzipora. *See* Tzipora. HEBREW EQUIVALENT: Tzipi.

Tzipiya From the Hebrew, meaning "hope." HEBREW EQUIVALENT: Tzipiya.

Tzipora, Tziporah From the Hebrew, meaning "bird." HEBREW EQUIVALENT: Tzipora.

Tzipori From the Hebrew, meaning "my bird." HEBREW EQUIVALENT: Tzipori.

Tziporit A variant form of Tzipora. HEBREW EQUIVALENT: Tziporit.

Tziril A Yiddish form of Sara.

Tzivia, Tzivya From the Hebrew, meaning "deer, gazelle."
HEBREW EQUIVALENT: Tzivya.

Tziyona From the Hebrew, meaning "excellent." HEBREW
EQUIVALENT: Tziyona.

Tziyonit A variant form of Tziyona. HEBREW EQUIVALENT:
Tziyonit.

Tzofit From the Hebrew, meaning "scout."

Tzofiya From the Hebrew, meaning "watcher, guardian,
scout." HEBREW EQUIVALENT: Tzofiya.

Tzurit From the Hebrew, referring to a plant that grows on
walls and rocks. HEBREW EQUIVALENT: Tzurit.

Unita From the Latin, meaning "one, united." HEBREW
EQUIVALENT: Achva.

Uranit From the Hebrew, meaning "light." HEBREW EQUIVA-
LENT: Uranit.

Uriela, Uriella From the Hebrew, meaning "light [flame] of
the Lord." HEBREW EQUIVALENT: Uriela.

Urit From the Hebrew, meaning "light" or "fire." HEBREW
EQUIVALENT: Urit.

Ursala From the Latin, meaning "a she-bear." HEBREW
EQUIVALENT: Duba.

Uza, Uzza From the Hebrew, meaning "strength." HEBREW
EQUIVALENT: Uza.

Uziela, Uziella From the Hebrew, meaning "My strength is
the Lord." HEBREW EQUIVALENT: Uzi'ela.

Uzit From the Hebrew, meaning "strength." HEBREW
EQUIVALENT: Uzit.

Val A pet form of Valerie.

Valeria, Valerie Variant forms of the Latin, meaning "to be strong." HEBREW EQUIVALENT: Gavriela.

Vana, Vanna Pet forms of Vanessa.

Vanessa From the Middle English, meaning "to fan, to agitate with a fan," an old method of winnowing grain. HEBREW EQUIVALENT: Garnit.

Varda From the Hebrew, meaning "rose." HEBREW EQUIVALENT: Varda.

Vardia A variant spelling of Vardiya.

Vardina A variant form of Varda. HEBREW EQUIVALENT: Vardina.

Vardit A variant form of Varda. HEBREW EQUIVALENT: Vardit.

Vardiya A variant form of Varda. HEBREW EQUIVALENT: Vardiya.

Veda From the Sanskrit, meaning "sacred, understanding." HEBREW EQUIVALENT: Tushiya.

Valentina The feminine form of Valentine. HEBREW EQUIVALENT: Aziza.

Velma A pet form of Wilhelmina.

Ventura From the Spanish, meaning "good fortune." HEBREW EQUIVALENT: Mazala.

Venus From the Latin, meaning "to love." In Greek mythology, the goddess of love and beauty. HEBREW EQUIVALENT: Ahuva.

Vera From the Latin, meaning "truth." Also, from the Russian, meaning "faith." HEBREW EQUIVALENT: Amita.

Vered From the Hebrew, meaning "rose." HEBREW EQUIVALENT: Vered.

Verena, Verina From the Latin, meaning "one who venerates God" or "sacred wisdom." HEBREW EQUIVALENT: Tehila.

Verita From the Latin, meaning "truth." HEBREW EQUIVALENT: Amita.

Verity A variant form of Verita.

Verna, Verne From the Latin, meaning "springlike" or "green-growth." HEBREW EQUIVALENT: Yarkona.

Veronica A variant form of Berenice, meaning "bringer of victory," or from the Latin, meaning "truthful, faithful." HEBREW EQUIVALENT: Amnona.

Vesta, Vestal In Roman mythology, the goddess of fire and purification. HEBREW EQUIVALENT: Avuka.

Vi A pet form of Violet and Victoria.

Vici, Vicki, Vicky Variant pet forms of Victoria.

Victoria From the Latin, meaning "victorious." HEBREW EQUIVALENT: Nitzchit.

Victorina, Victorine Pet forms of Victoria.

Vida A pet form of Davida.

Vikki, Vikkie, Vikky Pet forms of Victoria.

Viola A Middle English flower-name, from the Latin, meaning "violet." HEBREW EQUIVALENT: Varda.

Violet A variant form of Viola.

Virginia From the Latin, meaning "virgin, pure" or "maiden." HEBREW EQUIVALENT: Berura.

Vita From the Latin, meaning "life, animated." HEBREW EQUIVALENT: Chava.

Vittoria The feminine form of Victor, meaning "conqueror." HEBREW EQUIVALENT: Gevira.

Viveca An Italian pet form of Vivian.

Vivi From the Latin, meaning "alive." HEBREW EQUIVALENT: Chava.

Vivian, Viviana, Vivianna Variant forms of Vivi.

Vivien, Vivienne French forms of Vivian.

Vyvyan A variant spelling of Vivian.

Walda From the Old High German, meaning "to rule."
  HEBREW EQUIVALENT: Sara.
Wanda From the Old Norse, meaning "young tree," or from
  the Anglo-Saxon, meaning "wanderer." HEBREW EQUIVA-
  LENT: Hagar.
Wende, Wendey, Wendi, Wendy Pet forms of Genevieve,
  Gwendaline, and Winnifred.
Wilhelmina The English and Dutch form of Wilhelm,
  meaning "protector." HEBREW EQUIVALENT: Magena.
Willa A pet form of Wilhelmina.
Willene A pet form of Wilhelmina.
Wilma A pet form of Wilhelmina.
Winifred From the Anglo-Saxon, meaning "friend of
  peace." HEBREW EQUIVALENT: Menucha.
Wynette A variant form of Wynna.
Winnie A pet form of Winifred.
Wynna, Wynne Pet forms of Gwendaline and Winifred.

Xena From the Greek, meaning "great" or "stranger."
  HEBREW EQUIVALENT: Avishag.

Yaakova From the Hebrew, meaning "to supplant." HEBREW EQUIVALENT: Ya'akova.

Yaala A variant form of Yael. HEBREW EQUIVALENT: Ya'ala.

Yaalat A variant form of Yael. HEBREW EQUIVALENT: Ya'alat.

Yaalit A variant form of Yael. HEBREW EQUIVALENT: Ya'alit.

Yaanit A variant form of Yaen. HEBREW EQUIVALENT: Ya'anit.

Yaara From the Hebrew, meaning "honeysuckle" or "forest." HEBREW EQUIVALENT: Ya'ara.

Yaarit From the Hebrew, meaning "pertaining to the forest." HEBREW EQUIVALENT: Ya'arit.

Yael From the Hebrew, meaning "to ascend" or "mountain goat." HEBREW EQUIVALENT: Ya'el.

Yaela, Yaella Variant forms of Yael. HEBREW EQUIVALENT: Ya'ela.

Yaen From the Hebrew, meaning "ostrich." HEBREW EQUIVALENT: Ya'en.

Yafa, Yaffa From the Assyrian and the Hebrew, meaning "beautiful." HEBREW EQUIVALENT: Yafa.

Yafit A variant form of Yafa. HEBREW EQUIVALENT: Yafit.

Yaira From the Hebrew, meaning "to enlighten." HEBREW EQUIVALENT: Ya'ira.

Yakira From the Hebrew, meaning "valuable, precious." HEBREW EQUIVALENT: Yakira.

Yama From the Hebrew, meaning "toward the sea" or "westward." HEBREW EQUIVALENT: Yama.

Yamit From the Hebrew, meaning "pertaining to the sea." HEBREW EQUIVALENT: Yamit.

Yara A variant spelling of Yaara.

Yardaena A variant spelling of Yardena.

Yardena The feminine form of Yarden (Jordan), meaning "to flow down." HEBREW EQUIVALENT: Yardena.

Yardenia A variant spelling of Yardeniya.

Yardeniya From the Hebrew, meaning "garden of the Lord." HEBREW EQUIVALENT: Yardeniya.

Yarkona The feminine form of Yarkon, meaning "green." HEBREW EQUIVALENT: Yarkona.

Yarona From the Hebrew, meaning "sing." HEBREW EQUIVALENT: Yarona.

Yasmin, Yasmine Jasmine

Yatva Fromt the Hebrew, meaning "good." HEBREW EQUIVALENT: Yatva.

Yechiela From the Hebrew, meaning "May God live." HEBREW EQUIVALENT: Yechiela.

Yedida, Yedidah From the Hebrew, meaning "friend" or "beloved." HEBREW EQUIVALENT: Yedida.

Yedidia, Yedidiah Variant spellings of Yedidya.

Yedidela From the Hebrew, meaning "friend of God" or "beloved of God." HEBREW EQUIVALENT: Yedidela.

Yedidya From the Hebrew, meaning "friend of God." HEBREW EQUIVALENT: Yedidya.

Yehiela A variant spelling of Yehchiela.

Yehudit From the Hebrew, meaning "praise." HEBREW EQUIVALENT: Yehudit.

Yeira, Yeirah From the Hebrew, meaning "light." HEBREW EQUIVALENT: Ye'ira.

Yekara, Yekarah Variant forms of Yakira. HEBREW EQUIVALENT: Yekara.

Yemima Possibly from the Arabic, meaning "dove." HEBREW EQUIVALENT: Yemima.

Yemina From the Hebrew, meaning "right hand," signifying strength. HEBREW EQUIVALENT: Yemina.

Yeshisha From the Hebrew, meaning "old." HEBREW EQUIVALENT: Yeshisha.

Yetta A pet form of Henrietta.

Yifat From the Ugaritic and Akkadian, meaning "beauty." HEBREW EQUIVALENT: Yifat.

Yigala From the Hebrew, meaning "to redeem." HEBREW EQUIVALENT: Yigala.

Yimna From the Hebrew and Arabic, meaning "right side," signifying good fortune. HEBREW EQUIVALENT: Yimna.

Yisraela The feminine form of Yisrael. HEBREW EQUIVALENT: Yisraela.

Yisr'ela A variant form of Yisraela. HEBREW EQUIVALENT: Yisr'ela.

Yitra From the Hebrew, meaning "wealth, riches." HEBREW EQUIVALENT: Yitra.

Yitta A Yiddish form of Yetta.

Yitti A Yiddish form of Yetta.

Yoanna From the Hebrew, meaning "God has answered." HEBREW EQUIVALENT: Yo'ana.

Yochana From the Hebrew, meaning "God is gracious." HEBREW EQUIVALENT: Yochana.

Yochebed A variant spelling of Yocheved.

Yocheved From the Hebrew, meaning "God's glory." HEBREW EQUIVALENT: Yocheved.

Yoela From the Hebrew, meaning "God is willing." HEBREW EQUIVALENT: Yo'ela.

Yoelit A variant form of Yoela. HEBREW EQUIVALENT: Yo'elit.

Yolanda, Yolande From the Latin, meaning "modest, shy." HEBREW EQUIVALENT: Anuva.

Yona, Yonah From the Hebrew, meaning "dove." HEBREW EQUIVALENT: Yona.

Yonat A variant form of Yona. HEBREW EQUIVALENT: Yonat.

Yonata A variant form of Yona. HEBREW EQUIVALENT: Yonata.

Yonati From the Hebrew, meaning "my dove." HEBREW EQUIVALENT: Yonati.

Yoni A pet form of Yonina.

Yonina A variant form of Yona. *See* Yona. HEBREW EQUIVALENT: Yonina.

Yonit A variant form of Yona. HEBREW EQUIVALENT: Yonit.

Yonita A variant form of Yona. HEBREW EQUIVALENT: Yonita.

Yosefa, Yosepha A variant form of Yosifa. HEBREW EQUIVALENT: Yosefa.

Yosifa A feminine form of Yosef (Joseph). HEBREW EQUIVALENT: Yosifa.

Yudi A pet form of Yehudit. HEBREW EQUIVALENT: Yudi.
Yudit A short form of Yehudit. HEBREW EQUIVALENT: Yudit.
Yvette A Welsh form of Evan. HEBREW EQUIVALENT: Yochana.
Yvona A variant spelling of Yvonne.
Yvonne A French form of Yvette.

BEST BABY NAMES BEST BABY NAMES

Zahara From the Hebrew, meaning "to shine." HEBREW EQUIVALENT: Zahara.
Zahari A variant form of Zahara. HEBREW EQUIVALENT: Zahari.
Zaharit A variant form of Zahara. HEBREW EQUIVALENT: Zaharit.
Zahava A variant spelling of Zehava. HEBREW EQUIVALENT: Zahava.
Zahavi A variant form of Zahava. HEBREW EQUIVALENT: Zahavi.
Zaka, Zakah From the Hebrew, meaning "bright, pure, clear." HEBREW EQUIVALENT: Zaka.
Zakit A variant form of Zaka. HEBREW EQUIVALENT: Zakit.
Zandra A variant form of Sandra.
Zara, Zarah Variant forms of Sarah.
Zariza, Zarizah Variant forms of Zeriza. HEBREW EQUIVALENT: Zariza.
Zayit From the Hebrew, meaning "olive." HEBREW EQUIVALENT: Za'yit.
Ze'eva From the Hebrew, meaning "wolf." HEBREW EQUIVALENT: Ze'eva.
Zehara From the Hebrew, meaning "light, brightness." HEBREW EQUIVALENT: Zehara.
Zehari A variant form of Zohar. HEBREW EQUIVALENT: Zehari.

Zehava From the Hebrew, meaning "gold, golden." HEBREW EQUIVALENT: Zehava.

Zehavi A variant form of Zehava. HEBREW EQUIVALENT: Zehavi.

Zehavit A variant form of Zehava. HEBREW EQUIVALENT: Zehavit.

Zehira From the Hebrew, meaning "guarded, cautious." HEBREW EQUIVALENT: Zehira.

Zehorit A variant form of Zehara. HEBREW EQUIVALENT: Zehorit.

Zehuva From the Hebrew, meaning "gilded." HEBREW EQUIVALENT: Zehuva.

Zehuvit A variant form of Zehava. HEBREW EQUIVALENT: Zehuvit.

Zeira From the Aramaic, meaning "small." HEBREW EQUIVALENT: Ze'ira.

Zeita An Aramaic variant form of Zayit. HEBREW EQUIVALENT: Zayta.

Zeitana A variant form of Zeita. HEBREW EQUIVALENT: Zeitana (Zaytana).

Zelda A variant spelling of Selda.

Zemira From the Hebrew, meaning "song, melody." HEBREW EQUIVALENT: Zemira.

Zemora, Zemorah From the Hebrew, meaning "branch, twig." HEBREW EQUIVALENT: Zemora.

Zena A variant spelling of Xena.

Zeriza From the Hebrew, meaning "energetic, industrious." HEBREW EQUIVALENT: Zeriza.

Zeta A variant form of Zeita.

Zetana A variant spelling of Zeitana.

Zetta A variant spelling of Zeta.

Zeva A variant spelling of Ze'eva.

Zevida From the Hebrew, meaning "gift." HEBREW EQUIVALENT: Zevida.

Zevuda A variant form of Zevida. HEBREW EQUIVALENT: Zevuda.

Zevula From the Hebrew, meaning "dwelling place" or "palace." HEBREW EQUIVALENT: Zevula.

Zila, Zilla From the Hebrew, meaning "shadow." HEBREW EQUIVALENT: Tzila.

Zimra From the Hebrew, meaning "choice fruit" or "song of praise." HEBREW EQUIVALENT: Zimra.

Zimrat A variant form of Zimra. HEBREW EQUIVALENT: Zimrat.

Zimria, Zimriah Variant spellings of Zimriya.

Zimriya From the Hebrew, meaning "songfest" or "the Lord is my song." HEBREW EQUIVALENT: Zimriya.

Ziona A variant spelling of Tziyona. HEBREW EQUIVALENT: Tziyona.

Zipora, Zippora Variant spellings of Tzipora.

Zipori A variant spelling of Tzipori.

Zira From the Hebrew, meaning "arena." HEBREW EQUIVALENT: Zira.

Zita A pet form of Theresa.

Ziva From the Hebrew, meaning "brightness, brilliance, splendor." HEBREW EQUIVALENT: Ziva.

Zivit A variant form of Ziva. HEBREW EQUIVALENT: Zivit.

Zlata A Polish-Yiddish form of Golda.

Zlate A variant form of Zlata.

Zoe From the Greek, meaning "life." HEBREW EQUIVALENT: Cha'ya.

Zofi A variant spelling of Tzofi.

Zohar From the Hebrew, meaning "light, brilliance." HEBREW EQUIVALENT: Zohar.

Zohara From the Hebrew, meaning "light." HEBREW EQUIVALENT: Zohara.

Zoheret A variant form of Zohar. HEBREW EQUIVALENT: Zoheret.

Zonya A variant spelling of Sonya.

Zophia A variant spelling of Sophia.

Zora A variant form of Zara.

Zvia A variant spelling of Tzeviya.

ABOUT
THE AUTHOR

ALFRED J. KOLATCH, a graduate of the Teacher's Institute of Yeshiva University and its College of Liberal Arts, was ordained by the Jewish Theological Seminary of America, which subsequently awarded him the Doctor of Divinity Degree, *honoris causa*. From 1941 to 1948 he served as rabbi of congregations in Columbia, South Carolina, and Kew Gardens, New York, and as chaplain in the United States Army. In 1948 he founded Jonathan David Publishers, of which he has since been president and editor-in-chief.

Rabbi Kolatch has authored numerous books, the most popular of which are *Great Jewish Quotations*, *The Jewish Home Advisor*, *This Is the Torah*, and the best-selling *Jewish Book of Why* and its sequel, *The Second Jewish Book of Why*. Several of the author's works deal with nomenclature, about which he is an acknowledged authority. *The New Name Dictionary* and *The Complete Dictionary of English and Hebrew First Names* are his most recent books on the subject. Other books by the author include *The Jewish Child's First Book of Why*, *Classic Bible Stories for Jewish Children*, *The Jewish Mourner's Book of Why*, and *The Family Seder*.

In addition to his scholarly work, Rabbi Kolatch is interested in the work of the military chaplaincy and has served as president of the Association of Jewish Chaplains of the Armed Forces and as vice-president of the interdenominational Military Chaplains Association of the United States.